# THE SATANIC SCRIPTURES
## Peter H. Gilmore

UNDERWORLD AMUSEMENTS

Contents ©2007 & ©2016 Peter H. Gilmore.

ISBN13: 978-1-943687-08-4

This 10TH ANNIVERSARY edition contains an additional essay and is the first to be published by Underworld Amusements.

Goat of Mendes Painting by Peter H. Gilmore
Interior Illustrations by Timothy Patrick Butler
Author Portrait by Christopher R. Mealie
Typesetting and Design by Kevin I. Slaughter

UNDERWORLD AMUSEMENTS
Baltimore, MD
UNDERWORLDAMUSEMENTS.COM

**FOR PEGGY**
*my beloved*

To:

*Anton Szandor LaVey, Satanism's Prime Mover.*

*Blanche Barton, whose strength is legendary.*

*Those who have been with me from the beginning:*
*Ruth Waytz, Chris Cooper—stalwart co-conspirators, the found-*
*ing members of the Order of Fenris—Magister Diabolus Rex, Ma-*
*gister Nemo, Magistra Isabel, and Reverend Manning.*

*Charles Addams, who rendered our kin*
*and Arthur Fellig, a romantic realist.*

*Bela Lugosi, Boris Karloff, Vincent Price,*
*and Christopher Lee, who gave eternal life*
*to multifaceted monsters.*

*Ayn Rand and Madalyn Murray O'Hair,*
*women of monumental courage.*

*Jim Knipfel and George Carlin,*
*fellow misanthropes.*

*Eiji Tsuburaya and Akira Ifukube,*
*who gave form and voice to the classic Daikaiju.*

*Joi Lansing and Mamie Van Doren, bountiful bombshells.*

*Jackie Gleason, Oscar Levant, and Orson Welles,*
*remarkable polymaths who unleashed their dark sides.*

*John Kennedy Toole and Mel Brooks, who show us*
*how deeply funny the human animal can be.*

*Frank Herbert, who saw potential and Gene Roddenberry,*
*who created an Is-To-Be.*

And to:

*The magnificent Magisters and Magistras,
profound Priests and Priestesses, wondrous Witches
and Warlocks, astounding Agents, and the ever-inspiring
loyal cohort that makes up the Citizenry of our Infernal Empire—
you are an aristocracy of achievers, many of whom are
cherished friends, and cannot know how very much
you each mean to me.*

Special thanks to the esteemed Reverends
who gave form to my content in this volume:
*Kevin I. Slaughter, Timothy Patrick Butler, Christopher Mealie,
Steven J. Everitt, and Chris X.*

# Contents

**Prelude** by Blanche Barton                                    IX
Overture                                                         XV
The Essays                                                       XXIII
  Satanism: The Feared Religion. . . . . . . . . . . . . . . . . . 25
  We Are Legion. . . . . . . . . . . . . . . . . . . . . . . . . . 40
  Alienation . . . . . . . . . . . . . . . . . . . . . . . . . . . 42
  A Primer for Fledgling Misanthropologists . . . . . . . . . 45
  The Tide Turns. . . . . . . . . . . . . . . . . . . . . . . . . 53
  Apocalypse Now. . . . . . . . . . . . . . . . . . . . . . . . . 58
  I Am The Light and The Way . . . . . . . . . . . . . . . . . . 60
  On the First Anniversary of 9/11 . . . . . . . . . . . . . . . 65
  Victors and Victims: From West Memphis to Columbine . . 67
  Pervasive Pantywaistism. . . . . . . . . . . . . . . . . . . . . 79
  The Fascism Question . . . . . . . . . . . . . . . . . . . . . . 82
  Eugenics . . . . . . . . . . . . . . . . . . . . . . . . . . . . 92
  Iron Youth . . . . . . . . . . . . . . . . . . . . . . . . . . . 95
  Founding Family: "Morality" versus Same-Sex Marriage . . 98
  Intellectual Black Holes . . . . . . . . . . . . . . . . . . . . 101
  Green-Eyed Hamsters . . . . . . . . . . . . . . . . . . . . . 104
  Satanic Aesthetics. . . . . . . . . . . . . . . . . . . . . . . . 108
  Diabolus In Musica . . . . . . . . . . . . . . . . . . . . . . . 112

Idol Pleasures . . . . . . . . . . . . . . . . . . . . . . . . . . 136
Hell of a Town  . . . . . . . . . . . . . . . . . . . . . . . . . 141
ANTON SZANDOR LaVEY: A Tribute . . . . . . . . . . 147
Farewell, Dark Fane. . . . . . . . . . . . . . . . . . . . . . 151
On Elaboration and Justice. . . . . . . . . . . . . . . . . . 152
Natural Hierarchy: As Above, So Below . . . . . . . . . . 158
Masterful Slaves. . . . . . . . . . . . . . . . . . . . . . . . 166
The Myth of the "Satanic Community"  . . . . . . . . . . 170
Rebels Without Cause . . . . . . . . . . . . . . . . . . . . 186
The Magic of Mastery. . . . . . . . . . . . . . . . . . . . . 195
Every Man and Woman is a Star... . . . . . . . . . . . . . 197
Time Travel—Cheap and Easy. . . . . . . . . . . . . . . . 201
What, the Devil?. . . . . . . . . . . . . . . . . . . . . . . . 207
Walpurgisnacht LI A.S.. . . . . . . . . . . . . . . . . . . . 217
**The Rituals**                                        **223**
Satanic Ritual . . . . . . . . . . . . . . . . . . . . . . . . . 225
A Satanic Wedding . . . . . . . . . . . . . . . . . . . . . . 235
A Satanic Funeral Rite . . . . . . . . . . . . . . . . . . . . 255
Rite of Ragnarök. . . . . . . . . . . . . . . . . . . . . . . . 279
**Nocturne: To The Devil Born** by Peggy Nadramia      **297**

# Prelude

OR MANY YEARS, I've been anxiously awaiting the book you now hold in your hands. It is full of fire, conviction, depth and intellectual power—as well as some devilish winks. When people ask me, "What kind of man is Peter H. Gilmore? Why did you appoint him High Priest?" I'd wish there was one book I could give them that would effectively showcase this multi-faceted individualist. Yes, I could easily direct inquirers to our website where one can find many terrific edicts and essays written by our new High Priest, or to back issues of *The Black Flame*, where earlier versions of many of these essays were incarnated, or I could just be a dictatorial ass and respond (preferably with a thick, fake-Hungarian/Germanic accent), "Because I know what is in his soul and I appointed him to the role he had earned! How dare you question my judgment!" That last bit would be a tad out of character, and not very Satanic. We aren't too keen on taking things "on faith" and, while we all enjoy wicked posturing once in awhile, members of the Church of Satan deserve more than that.

What kind of man is Peter H. Gilmore? Dr. LaVey and I met Magus Gilmore, and his magically-adept wife (now High Priestess) Peggy Nadramia, at Izzy's chophouse one drizzly autumn night in San Francisco in 1986. They were poised, articulate, respectful. They both seemed to have a solid grasp of the dark evocations of Satanism, as well as the flashier, Coney Island aspects that blended so naturally in Anton LaVey's heart, and impressed themselves on his Church. Dr. LaVey was intrigued enough to invite them back to the Black House after dinner for conversation and music until the wee hours...and that was just the first of many long nights together over the next 11 years. The "Satanic Panic" was just beginning to rumble, and, after a short probation, we assigned our new cohorts in the East various administrative and publicity tasks to test their mettle. They rose to the occasion at every turn, facilitating but never intruding, following our High Priest's lead, having the ego strength to never chafe under his direction. Together with other representatives around the globe, we weathered the Panic. Dr. LaVey welcomed Peter and Peggy as valuable and unfaltering assets to his organization. Early on, Peggy Nadramia understood the power and potential of the Internet and created a presence for us there. Quite seamlessly over time, they became our Media Coordinators, designed our website and developed the Special Interest Groups, which, with the reinvigoration of the Grotto system, allowed fellow Satanists the focused, productive contact we all find so enlivening. Already publishing the excellent horror fiction magazine *Grue*, they began publishing *The Black Flame*, which quickly developed into the premiere forum for Satanic thought. Through the years, Peter revealed himself to be anachronistic, almost courtly, betraying manners and sensibilities not of this era, yet very much suited to it. As you'll see in his writings, he shares an element of genuine idealism many Satanists harbor, contrasting starkly with the various and vocal Goodguy-badge victimization cults rampant in our wider society.

When the time came for fresh, invigorating blood five years ago, the choice for High Priest became obvious to me. Years ago, when some young Turk would come on the scene, claiming to be the great black hope of Satanism, Dr. LaVey used to say, "Can he come up with the goods?" Not ego. Ego is easy—we're Satanists! But the man I needed had to have much more substance than that. He couldn't just be another guy in a swirling black cape looking to get his face in front of the cameras. What goes on in front of the cameras is only a mere sliver of what actually has to get done to keep this organization going. The new High Priest has to be the Head Administrator, making sure all the jobs are getting done at the same time. He has no time for snoozing comfortably on his diabolical throne or preening in front of the glass. Questions have to be answered, attacks must be deftly parried. And the impetus to keep the organization going has to come from extraordinary conviction that what you are advocating is right. Peter H. Gilmore has fulfilled these requirements nine-fold. The strength and resonance you read in these essays doesn't come from empty ego and posturing—it comes from deep understanding and hard-won wisdom.

In a way, Peter has both the best and the worst job in the world. On the one hand, he has, through years of dedication, risen to the position of being the foremost representative of Satanic principles on Earth. He has the satisfaction of contributing substantially every day to a philosophy that he has held deep allegiance to since he was 13 years old. On the other hand, he is following in the footsteps of the founder of our religion. He has precepts he is bound to adhere to, yet must also follow his own heart to guide us into virgin territory, forming new policies and exploring new attitudes as we move forward. World situations change. How does Satanism apply in these new circumstances? Anton LaVey gave us a philosophy that allows for evolution and constant change. We require a confident leader who can get past spewing party line rhetoric and dogma, who can take the themes and courageously refine as needed. He cannot be constrained by the past, but he should build constructively on our foundations. Inevitably, he must fend off criticism both from within and without. Few would dare question Anton LaVey's judgment; he's the founder, he must know what he's doing. But those after him are fair game for armchair advice. Magus Gilmore has risen to the task admirably, proving himself a steady and capable leader. As he himself brings out in his "Overture", our High Priest sees his role not as dictator but as Director, patiently recognizing and drawing forth the best in each of us (unless some upstart deserves a firm kick in the keister—he's enthusiastically committed to that form of therapy, as well).

One magical skill Anton LaVey possessed was a keen perception of people. As Peter has matured over the past twenty years I've known him, he's grown quite worldly, as well—not that he was anyone's fool to begin with. But being a Church of Satan administrator places one in an unequalled position to meet some vital, driven human beings, as well as some uniquely scabrous rogues. Sorting the wheat from the chaff is essential, and Peter Gilmore has become a master. Because the cohesion of our philosophy is at stake, his efforts (though they may at times seem ruthless and uncompromising to others) are central to our continued survival. Under his leadership, concentrating his attentions on those who deserve it and giving the bum's rush to those dissonant few, the Church of Satan has flourished. He has encouraged and orchestrated significant aboveground events, given thought-provoking interviews to appropriate venues and networked with valuable, productive members, creating projects of Satanic significance, some obvious, some not so apparent. I feel more connection, invigoration and clarity vibrating throughout our ranks than I have felt for many years.

THE SATANIC SCRIPTURES

Dr. LaVey poetically felt he conjured certain people to fulfill key roles at specific times, including myself. I like to think the High Priest and High Priestess were brought forth to fulfill their destinies at exactly the right time in history. I present this magical tome you now hold in your hands as evidence. It reflects a mature voice, distinct and rich. Magus Gilmore has developed his own sinister style of command, separate from Anton LaVey, but has proven himself in myriad ways worthy to stand proudly in this succession and guide us in our continuing diabolical unfolding. May these essays illuminate and inspire you on your path to fulfilling your Satanic destiny, and may you add body and excitement to our ever-evolving *Sinfonia Diabolica*.

**Blanche Barton, Magistra Templi Rex**
Hallowe'en, XLI A.S.

# OVERTURE

O N April 8ᵀᴴ of 1966, *TIME* magazine emblazoned its black cover with the stark question, "Is God Dead?" On April 30ᵗʰ, Anton Szandor LaVey delivered the answer by proclaiming the birth of the Age of Satan with the founding of the Church of Satan. Both events impacted the world of religion, revitalizing Nietzsche's vision of the liberation of humanity from the dominance of Christian morality. LaVey noted in *The Satanic Bible*, published in December of 1969, a number of pieces of evidence for this new Satanic age. Over the succeeding years, corroboration has continued. The perceptive have been enjoying that show.

In 1998, Episcopalian Bishop John Shelby Spong published a book entitled *Why Christianity Must Change or Die*. It acknowledges the irrationality of past Christian beliefs and argues for a new image of God as simply the "Ground of Being for the Universe," and for Christ as a **symbolic** gateway to this inactive God. I relished seeing a prominent member of a major Christian denomination admitting that the past model of God must perish or their entire religion will wither because it is against human nature. Dr. LaVey's joke about God needing MEDICARE and his prediction that the "Jesus character" would be considered a well-known folk myth by 2000 c.e. seem to have been on target.

While topless nuns have yet to perform the "Missa

Solemnis Rock," there have been other concerts of equivalent blasphemy. I stood on a steel balcony, in the nave of what was once an elegant stone church in the heart of midtown Manhattan. Below me a stage replaced the consecrated space previously supporting a Christian altar. On that now carnal precinct, members of The Electric Hellfire Club, a band of Satanists who use the techno-magic of electricity in their sonic evocations, proudly celebrated their Luciferian heritage. Lead singer Thomas Thorn, a Priest in the Church of Satan, was the commanding front man. His muscular tattooed arms gleamed in the infernal flashing of the laser lights. The plastic red horns stuck to his forehead gave the proper tone of mockery to his presence. He shouted out "God Is Dead, Satan Lives!" and this gruff incantation was echoed through the speakers by the sampled voices from the soundtrack to Roman Polanski's "Rosemary's Baby"—a film with connections to Magus LaVey and the early years of our Church. The resonance was powerful.

As Thorn capered about the stage, the black-garbed audience swayed to the savage dance beat supporting these impious incantations. Thorn raised his left arm and thrusted forth his fingers in the *cornu*—the Devil's salute. "Hail SATAN!" was his primal scream. The throng smartly returned this gesture, joining in on the chorus enthusiastically celebrating the triumph of Satan. I smiled.

On Walpurgisnacht of XXXVI A.S., I was consecrated as the second High Priest of the Church of Satan by Magistra Blanche Barton, the High Priestess since the passing of Magus LaVey in XXXII A.S. A year following that date my wife, Magistra Peggy Nadramia become High Priestess while Magistra Barton assumed Magistra Nadramia's former role as chairperson of the Council of Nine. The camaraderie I've shared with these two brilliant and powerful Satanic Witches has enriched me immeasurably. On the night that my wife took her place at my side as High Priestess, I shared with our members a metaphor I have used to explain my conception of my position and duties as High Priest.

Since I am a musician, having studied both conducting and composition, I often tend to cast my imagery based on this significant part of my creative practice. I see the Church of Satan as resembling a vast symphony orchestra of diabolical virtuosos, each with skills in playing their unique "instruments"—their talents. I am now the conductor and music director of this esteemed ensemble, and the "score" of which I lead us in performance is the philosophy of Satanism composed by Anton LaVey and embodied in his many works. As is the regular practice of conductors, I have studied both the historical context as well as made an in-depth analysis of Dr. LaVey's score, so that my interpretation is authoritative. Having worked for many years directly with the composer himself has also provided me with necessary insights into his unique methods and means.

This *Sinfonia Diabolica*, which we perform with the maximum engagement of our passions, is one with many *concertante* passages, calling for players to come forth from the texture of the ensemble and "sing solo" with great ardor. It is a score that also allows for cadenzas—passages wherein soloists soar in brilliant improvisation supported by the ground base of Satanism's carnal philosophy. And also it is a score that allows for continued expansion—ever more colorful elaborations of its orchestration as conditions change and evolving possibilities present themselves. Those who are not well-versed in classical music performance might not be aware that it has long been the practice of conductors to adjust the scores they are playing to take advantage of the continuing development of the instruments in the orchestra, facilitating greater expression of the intentions of the composer. And so it is my task to evolve the implementation of Maestro LaVey's philosophical masterpiece, as I do my utmost to galvanize you all in this continuing "concert of Promethean music" arising from the very heart of the Inferno.

This book is a collection of my essays written from 1987 C.E. to 2006 C.E., many of which were published in *The Black Flame*. I've made expansions and contractions in an effort to sharpen their focus. You should note that some pieces refer to incidents that occurred proximate to their creation. There are a number of pieces written as rabble-rousing rhetoric during the "Satanic Panic," when we had to defend ourselves almost daily from accusations spread by Christian fundamentalist fanatics that Satanism was a conspiracy of devil-worshiping child murderers. We were under fire and legislation had been proposed to make Satanism illegal, based on these nonsensical claims. Those laws were not passed. We survived and have thrived.

The title, *The Satanic Scriptures*, is an intentionally theatrical oxymoron. Scriptures are generally "sacred texts" and being Satanic in nature these scribblings of mine are not meant as dogmatic proclamations. They are observations made from my unique perspective as a member of the Church of Satan who came to be an administrator and trusted friend and colleague of Magus LaVey. I've spent close to two decades as a spokesperson for our cherished philosophy and during that time have developed principles that I think may be of use to other Satanists. The subjects covered are varied, and you'll find herein metaphors that have helped me leverage the world in interesting ways.

Beginning with the piece approved by Dr. LaVey as the best condensed introduction to our philosophy, "Satanism: The Feared Religion," I've sequenced the essays in a flow which I trust will make for enhanced understanding. They move through issues delineating Satanism in contradistinction to other perspectives extant for approaching human society. You will find several recurring themes that I tackle from differing angles. I define particular types of human animals that you might encounter and then move on to more personal concerns regarding my aesthetic choices.

Over the years I have often been asked about orchestral music, since it is my passion, and so I've created a guide to some of the composers and works which I consider to be among the greatest in the history of Western music. The Devil always has the best tunes, and I suspect that could be extended to encompass the idea that he'd also have a damned fine Hades Philharmonic to conduct.

It is then time to open those adamantine gates and tour the Church of Satan itself. I celebrate our founder and discuss important milestones in our Church's history. I next reveal some of the mechanisms and structures which form the architecture of our organization. The essays conclude by offering an insider's view toward the application of our philosophy, respectfully submitted as "words to the wise."

To end this volume I give forbidden rites to thee. While Dr. LaVey was alive, I created several rituals that became standard liturgy in the Church of Satan. These were circulated only amongst members of our Priesthood of Mendes, and they have been "chamber tested" for a number of years. It is now time to unleash some of them. Others remain secret.

I am so very proud of all the extraordinary people I've met through the Church of Satan. They are abundant proof that Dr. LaVey was accurate in naming our kind, and I know that there are more brave and talented individuals yet to cross my path. That my work may in some way continue to expand upon the brilliant pioneering of our founder for some of you is ample reward. I salute you, fellow Satanists, and look forward to your perfervid works to inspire me as I continue to forge my own creations in the infernal foundry of my Stygian passions.

Some fearful folk have questioned Dr. LaVey's initial proclamation of the new Age of Fire, but I know he was correct. As the Church of Satan passed its second Working Year in 2002 c.e., it certainly had fulfilled his prediction of attaining maturity. As we continue to move forward, the fervor increases on a global scale. We bear a legacy, crystallized and identified by Anton Szandor LaVey, which has come forth from the shadows to claim its due. It is a glorious time to be a Satanist. Now *TIME* should be ready for a new cover: "SATAN LIVES!" Mine eyes have seen the dark glory. I know that you share my vision.

✠ **Magus Peter H. Gilmore**
Friday, 13 October, XLI A.S.
Hell's Kitchen, New York City.

O Man, take heed!
What does the deep midnight say?
The world is deep,
More profound than the day had thought!
Deep is its woe.
Pleasure is deeper still than heartache.
Woe says: "Begone!"
But all pleasure wills eternity.
Wills deep, deep eternity.

From *Thus Spake Zarathustra*
by Friedrich Nietzsche

# THE ESSAYS

# Satanism: The Feared Religion

WHEN ANTON SZANDOR LAVEY shaved his head and created the Church of Satan on April 30, 1966, he knew that soon he would be the focal point of attention for people throughout the globe. Now that we have passed the fortieth anniversary of that fateful night, has the world begun to understand the real meaning behind the only organized religion in history to take as its symbol the ultimate figure of pride and rebellion, and to many, of Evil? And are there truly some grounds for people to feel fear at the evergrowing phenomenon of contemporary Satanism? As the High Priest of the Church of Satan, I can candidly say, "Yes!" However, what the general populace has decided to fear is a ludicrous portrait that has been painted in lurid Technicolor by media hypesters intent on titillation, unscrupulous evangelists struggling to fill their coffers and keep their mistresses in jewelry, and most distressingly by a segment of the therapeutic community who have found a goldmine in the treatment of so-called "ritual abuse survivors" who provide no evidence of their tales of terror, save for their fervent belief that they were victimized. These fictions are remarkably similar to stories told by women labeled by Freud as hysterics. I shall not waste time in refuting the absurd claim that there is an international conspiracy of generational Satanists bent on enslaving the world through drug use and the sacrifice of babies bred for that purpose by emotionally unstable women. That mythology has been thoroughly exploded by other sources[I]. Let us instead look at contemporary Satanism for what it really is, a religion of elitism and Social Darwinism that seeks to re-establish the reign of the able over the idiotic, of swift justice over sluggish injustice, and for a wholesale rejection of egalitarianism as a myth that has crippled the advancement of the human species for the last two thousand years. Is that something to fear? If you're one of the majority of human mediocrities merely existing as a media-besotted drone, you bet it is!

The philosophy of Satanism is delineated in the writings of Anton Szandor LaVey. His books include *The Satanic Bible*, *The Satanic Rituals*, *The Satanic Witch*, *The Devil's Notebook* and *Satan Speaks*. All are currently in print and should be consulted by anyone interested in a complete picture of the views held by the Church of Satan. One can obtain further information by reading *The Secret Life of a Satanist, the authorized biography of Anton LaVey* (Feral House) and *The Church of Satan* (Hell's Kitchen Productions), two books by Blanche Barton, the biographer and longtime companion to Dr. LaVey and a member of the Council of Nine. These works present abundant material regarding the history and contemporary practices of the Church of Satan.

For those who have yet to study this literature there are three sets of brief guidelines[II] issued over the years by the Church, authored by LaVey, which can give the uninitiated

---

I　　The FBI's National Center for the Analysis of Violent Crime: *Investigator's Guide to Allegations of Ritual Child Abuse*, January 1992; the Committee for Scientific Examination of Religion's report *Satanism in America*, October 1989; the British Government's Department of Health report: *The Extent and Nature of Organised and Ritual Abuse*, HMSO, 1994.

II　　The "Nine Satanic Statements," "The Eleven Satanic Rules of the Earth," and "The Nine Satanic Sins" are copyrighted by Anton Szandor LaVey and have been reproduced here with his permission.

a capsulized version of Satanic philosophy. The first are the "Nine Satanic Statements" (copyright 1969) which open *The Satanic Bible* and give a firm foundation for the Satanist. They are:

1. Satan represents indulgence, instead of abstinence!
2. Satan represents vital existence, instead of spiritual pipe dreams!
3. Satan represents undefiled wisdom, instead of hypocritical self-deceit!
4. Satan represents kindness to those who deserve it, instead of love wasted on ingrates!
5. Satan represents vengeance, instead of turning the other cheek!
6. Satan represents responsibility to the responsible, instead of concern for psychic vampires!
7. Satan represents man as just another animal, sometimes better, more often worse than those that walk on all-fours, who, because of his "divine spiritual and intellectual development," has become the most vicious animal of all!
8. Satan represents all of the so-called sins, as they all lead to physical, mental, or emotional gratification!
9. Satan has been the best friend the church has ever had, as he has kept it in business all these years!

The next statements, "The Eleven Satanic Rules of the Earth" (copyright 1967), were written at about the same time, but were then considered too frank and brutal for general release and issued only to the membership. Here is the *Lex Satanicus*, a law of the jungle for social interaction:

1. Do not give opinions or advice unless you are asked.
2. Do not tell your troubles to others unless you are sure

they want to hear them.

3. When in another's lair, show him respect or else do not go there.

4. If a guest in your lair annoys you, treat him cruelly and without mercy.

5. Do not make sexual advances unless you are given the mating signal.

6. Do not take that which does not belong to you unless it is a burden to the other person and he cries out to be relieved.

7. Acknowledge the power of magic if you have employed it successfully to obtain your desires. If you deny the power of magic after having called upon it with success, you will lose all you have obtained.

8. Do not complain about anything to which you need not subject yourself.

9. Do not harm little children.

10. Do not kill non-human animals unless you are attacked or for your food.

11. When walking in open territory, bother no one. If someone bothers you, ask him to stop. If he does not stop, destroy him.

Since we have been issuing statements of what we are seeking, it was considered time to make a list of behaviors that we wish to see avoided. Satanists acknowledge that we are human and work towards perfection, but can sometimes fall into negative patterns of action. Thus was born the list of the "Nine Satanic Sins" (copyright 1987), guidelines for what Satanists consider to be non-productive behavior to be recognized and eliminated from one's daily existence.

1. **Stupidity**—The top of the list for Satanic Sins. The Cardinal Sin of Satanism. It's too bad that stupidity isn't

painful. Ignorance is one thing, but our society thrives increasingly on stupidity. It depends on people going along with whatever they are told. The media promotes a cultivated stupidity as a posture that is not only acceptable but laudable. Satanists must learn to see through the tricks and cannot afford to be stupid.

2. **Pretentiousness**—Empty posturing can be most irritating and isn't applying the cardinal rules of Lesser Magic. On equal footing with stupidity for what keeps the money in circulation these days. Everyone's made to feel like a big shot, whether they can come up with the goods or not.

3. **Solipsism**—Can be very dangerous for Satanists. Projecting your reactions, responses and sensibilities onto someone who is probably far less attuned than you are. It is the mistake of expecting people to give you the same consideration, courtesy and respect that you naturally give them. They won't. Instead, Satanists must strive to apply the dictum of "Do unto others as they do unto you." It's work for most of us and requires constant vigilance lest you slip into a comfortable illusion of everyone being like you. As has been said, certain utopias would be ideal in a nation of philosophers, but unfortunately (or perhaps fortunately, from a Machiavellian standpoint) we are far from that point.

4. **Self-deceit**—It's in the "Nine Satanic Statements" but deserves to be repeated here. Another cardinal sin. We must not pay homage to any of the sacred cows presented to us, including the roles we are expected to play ourselves. The only time self-deceit should be entered into is when it's fun, and with awareness. But then, it's not self-deceit!

5. **Herd Conformity**—That's obvious from a Satanic stance. It's all right to conform to a person's wishes, if it

ultimately benefits you. But only fools follow along with the herd, letting an impersonal entity dictate to you. The key is to choose a master wisely instead of being enslaved by the whims of the many.

6. **Lack of Perspective**—Again, this one can lead to a lot of pain for a Satanist. You must never lose sight of who and what you are, and what a threat you can be, by your very existence. We are making history right now, every day. Always keep the wider historical and social picture in mind. That is an important key to both Lesser and Greater Magic. See the patterns and fit things together as you want the pieces to fall into place. Do not be swayed by herd constraints—know that you are working on another level entirely from the rest of the world.

7. **Forgetfulness of Past Orthodoxies**—Be aware that this is one of the keys to brainwashing people into accepting something new and different, when in reality it's something that was once widely accepted but is now presented in a new package. We are expected to rave about the genius of the creator and forget the original. This makes for a disposable society.

8. **Counterproductive Pride**—That first word is important. Pride is great up to the point you begin to throw out the baby with the bathwater. The rule of Satanism is: if it works for you, great. When it stops working for you, when you've painted yourself into a corner and the only way out is to say, I'm sorry, I made a mistake, I wish we could compromise somehow, then do it.

9. **Lack of Aesthetics**—This is the physical application of the Balance Factor. Aesthetics is important in Lesser Magic and should be cultivated. It is obvious that no one can collect any money off classical standards of beauty and form most of the time so they are discouraged in a consumer society, but an eye for beauty, for balance, is

an essential Satanic tool and must be applied for greatest magical effectiveness. It's not what's supposed to be pleasing—it's what is. Aesthetics is a personal thing, reflective of one's own nature, but there are universally pleasing and harmonious configurations that should not be denied.

This material sums up the rudiments of Satanic philosophy. It certainly has nothing to do with the prevailing Judeo-Christian outlook of altruism and self-sacrifice, and can thus seem quite alien and frightening to one brought up in that worldview. Realistically, the Satanic code of behavior is based on human nature as it is and thus comes naturally to most carnal people who have not been deeply indoctrinated in anti-life and anti-rational belief systems. It is a fact that many people today call themselves Christians but really have no clear concept as to what that philosophy fully entails, so they generally behave in a Satanic fashion. We think that it is high time that this is recognized and that people call themselves what they truly are, not what is socially convenient for them.

As you can see, there are no elements of devil worship in the Church of Satan. Such practices are looked upon as being Christian heresies. Believing in the Christian worldview of God vs. the Devil and choosing to side with the Prince of Darkness is pointless to the Satanist as neither exists. Additionally, we do not believe in the supernatural. To the Satanist, he is his own God. Satan is a symbol of Man living as his prideful, carnal nature dictates. Some Satanists extend this symbol to encompass the evolutionary "force" of entropy that permeates all of nature and provides the drive for survival and propagation inherent in all living things. To the Satanist, Satan is not a conscious entity to be worshiped, rather it is a name for the reservoir of power inside each human to be tapped at will. Thus, the practice of sacrifice is rejected by Satanists as being a Christian aberration—in Satanism there's no deity to which one can make a sacrifice.

Satanists do at times have experience of the super-normal in their practice of ritual or Greater Magic. This is a technique intended primarily as self-transformational psychodrama, but which may be used as an attempt towards influencing the outcome of human events to desired ends. In the context of a theatrical, stimulating ritual an extreme emotional state is reached, sending forth a vision of what you want to occur (the Is-To-Be), which, if your levels of adrenaline are high enough, might permeate the unconscious minds of those you wish to influence, causing them to behave as you desire when the time is right. This does not mean that anything is possible, for it takes a great deal of energy to make a strong sending, and it is often difficult to influence events from the inertia of their present directions. Satanists consider that effective Greater Magic may be a talent, and that different individuals may have varying capacities for "sending and receiving." Awareness of your abilities and what is possible to achieve is one of the hallmarks of a successful Satanic magician. Additionally, Satanists do not use faith as a tool of cognition, hence there is no requirement to accept Greater Magic as anything more than self-therapy. It is up to each Satanist to examine any "interesting coincidences" following their rituals and based on evidence decide whether more is in motion. Satanists also practice Lesser Magic, which is basically the day-to-day manipulation of your fellows to obtain your ends. Detailed techniques are given in *The Satanic Witch*.

In the recent past we have seen certain evangelists and even misinformed academics calling Satanism a neo-Nazi movement. This is an inaccurate label. The Nazi movement drew much of its power from a racist doctrine of Aryan superiority. Satanism is far more discerning than that. While there are provable biological differences between the races and statistically demonstrable performance levels in various activities, it is quite irrational to think that someone can be advanced or not simply because of the color of their skin. Even if one comes from promising genetic stock, and by that we mean from ancestors who have proven their abilities to be superior in performance, this does not guarantee an individual's advancement. We recognize individual merit, and ascribe no value to bloodlines. Satanists only deem individuals as being "elite" if they prove it by cultivating their naturally endowed abilities to the highest extent possible. This is something that requires the Satanic virtue of discipline, a quality we try to instill in our own "iron youth." There are thus outstanding individuals from all ethnic backgrounds, and they are embraced by Satanism for the superior beings that they are—creating a uniquely trans-cultural tribe of carnal people.

Satanists treasure individualism, hardly something to be gained by goose-stepping *en mass* down the street. Yet we do not embrace an "anything goes" atmosphere wherein all values are relative and nothing rises above the sludge of commonality. Satanism encourages a return to more traditional values in art and literature such as mastery of technique and emotional communication, of form and function, design and execution. Satanists find a wealth of material in Western culture to be treasured for the pinnacle of human achievements that they are, and not to be buried under the swill of multi-culturalist attempts to displace them with dubious achievements simply because they are non-Western as has become rampant in some academic and artistic circles. We call to each individual to seek human greatness wherever it can be found, from the vaults of history and from the talented producers of the present, and to deride the trendy shams for the shallow façades that they are. Since Satanism stands for acceptance of Man as an animal, there have often been creators in many past cultures who embraced this insight and explored it in the context of their society, thus Satanists seek out these artistic and philosophical expressions and see them to be the "roots" of our current awareness of our human type.

Satanists see the social structure of humanity as being stratified, thus each person reaches a level commensurate with the development (or lack thereof) of their natural talents. The principle of the survival of the strong is advocated on all levels of society, from allowing an individual to stand or fall to even letting those nations that cannot handle themselves take the consequences of this inability. Any assistance on all levels should be on a "quid pro quo" basis. There would be a concomitant reduction in the world's population as the weak are allowed to experience the consequences of Social Darwinism if this rational and just principal were put into operation. Thus has Nature always acted to cleanse and strengthen her children. This is harsh, but that is the way of the world. We embrace reality and do not try to transform it into some utopia that is contrary to the very fabric of existence. Practical application of this doctrine would see the complete cessation of welfare systems, an end to no-strings attached foreign aid and new programs to award and encourage gifted individuals in all fields to pursue personal excellence. A meritocracy would replace the practice of such injustices as affirmative action and other programs designed to punish the able and reward the undeserving. The natural generosity of some of the successful and affluent would not be curtailed, but it would also not be state-mandated.

Satanists also seek to enhance the laws of nature by concentrating on fostering the practice of eugenics. This is not some exotic doctrine hatched in the brains of Third Reich medical madmen. It is the practice of encouraging people of talent and ability to reproduce, to enrich the gene pool from which our species can grow. This was commonly practiced throughout the world as even a text on eugenics endorsed by the Women's Christian Temperance Union proves, until it was given a bad name by Nazi excesses. Until the genetic code is fully manipulable and we can choose the character of our offspring at will, Satanists seek to mate the best with the best. Satanists who know that they can pass on genetic defects would refrain from reproducing. Again, this is a practice that is a personal option, not a governmentally enforced dictate.

Most Satanists are particularly disgusted by the extraordinary level of criminal activity that abounds today, thus they advocate a return to the Roman *Lex Talionis*—let the punishment fit in kind and degree the crime. To achieve this, we would be pleased to see the institution of an elite police force, of men and women in peak physical and mental condition, trained in advanced techniques of crime fighting who would be ably equipped to handle the vermin that make so many of our cities into little more than concrete jungles. Man is by nature a social creature and makes his social contract with his fellows, thus rules of conduct are established to allow maximum freedom for individuals to interact. Disobey those rules and punishment must be swift and sure, and most probably public as well. This does not mean the incarceration of individuals in institutions at the expense of the victims for so-called "rehabilitation." No, these criminals should be put to some use, perhaps as forced labor to even clean up the environment that has so carelessly been soiled under the dominance of Christian spiritual philosophy that sees man as superior to other living creatures with a "God-given right" to abuse them at will. Man is an animal, and must go back to acting like one—not soiling his own lair as only twisted humans do.

The Church of Satan pursues a five-point plan to move society in directions that are considered to be beneficial to Satanists. The first point is the advocacy of general recognition and acceptance of stratification, which is no less than the elimination of egalitarianism wherever it has taken root. Mediocrity shall be identified and despised. The stupid should suffer for their behavior. The truly beautiful and magnificent are to be cherished. Each individual must choose for himself his own aesthetic standards, but we think that there are certain elements of achievement that are undeniable, even if they are not satisfying to everyone. For example, one cannot deny the superior accomplishment inherent in a Beethoven symphony, a Michelangelo sculpture, a da Vinci painting, or a Shakespeare play. Many Satanists are working to create their own citadels of excellence outside of the cultural mainstream and have preserved the worthy from the past and continue to create new works of power to be revealed to those who will be appreciative.

The second point is the enforcement of strict taxation of all churches. This would remove the government sanction of religion and force these parasites to live off of their own members alone, and if they can't, then they will perish as they should. The Church of Satan has never pursued tax-exempt status and challenges all the rest of the world's churches to stand on their own feet. Let us expose the vampiric nature of the organized religions and see if they can cease their parasitism.

Third, we call for the re-establishment of *Lex Talionis* throughout human society. The Judeo-Christian tradition, which exists secularly under the guise of "liberal humanism," has too often exalted the criminal over the victim, taking responsibility away from the wrong-doer with their doctrine of forgiveness. Such thinking is a disgrace towards the ideal of justice. This must stop. Individuals must be held accountable for the consequences of their actions, and not be allowed to scapegoat society, history, or other supposed "outside" influences. It should come as no surprise that many Satanists are part of law enforcement agencies, and that there are a large number of people throughout this and other criminal justice systems who fully agree with Satanic philosophy on this point. If the law is not being enforced, Satanists advocate the practice of seeking personal justice, but you are warned to be fully aware of the consequences of such actions in today's corrupt society. With the present state of affairs, the outcry may yet come to welcome justice back to stay.

Fourth, Satanists advocate a new industry, the development and promotion of artificial human companions. These "humanoids" will be constructed to be as realistic as possible, and available to anyone who can afford one. Recognizing that the human animal often raises himself up through the denigration of another, this would provide a safe outlet for such behavior. Have the lover of your dreams, regardless of your own prowess; every man a king who can purchase his own subject; or contrary-wise, buy the master you wish to serve. Freedom of choice to satisfy your most secret desires with no one to be bothered is now at hand. What could be better for blowing-off the tension that exists throughout our society, and promoting healthier interaction?

Finally we advocate the construction of total environments, technologically up-to-date but theatrically convincing, to be literal pleasure domes and places of amusement and delight. We have seen the beginnings in some of the major theme parks, but let us take them on to the heights depicted in films like *Westworld*. Here you would be able to indulge in whatever environment you can imagine. Recreation of past history would not only be ripe for these constructions, but science fiction and fantasy will provide fertile sources for many of these playgrounds. Resorts of this nature grow more abundant every year.

Would the average person be able to spot a member of the Church of Satan? Since Satanists cover the total spectrum of economic and professional achievement, unless someone is sporting a Sigil of Baphomet medallion, or wearing the Baphomet lapel pin signifying an official representative, you really cannot pin down a Satanist by appearance and behavior alone. In their daily practices, Satanists are individuals who are enjoying their lives in the here and now. They eat what they please, dress as they please, and generally follow whatever life style suits them best, so long as it is within the laws of their country of residence.

There is no requirement for participation in ritual activity. The techniques presented in our literature are for members to make use of as they so desire. Some Satanists enjoy the social atmosphere of group ritual and seek out others for this purpose. Many Satanists find their ritual activity to be very personal and prefer to remain solitary. Either path is acceptable to the Church of Satan. Indeed, there are no rules for frequency of ritual activity. Some traditionally celebrate the equinoxes and solstices as holidays, but of course one's own birthday is the highest Satanic holiday of the year. The ritual process is often used as a cathartic, to cleanse the individual of desires that could turn into compulsions if they remained unfulfilled, thus such practices take the place of therapy. Satanists cherish their individuality and do not try to conform to others' standards of normality. Also, Satanists do not proselytize, so you will not find yourself approached by someone in a black cloak waving tracts in your face. We have our literature readily available, and should some find the philosophy to be to their liking they may approach us to

THE SATANIC SCRIPTURES

investigate the possibility of affiliation (www.churchofsatan. com). The general public would probably be surprised to find that they have been interacting with Satanists for many years, and that these Satanists will be some of the most interesting, fair, trustworthy, and enjoyable people that they know.

The world, when more fully permeated by the primary values of Satanism, will provide a challenging environment wherein you can achieve much, or little, based on the level of input you can muster and the extent of your natural abilities. Yes, this is frightening to the masses wishing to sit back and be herded from one media-hyped product to the next. Our worldview challenges you to think, and do something with those thoughts! As ultimate realists, we do not expect a large percentage of the human population to have the energy and discipline needed to excel, nor would a Satanic society attempt to force people to do that which is beyond their capabilities—but we will not refrain from judging these people by our standards. Those who wish to lead a drugged existence, whether the addictive element is chemical or media, shall be recognized for the slaves that they are and held in contempt. They can continue their self-destructive paths if so desired, but they shall not be allowed to hold back those who want to achieve greatness.

Don't worry, you who have been fooled into believing the paper tiger displayed by today's media; we Satanists aren't after your children, for they are probably as hopelessly mediocre as their parents. But we are moving the world towards a state wherein the freeloaders will either work or starve, and the parasites will be removed to wither and die. So, you need only fear real Satanism if you are a criminal, a parasite, or a wastrel. Are *you* afraid?

# WE ARE LEGION

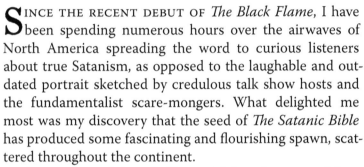

Since the recent debut of *The Black Flame*, I have been spending numerous hours over the airwaves of North America spreading the word to curious listeners about true Satanism, as opposed to the laughable and outdated portrait sketched by credulous talk show hosts and the fundamentalist scare-mongers. What delighted me most was my discovery that the seed of *The Satanic Bible* has produced some fascinating and flourishing spawn, scattered throughout the continent.

I encountered the rabidly stupid, but also many fellow travelers who appreciated, often agreed with and even embraced our philosophy of rational self-interest. True to form, the most Satanic individuals who called in to chat did so during late night shows. Yes, we Satanists *are* the men in black, vampires and werewolves that raven in the night.

With tongue in cheek, I deflected the rumors that the Satanic research labs deep beneath the Pentagon are even now perfecting the virus that will make stupidity painful to the perpetrator. Would that their efforts could be hurried.

I witnessed the evidence that there is a diversity among our kind that is a sure sign of the health of our ever-growing movement. Satanism promotes the myriad personal pathways developed by the compleat Satanists who have risen above the herd of sheeple. The Satanist sees himself as different, experiences a sense of alienation from those surrounding him. This is the first step of individuation. One first looks to his neighbors and questions the very foundations of their values. The true Satanic question is "Why?" Are you a person of self-made identity, or have you simply absorbed what is being hawked in the cultural market place? Are you self-aware? Do you feel proud that you are not embraced by the teeming masses? How do you view those people whom you encounter in your daily existence who are also in some sense outcast?

The true Satanist will deal with people as individuals, eschewing collectivist doctrines such as racism. Satanists do not simply tolerate the freaks and misfits of society, they seek them out to gain wisdom from their fellow eccentrics. We are truly lone wolves, howling our songs of *noir* melancholy in the night. But sometimes we choose to run in packs. We might even try to shake up the complacency of those who thoughtlessly embrace consensus-reality by demonstrating that there is far more in Hell and on Earth than could ever be dreamt of in their philosophies.

And sometimes we find those feral children, wolflings who are abandoned because their alien natures are sensed by others who reject them. They have yet to comprehend their uniqueness, and we embrace these fellow children of the night, lighting their way along the Left-Hand Path with the Black Flame. What wonders we have to show you, who would cast off your mantle of self-righteousness to enfold yourself in the cloak of Luciferian understanding. These heights are not for the timid. Do you dare to look into the black, smoking mirror of Tezcatlipoca? Care to join us?

# Alienation

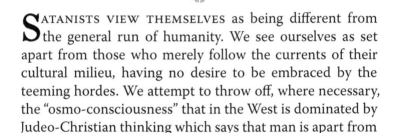

Satanists view themselves as being different from the general run of humanity. We see ourselves as set apart from those who merely follow the currents of their cultural milieu, having no desire to be embraced by the teeming hordes. We attempt to throw off, where necessary, the "osmo-consciousness" that in the West is dominated by Judeo-Christian thinking which says that man is apart from the natural world and should purge himself of the material to embrace the spiritual.

Balderdash! Satanists embrace the fleshly, are at one with their animal nature and work to recapture the beast within that has been sterilized by those who hate themselves. One of the root causes that have led to the proliferation of anti-carnal thinking is the fact that there are two types of humans, and one type has come to dominate through sheer numbers. There are those who feel at one with themselves, comfortable with their emotions and their reason, finding no contradictions between their thoughts and feelings, which we can call the Carnal type. The other strain feels at war with itself, suffering from a profound personal disharmony of mind vs. emotions, body vs. soul, and a longing for a heaven and a rejection of earthly life—the Ethereal type.

It is this second type that feels a self-alienation that is the cause for self-hatred, leading to disgust for the body which is constantly being thwarted in its natural desires. This Ethereal impulse is behind the major spiritual religions that have spread their loathing for life over our globe. The Carnal individuals have difficulty perceiving what the Ethereal wishes to purge from himself. Indeed, the Carnals are usually too busy enjoying life to worry about such illusory concerns. But to the Ethereal, this is a very tangible dichotomy, one that must be remedied. Often they employ asceticism to rid themselves of fleshly impurities, stifling any pleasure they feel. Ultimately this results in universal masochism, a reveling in the agony of "purification." Since the Carnal types can't even begin to split themselves in this fashion, the Ethereal sees them as incurably impure and will often exterminate such individuals to rid themselves of reminders of what they cannot be: harmoniously in tune with their nature as living beings.

The Ethereals won a significant victory with the overwhelming of the West by Christianity. This is the broadly accepted outlook promoted by many religions and philosophies held up as the standard for human behavior. The Satanist is naturally of the Carnal type, and finds himself completely at odds with this prevailing value system, thus he is alienated from the cultural norm. This is a healthy form of detachment leading to a strong sense of Ego and the growth of individualism. The Ethereal is estranged from himself, a truly dangerous and destructive alienation that has caused centuries of pain and devastation. The Ethereal types when governing often advocate genocide against the Carnals, because they cannot stand to see individuals who live in joy, rather than the constant agony they experience.

The time is now for the re-emergence and triumph of the Carnal type. We have unleashed the fleshly beast that will tear the wizened flesh of those who feel at odds with the natural order. Their desiccated and poisoned tissues will be buried with the other refuse whose decomposition will provide fertilizer for the new generations of integrated, self-aware and self-embracing humans. Nature *will* claim its victory over those who would deny it.

# A Primer
# for Fledgling
# Misanthropologists

Satanists are pragmatists, who do their best to see the world around them in as unclouded a manner as is possible; we call that "undefiled wisdom." Then we use this understanding to make the best from life for ourselves as well as those whom we cherish. Being filled with disgust at the spectacle of the milling hordes that cover our lovely globe and soil it with their presence, we try to minimize our contact with those gullible denizens whom we call "the herd." Human life, in and of itself, is *not* considered valuable; it is the worth of *particular* humans that matters to the Satanist. Most people go about their middling ways and thus rate only indifference, while we are engaged with those who *truly* matter to us: the worthy and the accomplished. Misanthropy is thus the basis for a Satanic lifestyle. Since we generally feel that just about everything on this planet is ruined by an over-abundance of people, we who study the beast called Man call ourselves, with a nod and a wink, "misanthropologists." I salute a colleague, Carl Abrahamsson, who travels the word to explore various cultures, as he first used that term to describe his activities.

From the Satanist's perspective, an important characteristic of our species can be visualized in the shape of a pyramid. We see a small capstone at the top defining those few individuals who have the ability to create. These precious beings synthesize a unique combination of select ideas in chosen fields of human endeavor, or define some principles that reveal a deeper understanding of the landscape of existence and thus enrich the rest of the species. They move the world of human society. Charting the achievements of these individuals is often considered a depiction of a civilization's "progress." Below this rather small pinnacle is a far larger trapezoidal region that includes those people who have the ability to produce something. These are the folk who apply the breakthroughs of the creators. They sustain a civilization. The great mass of the pyramid below is the vast majority of the human race, people who can do naught but believe in what they are handed. They are the marching morons who flow with the current of their social reality, who do naught to affect it, and who are an ocean whose tides are generated by the gravitational efforts of those in the strata above them.

It is a fact gleaned from observation that most members of the species *homo sapiens* are incapable of looking at the world with anything that approximates a clear perception of its actuality. There is an objective reality, a totality of all that exists, but each individual's worldview is a subjective reality, a unique subset. This perspective is based on perceptions colored entirely by an individual's axiomatic structure of concepts. That foundation is the means through which these perceptions are organized. Religion or philosophy is thus what provides that bottom-line context for the synthesized perceptions of each person, whether it is consciously determined or simply absorbed through one's culture as an "osmo-consciousness."

Throughout human history, the dominant cultures have always found a means for controlling their populace. In the West, Christianity has occupied a great deal of time as one means for control. Its ideologues successfully duped the faithful into accepting the idea that their natural impulses were sinful to God (whom they conveniently couldn't contact for verification), and that the Church was needed to cleanse folk of what they can't help doing (they're *all* sinners) in preparation for some mythical afterlife which was guaranteed to be better than the one through which they currently suffered. This swindle worked, since life for most was, as has been said, generally rather miserable, brutish, and short.

Today, technology devised by our creators and manufactured by our producers has made this con game irrelevant. So, our corporate culture has found a new means for control. The proles have been taught that they are all individuals, unique and precious, and that it is their right to be free. As they nod their heads in unison the corporate hucksters set up their various wares, which are then peddled to these sheep. The masses rush to mortgage their lives to purchase pre-packaged symbols, which supposedly proclaim their freedom and individuality to the rest of the herd. Those who are truly aware laugh at the spectacle of people who actually think that they have evolved to be unique by purchasing a particular brand of running shoes or a sports utility vehicle. And it is fascinating to note that those two particular products are similar in design. They are bought by people who neither run, nor drive in terrains that require such means of transport. Consumerism is today just as powerful a device for enslavement as was Christianity. Nothing has really changed.

That plebians have a capacity for swallowing-whole myriad concepts without factual basis is what makes them so easily manipulated. It is their inability to check the doled-out illusions against reality that allows this to continue. All that a would-be leader needs to do is to tell his intended followers that they are somehow special, "elect," unique, or superior, and they will gleefully accept these false compliments. The leader simply tells the flock that they are elite, and points out some manifest destiny of his own choosing, and the sheep sprint to the slaughter. Never underestimate people's tendency to identify with something deemed superior by an authority figure in an attempt at self-elevation. Xenophobia is almost always the rule. Promoting the fear and denigration of alien societies serves leaders as an easy technique for herd unification.

There are also those who do have some native spark of brightness, but who will never be considered by their peers to be the acme of our species. They often ponder about the uniquely efficacious few in history, misidentify themselves with them, and then somehow think that they too ought to be treated as are these rare gems of our species. Our current culture is founded on such narcissism, and the extreme forms of self-deification now practiced by the mediocre have reached an astonishing level. The capacity for self-delusion in those with moderate talents and abilities is boundless. There is no self-evaluation present in this type, who enshrines each piddling thought as if it were the unified field theory. The rigorous self-criticism of the true creator is alien to these vacuoles, who generate nothing but excreta, yet think it gold, demanding your participation in maintaining their illusion. This is another symptom of the general masses' tendency to eschew discrimination and thus view the world from an idealistic, irrational point of view.

Idealism is one of the most dangerous practices to be found in our kind. It is a projection upon reality of an illusory "ought to be," which in many prevents acknowledgment of what actually "IS." This practice has most often been fostered by religions, which create systems of morality in an effort to make their particular "ought" a reality. They then must exterminate any who don't share allegiance to this paradigm, as they shatter the illusion of its "truth" by following a very different "ought" of their own. Curiously, human factions have distilled these "oughts" into symbols, and fight and die for the cloth versions of these icons called flags. The Satanist sees the act of dying for a symbol as a ludicrous waste of life.

Looking through history's annals, one can amply prove that blind idealism is the root cause of the slaughter of millions, as one group works to force another to accept its illusory formulations for their vision of what ought to be. This is what leads me to offer a principal that will help you to predict the outcome in all arenas of human competition: Might is Right.

This simple sentence is actually an equation, which stands for an axiomatic principle used for understanding the nature of human social interactions. Note that this is not a dictum that has any effect on the nature of objective reality. It is not pertinent to the inorganic, rather, it is a measure of forces and vectors found in the exchanges between members of our species, from the level of one-on-one up to that of nation versus nation. In the province of human interactions, it is inexorably true and cannot be avoided. So, to be a master in the realm of human society, it is required that one flow along with this principle. The idealistic fools may scream that it is not fair, but then, we Satanists know that justice is relative and only lasts as long as one has the power to maintain it, either personally or through an alliance with those who do. There is no exterior, superior "Big Daddy," or Karmic Laws, or "Balancer of the Scales" to maintain some objective standard in the games played on this small planet. Nobody is looking out for you, and Lady Luck is not going to drop by to make your number come up. We're on our own and unless we grasp and apply these house rules, we'll leave this joint with our pockets empty and asses reamed.

So let us examine the implications of this elegant little

A PRIMER FOR FLEDGLING MISANTHROPOLOGISTS

principle. We have two terms on the opposite sides of a verbal "equals" sign. "Might" is the first. Seems obvious. Does it refer to sheer brute force? Only to those with a simplistic point of view. What "Might" signifies, in this context of human interactions, is the position of power—and thus control—for the situation under analysis. In some contexts, the power position could be attained through brute force. But the rarity of this might shock the armchair theoretician.

Here's an example: you encounter a thug in an isolated location, both of you are unarmed, and all other factors are equal (and we know equality is but a myth found only in hypothetical situations). Both of you have the same level of fighting skills, endurance, and intelligence. The only element which we grant to be unequal is the strength of the opponents. Then, brute strength may be the deciding component in the outcome of this encounter. But, even in such a simple situation, the observer will note that there are quite a few factors that must be considered to determine who truly is in the position of power—who has the "Might." Only the naïve think such a determination is obvious.

In more elaborate social situations assessing the many factors that determine who indeed has the "Might" becomes rather a daunting task. Consider the complexities inherent in the event that one special interest group might be opposing another, or in an instance of intertribal warfare, or when one nation might come into conflict with another. However, attempting to see with clarity and accuracy is the lot of those who would understand the true nature of the human animal. We must be diligent and perceptive if we want to retain some modicum of control over our lives.

"Might" could mean superior weaponry, a larger body of armed troops, a better-trained corps of soldiers. It could also mean a populace who is more dogged in resisting attack, having an uncompromising will, or simply being so numerous that the aggressor cannot prevail against such a mass of animal bodies. And this barely scratches the surface of the many elements that are involved in human interactions on a societal level involving the elements of force. We haven't even begun to examine the levels of power inherent in cultures themselves, and the living ideas in them that can overwhelm other cultures that might seem to have superior military power.

Consider this: A well-armed man carrying grenades and an assault rifle is in the depths of a swamp. He wades through the muck in which there live hundreds of thousands of tiny leeches. One leech is clearly not a match for our soldier who doesn't even need to avail himself of his exotic weaponry—his mere fingers can make him the victor. Holding his gun overhead, he proceeds through the neck-deep ooze. Once he emerges and then soon stumbles in a weakened condition, he begins to strip his clothes from his body and finds that thousands of tenacious mouths are now draining him of his very life's blood. He tears them from himself, stomping them to death in his fury, but the wounds continue to bleed because of the anti-coagulant employed by the small feasters. He notes, as his consciousness fades, that he is now too weak to rip the rest of them from himself. He has been vanquished. Groups of humans can be like these leeches in having the ability to overwhelm what looks to be a superior aggressor. The "Might" in this encounter belongs to those little eager leeches, and they were merely trying to assert their view of what is "Right"—their individual nourishment.

And that brings us to the second half of the equation, the term "Right." "Right" in this context does not mean, "True," which I'd define as being wholly consistent with objective reality. "Right" simply means the subjective outcome desired by each of the participants in the conflict which is under observation. "Right" is a matter of value judgment, not of determining objective facts. Naturally, most humans would like to think that their value judgments really should be seen as being objectively factual, and many religions and political organizations do claim that such is the case.

We Satanists are well aware that such things are mere human convention, dependent upon culture and practice, not objective reality. We understand that all human values are subjective. They are based on each individual's axiomatic premises, his bottom-line concepts for his view of the universe and his place in it. Some claim these to be objective, but that is vanity, or fanaticism. From this foundation arises the person's hierarchy of values. It doesn't matter if people don't understand the "mechanics" of this process—most of them don't—but this is precisely how it works, and it is as unavoidable as the laws of physics.

So it becomes quite clear that the "Right" in this equation is determined by the desires of each of the human participants. It is their ideal, their "Is-To-Be."

Of what significance is this for Satanists? Knowing this unvarnished truth about the human species, the Satanist makes it his business to be acutely aware of the balance of power in any situation in which he is engaged. He must also ascertain to the best of his ability the REAL agendas of the participants—their actual desired outcomes, not merely their stated aims. He must see the subtleties and note the delicacies in the "war dance" controlled by this equation. If he can see the essence of the situation—to whom belongs the "Might"—he will then be in a position to make certain that his notion of "Right" will be the one favored by the outcome, providing that he can place himself in the position of being the bearer, or controller, of this "Might." The Satanist knows that the truly strong always triumph over that which is objectively weaker (taking ALL factors into account) and that the clever have the ability to rule the strong. As Satanists, we always choose to be counted among the clever. Here endeth the lesson.

# The Tide Turns

WE HAVE SEEN in the latter months of 1993 a trend on the part of academics, finally picked up by the media, towards refutation of the contemporary urban legend of "Satanic Ritual Abuse" which has been the foundation of entire "consultation" and "therapy" industries. The idiot fundamentalist effort to convince people that a worldwide conspiracy exists—to breed babies from dysfunctional women, spread drugs, pornography, and snuff films in an effort to dominate the globe—is finally being perceived to be a laughable fantasy. How long will it be until the McMartin trial joins the Salem debacle as a symbol of the American "justice" system gone wrong?

Yet during the entire hoohah, real Satanists have been untouched by this "witch hunt." Instead, children of Christian parents have come under the influence of their pastors and therapists and have accused family members and friends of being Satanists, often ruining their lives. And who can ignore the continuing media-touted scandal of child molestation perpetrated by Christian clergymen? This is all so well-deserved. Behold the utter desperation of Christianity in its last gasp to find an enemy that can frighten the sheep into their churches. This enemy is but a projection of their *own* misdeeds that stem from the heart of their anti-life creed. Let them feed on themselves, as followers of the flaccid Nazarene should.

Church of Satan spokespersons have been going on talk-shows for years, debunking this hysteria, yet now that "official" sources are coming to their senses does anyone look to us and say, "Gee, you were right all along?" Of course not. We were invited on these shows not as sources of truth, but as freaks, "real live Satanists" at whom the proles could gawk. However, we did not shrink from articulating the unvarnished truth of our beliefs which many label as brutal, fascist, animalistic. If people want to fear us, then let them fear us for the *correct* reasons. We made this effort so that there would be an accurate presentation of our beliefs, especially should the time come when we could face legal difficulties because of our affiliations.

The real danger lies in the remaining influence of this mythology on law enforcement agencies. Tax dollars are still being wasted on seminars run by self-proclaimed experts (often retired, moonlighting, or would-be law officers of a decidedly Christian slant) who spread completely bogus information. The gullible local cops, wowed by jargon-laden presentations, swallow this stuff whole as it comes from apparent "experts" and thus they help spread a panic by seeing signs of the Devil's work in minor and typical crimes. Just recently I was called in to examine evidence that "Satanic cult activity" was the basis for vandalism of a house up for sale that had remained vacant for about a year. Prior to examining the site, I was told that certain Satanic graffiti and an inverted cross had been found, proof positive that this had been done by a local cult.

When I got to the house, an old structure that is fairly isolated, I examined every room and the entire grounds. What I found was an old mattress in the living room, with a collapsed card table next to it as well as two candles—one green, one pink. A small gold cross pendant was hung on the edge of the table, which seemed to have been removed by the wearer before going to sleep on the aforementioned mattress. The cross had sharp edges, but was not inverted. The only graffiti were various slogans such as "Nicole loves Mark" (if there is hidden Satanic significance, it escapes me). And in an upstairs room, once belonging to a child as evidenced by the garish sports-figure wall paper, there was a copy of the Simon *Necronomicon* and a Ouija board. We all know that this paraphernalia is not part of authentic Satanic ritual.

Outdoors, the squatters had taken the lawn mower from the garage and cut a path through the overgrown grass to a section of the yard surrounded by pine trees. Here they mowed out a roughly circular patch, about eight feet in diameter, in which to sunbathe. There were no signs of ritualistic activity in this circle. So, here was, at most, teenage dabbler stuff, but hardly evidence of a cult. This sort of incident has been repeated across the nation and has been inflated by the overactive imaginations of the unworldly (often those with Christian beliefs) into evidence for a broad-based conspiracy. I don't particularly care about the paranoid fantasies of the dysfunctional, but when members of the police are convinced that there are Satanists with nefarious plans lurking under the beds of innocent Americans, that is when we must insistently stand up and tell the truth about our beliefs. And so we have been doing.

I have been active in recent months as a consultant and expert witness regarding the practice of Satanism in cases concerning the religious rights of prisoners—individuals who have become members of the Church of Satan after their incarceration. Numerous prisons are very "liberal" where religious observances are concerned and some even have multi-million dollar complexes to serve the needs of their inmate populations, yet when it comes to allowing

Satanists to ritualize, or even have their literature, there has been resistance from some institutional authorities. We have been making headway in this area by demonstrating our credentials as a legally recognized religious organization whose existence must be tolerated along with the other minority religions permitted. We do not seek special treatment for these incarcerated Satanists, simply that they be given equal treatment concerning religious practices. Also, we assist only those inmates who have joined our organization and professed Satanism that is consistent with our philosophy.

It has never been the goal of the Church of Satan to take its place among the other world religions, with dutiful followers and neatly labeled congregations. No, Satanism will permeate the societies of the globe as a secular lifestyle. Indeed, Satanism *has* penetrated the culture in many ways, and obvious imagery has particularly conquered the heavy metal world. Yet our religion is often not taken seriously. This can be used as a strength, for Satanists continue to influence larger cultural movement without being recognized as such, except by the astute—and some of our Christian enemies *do* know for what we really stand.

We do *not* intend to turn the vast insensate masses into Satanists. The masses will do as always and follow their inertia. However, in the growing Satanic Age, we shall find desired situations and objects a bit more easily obtainable, and have direct recourse to justice. In the interim, we will not be treated with any less respect than other religions.

While the Christians have been tilting at straw men, we have continued to extend our influence through society. We have defended real Satanism and our literature is widely available so that our fellows may discover the name that best describes them. Meanwhile, the altruist/egalitarians have continued to force situations into extremes so that even the dullard couch potatoes have come to see the error of this doctrine—*reductio ad absurdum* works again!

As always, we remain aloof from the hubbub with our cherished objects and individuals, and when the time comes we *push* and direct the currents as we think they should naturally go. Our victory is assured as we *are* in harmony with Nature—avatars of the Universe's order. We demand that those who are hired to administer justice, thus acting as agents of the state, must leave their religious prejudices at home. Not for nothing did our Satanic Founding Fathers create a Constitution that demands a separation of church and state.

So enjoy the ringside Colosseum seats and the spectacle of Christians being thrown to Christians, but keep an eye on those credulous constables. As our influence continues, we will see real order based on Natural law, not the criminal-favoring morass enshrined in today's "justice" system. And don't be surprised if some of those men and women in blue, who aren't the least bit gullible, put on Baphomets when their badges come off.

# Apocalypse Now

I N 1990 I SPENT SOME TIME with the media taping a two-hour version of *Cristina* in Los Angeles and chatting on the airwaves with Denver evangelist Bob Larson—Magistra Blanche Barton did the show the prior day. One particular point presented itself to me in crystal clarity: the fact that we are truly in the "end times," though things are not going according to white light prophecy. Christianity, now in its last gasp, is like a star about to end its existence, swollen with the consumption of the fuel that had kept it going. No longer the arbiter of Western thinking, it has been replaced by the new God, Television, which holds most of the herd in the thrall of its hypnotic single eye. Today's true believers are "videodrones."

As the new millennium draws near, we see about us the signs of a world teetering on the brink of vast changes. The old order has become a chaos of factions and fanaticism, no longer capable of meeting the demands of a globe festering with more humans than can be comfortably supported, many of whom are simply parasites fattening on the blood of the producers and achievers. The Earth is subject to natural laws and the rule of Nature is both just and harsh. The beast is awakening, throwing off two thousand years of slumber to once again clear the dross and re-establish the rule of fang and claw. Fenris' chains have been shattered and his jaws shall crush the feeble crucifix to splinters.

The Christian hysteria at their continuing loss of power has in the past decade fastened on Satanism as a scapegoat, bringing a remarkable return to the same tactics used in the late 1400's with the publication of the *Malleus Maleficarum*. "Official" statements create a popular picture of "evil" Satanists who are depicted as reversed Christians involved with worshipping the Devil, committing sacrifices (human or other) and promoting the use of drugs to enslave people to their cause. But things have changed since those dim and blood-drenched times.

Satanists now exist *for real*, and we talk back. The Church of Satan demonstrates a rational philosophy consistent with Man's nature, making Satanists truly dangerous to those who would enslave one with guilt for following his natural inclinations. We have exposed the so-called "prince of peace" as the agent of decay, through his championing of the weak at the expense of the strong. The pendulum is now swinging in the opposite direction. *Ragnarök* is witnessing an influx of extremism to work towards the re-establishment of meritocracy. Satanists are the accusers, not passive straw men used to frighten the stray sheep back into the fold.

The bloated star of Christianity is about to implode, forming a black hole of vileness sucking down into its depths the human refuse that has held back the evolution of our species. As James Blish said in his novel *Black Easter* regarding Biblical prophecy, "Each of the opposing sides in any war always predicts victory. They cannot both be right. It is the final battle that counts, not the propaganda." The rules of the earth are on our side. We are already the victors for they, and their God, are dead.

# I Am The Light
# and The Way

IT WAS INEVITABLE. For this generation, to whom the cathode ray tube is their monolithic deity, the time had to come for the birth of a savior. They all inhabit a tacitly accepted Christian frame of reference, so they are the ones who have this need for being saved. And lo, the virgin mother of the desktop PC was visited by the holy spirit of online communication and thus was delivered unto the herd the incarnation of their deity: The Internet. It is their God made flesh. They have forsaken worldly things for a virtual Heaven, here and now, but isolated from the abundance of the earth.

Of course, that leaves actual reality up for grabs for those of us who won't settle for ersatz existence. Now, the masses can sit at home, bathed in the glow from their monitor screens, while their hands work their keyboards, their mice, their trackballs, and their own nether regions. It keeps them out of our way. What more could we ask for?

And so the evolution of world society continues. All the world was a stage—and now it is but a monitor screen. Sets, costumes and performers have been replaced by an endless dance of glowing pixels. The threat of actually encountering someone, of being judged for what you are as they see you, has been subverted into allowing individuals to simply present masks-of-choice via whatever they choose to type or post from the safety of their keyboards. The portal to this cyberspace is a filter through which one sends that which is intended to be a simulacrum of oneself. Some quite consciously edit their postings to intentionally create one or several personae. Others are more guileless and just spew whatever comes to mind and fingers, but erroneously think that this is somehow a complete and honest representation of themselves. Overall, they who previously sat passively in front of their God Tube, worshipping whosoever appeared upon the screen as a sanctified member of the pantheon, can now actually appear upon the screens of other people's computers—they've found a means for self-deification! The kingdom of Heaven has been opened unto them!

But, as as those of us with some perspective can see, this is an arena which does not require anything to back up what is presented. Everyone has the same soapbox, the brain surgeon will have a soda-jerk telling him how to do his job. All are reduced to the same level—democracy in its vilest form as mob rule. Everyone here looms small on the PC monitor.

In the past, were one to produce an epic film, a cast of thousands was required. The few stars were supported by thousands of extras who filled-up the screen bringing spectacle. In films today, the milling throngs are now generated in computers with algorithmic programs controlling their appearance of individuality. Thus it has become with this virtual timid new world of the human species. Those who people the screen as mere set decorations do so through the virtual reality of their online activity, and they are little more, in the larger scheme of things, than those computer generated filler-folk.

Dr. LaVey predicted a new industry would arise for the creation and sale of artificial human companions. But being Epicurean he perhaps solipsistically projected too much of his own standards upon the human species. He thought that they would need, as he did, the tangible figures of other beings to satisfy their desires. He thought they'd need the tactile, the olfactory, the actual physical presence of a body co-existing in the same space. Ah, he gave them too much credit for taste. The standards of the herd are far lower. For them, they don't even need the visual stimulation of actual pornographic images, either moving or still. No, the simple misspelled words ephemerally flashing across their monitor screens are enough to give them satisfaction. Their common denominator, the ultimate herd wallowing point, is the chat room. Their artificial human companions are what passes before them on their screens. That some of this material actually comes from other living human beings is not relevant, as the caliber of the minds creating this "content" are less than that of software which currently can assist a writer to elaborate his own attempts at fiction.

Like other diversions embraced by the herd, we avoid this like the plague. We Satanists note that this "savior" is a diabolical device that shows the workings of stratification. It has seduced the herd and, like our thoughts concerning that "other savior," our response is to "just say no." Satanists won't settle for only interacting with people via words on a screen. We demand flesh and blood, and smell, taste, and touch. We are carnal animals and we will not settle for less.

For the Satanic entrepreneur, I advise you to aim low. Give the crowd the minimum, but just package it as something new and they'll beat your door down to get some. Those of us who use software know that we are always being hawked some upgrade, but those who pay attention have seen that often the new versions are actually less useful than the predecessors (though they are bloated, needing more memory, and as the public knows—"bigger is better!"). You can't go wrong with our current consumer society, as the throngs always want the "new and improved," demanding it, even. As always, the streets are paved with gold for those who know what vacuum lies in the hearts of men.

Some futurists postulate that complex virtual reality, such that it really fools the senses, will be the next immediate lure to be wrought by technology. I think they are wrong. The masses just aren't that discriminating. True visionary fetishists, techno-geeks, who want to create believable fantasy worlds will eventually develop the technology for this. The "holodecks" of Gene Roddenberry are certainly their Is-To-Be, and something like that may eventually come about due to such devout fantasists. But it won't get the masses' attention until it is cheap to purchase and easy to use. Now it is high-end expense wise, and very crude. But, should it be as common as the television or the PC, it will then be embraced. And of course, the first thing it will be used for is sexual gratification! And this too will be a boon for these many pent up folks who haven't evolved the social skills to get laid on a regular basis, and who do not fully enjoy the satisfaction of self-love. It will provide the means for a catharsis without them having to bother anyone else. We Satanists applaud, and promote, anything that keeps the herd occupied and out of our hair. The world is a beautiful place, once one subtracts a substantial amount of the human populace, so by essentially setting up the means for them to choose to imprison themselves in a virtual world that is at their fingertips in their own homes, we thus are doing the entire ecosystem of the globe a great service.

The rise of the virtual existence also has a bearing on the Church of Satan itself. We spawned a movement, filled with actual people, called Satanism. But now the Church itself stands above and apart from that movement, as many people are currently attracted to parts of our philosophy and symbolism yet do not grasp the integrated totality of our core ideas. They are generally desperate folk, seeking self-definition and satisfaction in a world in which they are ill-equipped for survival. They think they are instant supermen after reading but a few essays online. They no longer even have the attention span to read *The Satanic Bible* in its entirety, pithy as that volume is. But they do serve a purpose in our plan. Out there online, these many play the role of background extras filling up space like a gaggle wearing togas to populate a set of the Roman Colosseum. We can leverage that to our advantage, being masters of the art of misdirection. The real stars of the show will be on the sandy floor of the arena itself, or placed in the Emperor's private box, molding the emotions and providing the concepts that will inspire and motivate the attentions of this black-garbed mob. Of course, we know such herds are fickle, and will change their allegiance when the next trend is presented to them. So be it. We will be stronger still once this tide has receded. The authentic Satanists will endure while the extras move on to some other show.

The Church itself will remain the casting office for those who will be the stars of this ongoing show. Our members will be the characters who have more than just a walk-on part. Discrimination will always be our guiding principle. Those proud players with red cards shall be the productive few who get top billing. Our principles will be the script for the evolution of the movement, for anyone who claims to be a Satanist must now define himself in relation to our philosophy. Whether he embraces it or rejects it, we are the bottom line.

So dear Satanist, the world will be free for you to walk at will, to enjoy in all of its sensual reality. The masses will be deep in Holy Communion with their electronic messiahs, the glow from the screen lighting up their faces with a halo of beatitude. May their Lord's peace be with them.

# On the First
# Anniversary of 9/11

TODAY IS A DAY OF REMEMBRANCE. Many individuals are recalling relatives and friends who were murdered by terrorists a year ago today in the attacks on the Pentagon and the World Trade Center. Satanists understand and deeply empathize with their grief, as undeserved loss of life is a tragic part of human existence that can touch us all. Our hearts are with them.

However, we also remember something of greater significance. We understand that the source of this day of mourning is the conviction, held by fundamentalist fanatics, that any act of violence against those who do not share their devotion is championed by their God. The events of 9/11 are absolute proof of the danger of such spiritual belief systems, which maintain that only certain individuals have a direct connection to a deity, and that any who do not agree with their "truth" are to be seen as less-than-human, a threat to their "faith" which supernaturally sanctions their extermination.

While the sanctimonious of many spiritual religions will enter their sacred spaces today, thanking their God or Gods for acts of heroism performed by valiant individuals in response to that tragedy, they will smugly forget that their God did nothing to prevent these human-initiated disasters. Responsibility for what they deem to be good is assigned to their deity, while responsibility for what is deemed evil must, in their limited view, originate elsewhere, and probably from those holding different beliefs. They will fail to see that such a perspective is one shared by the terrorists. More significant than that, these people will also fail to recall that, over the centuries, far more people have been slaughtered by the followers of spiritual religions—including their own—than were killed by the Islamic terrorists on September 11 of 2001. There is blood on the hands of the ancestors of those who pray in their sanctuaries today, and that is a fact they should appreciate as fully as do we. Millions have died because fanatical worshippers refused to allow that values other than their own might have validity for those who hold them.

We Satanists, as well as others who grasp the importance of maintaining a secular society which allows for diversity of belief and non-belief, will recall this grim truth today. Fundamentalist fanatics, regardless of which deity they worship, are the greatest threat to human freedom in our civilization. September 11$^{th}$ should be sustained as a worldwide memorial to their victims, past and present. Remember this day in fury. Bow not your heads in prayerful attitude, but raise your chins in defiance. Hear the brazen clangor of the funerary bell. It shatters complacence, serving as memorial and as tocsin. We shall not forgive nor shall we forget.

# Victors and Victims: From West Memphis to Columbine

W̲E ARE NOT AS THEY ARE.

Satanists see themselves as being aliens when compared to what we perceive to be a herd of vapid simians who surround us. Whether they believe in Jesus or not, they are "Christers" to us. I'm not talking about those casual Catholics and Protestants, many of whom really only have their religion because it is passed along by their parents. I'm talking about those who have "personal relationships with God and Jesus," who really feel that they are soiled by sin and need to be "saved." These creatures are empty at heart, and seek an outside source to vampirize as they attempt to ease the perpetual pain of their existence. This type is typically found amongst the "born-again," but they don't always bear this label. They are, by our standards, "things" whom evidence shows have often previously tried to ease their life-pain with drug addiction, violence against human and non-human animals, and usually have lived for a time not by productive effort, but by crime. They are motivated by hatred for all who have joy in their lives, and, now that they are "Jesus-jockeys" riding on the back of their mythical savior, they consider themselves to be "elect" and superior to the rest, with their constant pain a testament to their elevated status.

In truth, it is we who are natural and they who are

alienated from Nature itself. And they too sense that we are different. And they hate us for it. We want to keep away from them, to be free to live in the pursuit of the wondrous indulgences of mind and body that our one and only life can hold for us. They hate us for our capacity to experience these pleasures, preferring to think that they will someday experience something akin to our joy, but only after life has ended. For them, life is not precious, as they believe their true awakening will come *post mortem*. They long for death to complete themselves. They also can see how much we love our lives, and so they want to take that away from us, using whatever means they have.

In the past, this hatred was empowered by the alliance of the state with organized Christianity. The two worked mailed-fist-in-velvet-glove as ecclesiastical and secular authorities cooperated to crush those of a Dionysian caste. The life-haters sought out any who had that spark burning brightly within, and in the end the vital ones were often tortured and murdered. Enough of our kind were sufficiently savvy to escape their attentions, but this war was waged by these living dead with the goal of making everyone else's life a misery equal to the one they experience.

Who won?

The Christians, as they killed thousands, but we gain some consolation from the fact that, in their lust for death, they accused many of their own and consigned them to the rack and flames.

Today you might ask: "How have things changed?" The answer, gentle Satanist, is that the means are different, but the motivation is the same and still pervasive. The institutional church has now been severed from the state, and it may no longer confiscate property and execute those it deems as heretical. But the Christian-by-nature is still in the majority today, and they cling together as a dull and brooding herd, ready to lash out at any who evince the Black Flame's lambent spark.

Observe our High Schools, particularly the public ones. I did. I survived the incarceration called "education" and can comment upon it first-hand as could any anthropologist analyzing a barbarian horde under his observation. Most of the students are dull and insipid. They seek to fit in with their peers, to obtain a place in some sort of hierarchy. They find certain types who rise above them: bullies who can physically intimidate them and students who come from wealthy families who socially intimidate them. These are their icons, their leaders—those whom they fear, upon whom they attend with metaphorical bended-knee, often with a sneer emblazoned on their lips, or the *rictus* of terror.

But our herd is not complete. They need another ingredient. The mediocre majority cannot abide being the lowest in their pecking order, though they accept their place as not being top of the food chain. They must also create a caste of untouchables who will be their scapegoats. They need someone to be a visible "bottom of the barrel" that they may safely deride. These will be the students who everyone picks on, who are universally despised, and it is clear who they will be: the ones who are "not like most." The Christian types can literally smell the difference. They mark those who are creative, who are studious. They brand those who do not share their values of slacking off or joining in on team sports. They condemn those who are more perceptive, for such is clearly a danger, and to them, unfathomable to an extent that it appears like magic. These outsiders do not grant the herd's icons sovereignty, so they are seditious to the accepted order. They are lead by their muses, and human icons who have achieved what they admire. Fear is not part of their equation, and their smiles are born of delight, not contempt or terror.

And it has ever been thus. The Christian types engage their deeply woven xenophobia to allow themselves to see these others as "not part of their tribe," and so not to be granted the status of being human by their definition. Most certainly they are denied any shred of empathy, and we know that the Christian type is capable of so little, if any. The Jesus-loving mob always correctly identifies those who are like you, dear Satanist, and they will do all they can to quench your spark. They always have.

Remember.

Columbine is a case in point. In this upscale Colorado high school, violence erupted which was shocking—to some people. Two students, Dylan Klebold and Eric Harris, brought weapons and bombs to their school and began to exterminate students and teachers. When the situation ended, the shocked world focused its attention and it was discovered that this deadly duo were the bright kids. They were more skilled with computers than anyone else in the school, and were even consulted by the faculty for their knowledge. They wrote poetry. They listened to music that was not the kind chosen by the majority of their peers. They dressed differently. They were clearly not "of the body" and were apparently marked by the other students for ostracism and the usual social cruelty so rampant amongst the fledgling herd that is commonplace in the fetid rookeries known as schools.

But here there seems to have been a difference. Klebold and Harris were intelligent, but something drove them to seek desperate recompense for something uncommonly painful to them. We may never know the truth regarding the actual motivations of these two killers, but it is conceivable that this school would be like so many others and supplies a context that provides a plausible explanation.

They may have been tortured at the hands of the

jocks, cheerleaders, and the common herd-spawn whose enshrined heroes gave them the needed approval for their daily performance of "hassle the nerds." As is typical, the mediocre want to be elevated in the eyes of their social "gods," so bullying the outcasts becomes a sort of "sacrifice" by which they hope to earn the favor of their capricious and mediocre idols. That may have been the case here. If it was, these "sacrificial lambs" refused to be lead to the altar of holocausts. Klebold and Harris came from families with money, so they had the wherewithal to purchase firearms and ammunition, as well as the materials needed for explosive devices—which they were smart enough to know how to construct, and, as everyone later discovered, to deploy. So it looks as though the alienated struck back at their oppressors, a lesson that history has taught us is often the consequence when such situations arise.

One thing might have helped defuse the situation: Satanism. If Klebold and Harris had understood real Satanism and chosen to live by it, their vengeance spree would not have happened. Satanism would have taught them that, indeed, they were not like these others, and that such is a positive attribute. Satanism would have taught them that they had only one life, and that their intelligence and talent would take them along paths which would lead to their drinking deeply from that cup which is offered but once. They would have known that Satanists practice *Lex Talionis*, making the punishment fit in *kind* and *degree* the crime. With their superior intelligence, they should have been able to respond to taunting with verbal wit, and made responsible administrators aware of their pain. They would see that the herd cannot help their nature, and that the human who really flows with Nature learns to walk nimbly between these ponderous golems, to snatch the bounties that the dullards will never even see. The Satanist finds a way to prevent the torture, and means to be free to prosper, as living well is truly the best revenge. If these two had a Satanist's perspective, they would not have seen the transitory period of High School as being such an insurmountable burden, and they would not have been compelled to commit heinous acts against innocent victims.

Instead, they saw no way out, and thus made their last stand, and perhaps did so as a gesture for those they thought to be like themselves. They are now icons for the alienated, and an example that sets up an Is-To-Be that desperate others may follow. Satanism can stop it. Satanism sees the futility of martyrdom, as what matter is it becoming a symbol while losing your own life? To the Satanist, his own life is the most precious. Let fools die and become symbols. Self-immolation is "herd think," Christian life's blood—the essence of their creed. And so in this siege, they essentially finally adopted the herd's premise that one's own life can and should be thrown away.

Who won at Columbine? The herd did.

They now felt justified in having feared these outsiders while they lived. The herd then deified those who had been killed by the outsiders, and when one listened to the praise being uttered on talk shows and throughout the media, canonizing the dead by exaggerating their achievements, it showed the true nature of the masses. Remember their faces, their righteousness. They absolved themselves of any guilt, and saw their world-view glorified. They will always continue on this path, as they are convinced that the killing was the fault of those outsiders alone, who embodied ultimate Evil by their difference to the mundane crowd. The possibility that the two killers might have felt that this was their only means for fighting oppression was dismissed. Satanists do not condone these acts, but we aren't so naïve as to be unaware of their possible causes.

I watched *Revelations: Paradise Lost 2*, the second documentary presented by HBO about Damien Echols and the other two boys who have come to be called "The West Memphis Three." It is a very educational piece concerning small town mentality, quite worth seeing. The following discussion is based upon data presented in this film. You may recall the case. Three young children were murdered in a manner that was savage beyond description. They were mutilated, emasculated, bitten, and two of the three were finally drowned, naked, in a wooded area. Since the murdered children had been killed in such an abundantly brutal manner, the "good Christian people" cried out for justice, for blood to be spilled to make right this dastardly act. And Satanists would agree that such just vengeance was called for. But the local denizens didn't seem particularly interested in finding out who actually did it, which would be the way to dispatch Satanic justice. Instead, they sought and found a quick fix to their distress, in time-honored lynch mob tradition.

Enter Damian Echols and pals. He and his friends were the town oddballs. Damian dabbled in Wicca, and was charismatic enough to have Jason Baldwin as a friend and Jessie Misskelley Jr. as a follower. Neither of his companions was as bright as he, with Misskelley actually having an IQ of only 72. Because they at times wore black clothing and nail polish, the local yokels thought that they must be devil worshippers. Damian was rather effete, so this added a whiff of possible homosexuality to the mix. Thereby came the reason for their guilt: the crimes were so horrendous, that the only explanation which the townsfolk could see was that Satan had to have inspired these obvious deviants to kill their own precious, non-deviant children.

The police arrested the boys and separated them. Misskelley was browbeaten by officers for 12 hours straight, after which he clumsily confessed to what they wanted him to, admitting not only to having witnessed the crime but finally to have been a participant. The officers only taped the last 45 minutes of this interrogation, once Misskelley was saying what they wanted him to say. He recanted the confession soon afterwards. The trial was a mockery, and in its course it demonstrated that the police work was, at the very least, inept. Leads were not followed up, since nobody even thought for a minute that the town weirdos might be innocent—they were considered guilty from the get go. Police ignored the highly anomalous fact that there was almost no blood at this "murder site," a certain indication that the wounding had been done elsewhere. This would mean that the killers would have needed to bring the bodies some distance through rough terrain to the place where they were found—a very difficult task. This important fact was ignored and never investigated.

And so, with victims chosen to appease their lust for vengeance, the mob failed to look elsewhere for suspects. According to the film there is one amongst them who looks like he's possibly the real culprit—the stepfather of one of the murdered children. John Mark Byers claims to be a devout Christian. And like many of those, he was previously a drug addict and a criminal. He married a heroin addict who already had a son, Christopher Byers—one of the boys who was killed. He is six feet eight inches tall, and has a long history of mental illness for which he is prescribed numerous psychoactive pharmaceuticals. He has a brain tumor. These details are presented as facts by the film. And when one watches his behavior on the screen, he appears to be a conniving monster.

Attention turned briefly to him during the trial, but his own knife which was covered with blood wasn't properly tested, so the blood couldn't be conclusively identified. Thus possible evidence was lost in the process of inexpert analysis.

Could three children, hardly much bigger than the dead boys, have transported on their bicycles through rough woods one dead and bleeding child and two who were mutilated and still alive? Unlikely. A large and strong adult is the likelier perpetrator. The Christian giant Byers seems far more plausible.

Ultimately, no reasons were given during the trial as to why the three accused would have been motivated to do these murders, except for their alleged interest in Satanism. The prosecutor spoke of how religion had been used for centuries to kill others—and he meant sacrifice, like the Aztecs and Druids had practiced. He failed to see the irony of his argument in that his own Christianity should have been added to that list of guilty forebears. So fey Damien was branded a Satanist, a deviant, and thus no other facts were needed by these people to justify his crime. This was more than enough for the blood-maddened rabble. Their anger and grief served to give them tunnel vision.

As seen in the documentary, what is truly chilling about Byers is that he appears very calculating. Every word has the feel of being spoken "on stage," and the filmmakers document his contradictions, and more damningly, his own ritual wherein he goes to the site where the bodies were found and symbolically buries, then immolates in effigy, the three incarcerated boys. Did anyone ever have any evidence of ritualistic behavior on the part of the accused? No. Did our malignant father display this behavior? In spades—and on camera.

So three apparent innocents are in jail, one waiting for his death sentence to be carried out, because they weren't like all of the others in their insular small town. They dared to be different, and oh how they have paid: two have life sentences in prisons, while Damian awaits the carrying-out of his death sentence, and is regularly raped on death row. It looks like a Christian murderer is left to sing hymns and curse those who don't believe in Jesus as devil worshippers who will go to Hell. There is some choice footage of Byers doing precisely this. That, my stunned reader, is what happens in a Christian community in the state of Arkansas. Let that be a warning.

Satanism again could have been of assistance in this case, since our philosophy teaches us to tolerate differing practices and not to pillory individuals whose tastes and beliefs are not ours. A Satanic investigator would not have jumped to conclusions concerning the guilt of suspects, but would have diligently assembled evidence and examined all likely possibilities. Rational investigation, as well as prosecution, would have been the Satanic approach. Simply sating the local desire for closure by laying blame on unlikely suspects would not have been the result.

In the unlikely event that these young men are released and Byers is brought to trial, a savvy prosecutor would have a unique opportunity: to use Christianity as the motivating factor behind these killings. Is not the essential image in Christianity the image of a son being tortured to death as a result of his father's will? If a disturbed individual was deeply obsessed with this iconography, might he be tempted to emulate his Most High? "What Would Jehovah Do?" The herd felt that pointing to deviance and the Devil was all the reason needed to give meaning to these appallingly horrific murders, but it is possible that it is *their* own God who is the ultimate inspiration for this tragedy. Jahweh could have been the inspirer of these deeds, having been "made flesh" by a disciple acting as his hand out of "Christian love and justice."

Who won in West Memphis? They did yet again, my now agitated reader.

The herd singled out the aliens, who were too innocent to realize that their outsider status was more than enough to incite killing bloodlust against them. And what of the devout Christian who, like Abraham, may have brought his own lamb to the slaughter? He seems to have escaped the law. The film implicates Byers via circumstantial evidence, and I think it shows a scenario for what happened that makes more sense than the judicially determined one. At the very least it casts reasonable doubt on the accusations against the three young men, which should have brought a "not guilty" verdict. Perhaps there are enough people from beyond that town who have chosen the label of "outsider," who will also see it and may motivate their kind to put a stop to this travesty of justice? I'm not holding my breath.

From West Memphis to Columbine, we've seen what can happen to those outsiders who don't have the Satanic perspective. They may be lead to desperate acts or are simply slaughtered to appease the fears of the masses. And people say there is no human sacrifice today, or they try to say that it is something we Satanists practice—what rubbish!

So, most cherished Satanist, you might finally ask, "Are we anti-Christian?" And I answer, "We are indeed." We hate their creed and all that it spawns from the very depths of our hearts and minds. They are welcome to this nauseating belief system, so long as they keep it amongst themselves.

It is they who seek to destroy our kind. It is they who will blame us for their own hideous actions. It is they who love death and torture, who believe in and practice sacrifice, and it is they who scorn the preciousness of life itself.

As I see it, if the face of their God has been incarnated in human form, it would resemble the face of John Mark Byers. Watch the film and look into his mad visage, the possible slaughterer of his own son, and of other's sons. That image is the God of the Christians—for real. That is the very essence of Christianity, and it is why we hate it with every fiber of our beings and see that only creatures that are truly damaged could embrace a faith that has such absolute vileness as its central cherished paradigm.

Any of you fanatical Jesus-lovers who might have stumbled onto these words—behold how we Satanists correctly identify you, and know full well that we understand your true nature. We know you will deny it, but you cannot change what you are. You have no alternative.

We Satanists have a choice: to be aware and hold the upper hand, or to be ignorant and thus fall to the ravenous Christer mob. Always bear the following in mind, my fellow tribesmen:

We are not as they are. They know it. Remember.

They believe in killing out of "love,"
and they "love" their enemies.
Remember.

It is within our power to be the victors, not the victims,
if we maintain our Satanic perspective.
Remember.

Never forgive. Never forget.

# PERVASIVE PANTYWAISTISM

**M**OLLYCODDLES ABOUND. Wimps are on the rise. Sissies hold sway. Our society is pervaded by a patronizing protectivity, shielding the timorous from ideas that might be inimical to egos fragile as sodden tissue paper. What ever happened to cultivation of strength and self-assurance, once the hallmark of American culture? The minions of "political correctness" and a new generation of whiner-spawn have attained the legislative power to enforce their pusillanimous intolerance for any difference in opinion. Behold the vile cowardice that reigns in just about every public forum. Witness censorship, based on the principle that individuals must be protected from any negativity or they will suffer irreparable trauma and thus deserve reparations from the state to satisfy their shattered self-image. Here is the new standard for behavior, ranging from universities to work places, from the printed word to cyber-space, and it is enshrined by the various media who have united to crush those who refuse to abandon their critical faculties.

People are deathly afraid of words; they can't bear anything being said against them. To be "dissed" is the equivalent of being destroyed. The contemptible contemporary credo is to seek the approval of all and sundry, while eliminating any critical commentary. It has become a thought-crime to voice the opinion that you don't embrace everyone in one sloppy hug of "brotherhood." Satanists deplore such weakness. It was once expected that one instinctively evaluated the gainsayer (as well as the flatterer), automatically reacting with either pleasure, disappointment or even indifference based on the relative merits of this individual. Now, all are required to tout everyone else without discrimination—a word that now has an "evil" connotation and previously meant the exercise of one's selectivity based on educated appraisal. Satanists have not lost this instinct; we welcome the conflict of ideas, and are excited by differences. It is by actions that we judge. Words are mere window-dressing.

We must cultivate a neo-Darwinian arena wherein opinions may clash in the bright glare of mid-day, light glinting off saber-sharp tongues that slam against the armor of cultivated wit and erudition in a true conflict of rip-roaring repartee. We expect to see the sands stained crimson and will be ready to wield our discrimination boldly, without stinting, to either raise a thumb in approval or give the sign of rejection. We will celebrate the victorious while the vanquished are carted off as refuse. This is the climate that will foster the re-emergence of intellectual rigor, and will present competing concepts for all to see and judge accordingly. It is time to end this childish insulation from the real world and go out to experience the invigoration to be had from a world of variety. If you come across that with which you don't agree, you'll be able to identify those who hold such values and deal with them as you will. Control of speech is not control of thought. The current climate has caused many to hold secret their true feelings, which often grow to strange shapes in their restraint, bursting forth in extremity that is shocking to the naive, but expected by the aware.

Let the triumphant strains of "My Way" sound the call to those who refuse to disguise their true thoughts beneath a grimace of false politeness. Enter into the fray with claws extended, flying your true color—winning friends and foes, or walk away and find another exchange more to your liking. You can soar, or crash and burn, but do so on your own. Don't go crying to some societal authority to wipe the snot off your nose and kick the ass of your betters. Perhaps you want to remain in diapers all of your life, but don't expect Satanists to stick around and smell the load. Manure is best when buried as fertilizer.

# THE FASCISM QUESTION

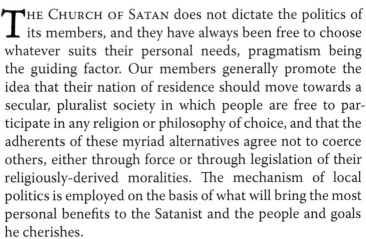

THE CHURCH OF SATAN does not dictate the politics of its members, and they have always been free to choose whatever suits their personal needs, pragmatism being the guiding factor. Our members generally promote the idea that their nation of residence should move towards a secular, pluralist society in which people are free to participate in any religion or philosophy of choice, and that the adherents of these myriad alternatives agree not to coerce others, either through force or through legislation of their religiously-derived moralities. The mechanism of local politics is employed on the basis of what will bring the most personal benefits to the Satanist and the people and goals he cherishes.

Those outside the Church of Satan have, from its inception, accused it of all manner of politics: communism, fascism, anarchism, liberalism, conservatism—and just about anything else you can think of, all of which are mutually exclusive. What IS clear, is that journalists who have an "axe to grind" against the Church of Satan have always accused it of advocating a political system which is one they personally abhor—thus casting the Church of Satan in the role of "devil" for them in whatever arena of human thought they wish to explore.

In the 1960's the radical left preached a philosophy of

"peace and love" which really boiled down to the concept of leveling everything to being "equal." This "philosophy" championed the abandoning of rational criteria for evaluation of anything, and the embracing of everything as being of equal value, thus fostering mediocrity on every level of human endeavor. We are still living in the fallout of this mode of thinking, as the people who espoused these ideas when young have grown to adulthood and are now the "establishment"—those adults whom they considered to be the enemy during the sixties. This "egalitarianism" was manifested in cultural domains with concepts such as: "Anything can be defined as being art and all such works must be considered to have equal validity." Thus, some random splashes on a canvas were considered an equal achievement to the Sistine Chapel; a mud hut was held up as being equivalent to Versailles. A janitor was dubbed the equivalent to a physicist; a novelist was now the peer of one who scrawled graffiti on a bathroom wall. This principle of "indiscrimination" was applied to all other fields of achievement. Those who opposed this leveling were accused of being "fascists" or "Nazis," without regard for what these terms might have meant in their actual historical origins and practice. After all, it was the mid-sixties, twenty years after the ending of a war that most of these folks weren't even alive to have experienced. How quickly past orthodoxies are forgotten.

The Church of Satan was created in 1966 and stood in contradistinction to these ideas, which were generally defined as being "liberal." From the time of the very foundation of the organization, Anton LaVey and the members of the Church of Satan were appalled at this ideology which preached that any kind of merit was illusory—and thus that the act of evaluation was an "evil" practice. Discrimination became a bad word, when previously it had denoted sound judgment. Well, the Church of Satan never shied away from embracing things that society considered evil, and thus it championed a rebirth of strict criteria for evaluation of all areas of human endeavor, and quite radically placed the responsibility for this squarely on the shoulders of each individual. There was no "appeal to authority" in Satanism since each person held the responsibility for being his own authority. For this reason, we were then called "fascists" and "Nazis"—NOT because of any advocacy of the sociopolitical ends of these historical movements.

The masses today still don't know what the terms "Nazi" and "fascist" really mean in their original sense. These words are now used as epithets against anyone with whom they don't agree. Most frequently they are employed by "politically correct" intellectuals in the same manner that Joe McCarthy used the word "communist" and the Christian Inquisitors used the word "witch"—to discredit the validity of the accused's point of view and brand them a "heretic" or "thought criminal." Because of the continuing decline in the level of education, even amongst those who pursue degrees at major universities, we can expect that there will be no broad understanding of what the terms "Nazi" and "fascist" really mean now and for some time to come. These will simply remain vague derogatory designations used against those perceived to be "the bad guys."

Satanists are aware of what impact words and images have on the herd, and thus use them to their advantage. It should be clear to anyone who has observed human society that there is an all-pervading interest on the part of the contemporary general public in the Third Reich. Anyone with cable television or who happens to visit movie theatres will see that the Nazis are the standard archetype in entertainment for what the masses deem to be evil, and they are fascinated with this dead government and fetishize it to no end. Do you watch "The History Channel" (whose emblem is a carved, angular letter "H")? We jokingly say that this really stands for "Hitler" not "History" as much of their programming concerns analysis of the Third Reich.

The herd's misconceptions establish how a Satanist uses symbols to influence these people. Would-be iconoclasts today who try to reclaim the swastika as a "good" symbol have failed to supplant the herd's identification of this as a sign of "ultimate Evil," far more potent to them than our Sigil of Baphomet. When dealing with mass consciousness, current meanings establish buttons that can be pushed.

Certain savvy Satanists who make their living entertaining the masses have used the public's obsession with this material for their own ends. Hence they have employed symbols and techniques derived from Third Reich spectacles (which were undeniably powerful means for motivating masses of people) for the purpose of stimulating their audiences and thus putting money in their pockets. Is this advocating political fascism? No, of course not.

Fascism is a doctrine that requires the submission of individuals to the goals of the state. This is a collectivist philosophy, suppressing individualism, which states that each person should sacrifice himself to an abstract principle, which is treated as a sacred entity: THE STATE. The past supposed "glories" of the state, usually mythological, become the sacred icons in what is in actuality a new religion. Fascism is clearly a means for controlling herds, and one that was effective. It took one of the largest wars to end the bid for world dominance by nations using this system.

The "sameness" of the masses serving THE STATE is the common ideology for unification of the populace, and such is the favored tool for totalitarians whether they are called fascists, or clergy, or commissars. Hence uniform modes of dress are frequent tools to bond the populace together.

Satanism advocates a different approach. Stratification

is a term coined by Anton LaVey to signify how nature allows everything to "seek its own level." It is not something that need be advocated—it happens of its own accord. Social orders are human constructs, artificial in nature. We Satanists think that if one were to apply Nature's principles to a society, in this context stratification would then be the concept that one's merit, evidenced by developed talent and productivity, decides one's position in society. That position could change, depending upon the shifting matrix of societal values for your abilities. Individuality is thus championed, and there will be a flux in class status rather than an imposed stasis creating a frozen hierarchy of hereditary aristocrats.

This was not the goal of the German fascists of the Third Reich. Their standards were racist. They sought political power and needed a scapegoat for the economic woes of many people. They chose the Jews, since many were economically successful as well as skilled arts practitioners, and Nazi propagandists galvanized much of the populace into following them through hatred of people they branded seditious monsters. They also targeted Communists, whom they felt were enemies to their system of National Socialism. Once the Nazis took power, their first order of business was to imprison political enemies, many of whom were Communists. These were the people first incarcerated in concentration camps. However, the need to continue identifying enemies, denigrating groups of people so that the "Aryans" could feel superior, lead to the imprisonment and extermination of the Jews, along with gypsies and even homosexuals, despite the homophile proclivities of some leading Nazis. They too were purged. "Decadent" was the smear used against them while the Nazis assumed the mantle of moral and aesthetic purity.

When fascist doctrine is placed into practice, regardless

of where or when, there has to be somebody who tells the herd what the needs of THE STATE are to be, since THE STATE is just an abstraction—it does not actually exist. Here enters the "Ruling Class," otherwise known as the Nazi Party, the Communist Party, the Khmer Rouge, and so on. These rulers claim to embody THE STATE, telling the masses what the will of THE STATE is. They reign much like the ancient priesthoods who held their power by being the only ones capable of communicating to people the "will of the Gods." These people are a *de facto* aristocracy, using THE STATE for its *raison d'être*, just as the latter-day heads of some of the communist states handed down THE WILL OF THE PEOPLE as their excuse for controlling their massed subjects. These rulers are not subject to sacrificing themselves to THE STATE, because they are the ones who, as embodiments of THE STATE, choose who is to be sacrificed. They don't pick themselves, though sometimes they do pick their cohorts who are getting a bit too cocky. These kinds of rulers now use terms more palatable to our century, whose masses won't buy such old excuses as "the divine right of kings," but their means are identical. Of course, these rulers are often foiled by subsequent "prophets," who convince the masses that they, rather than the current rulers, embody THE STATE, and so counter-revolutions occur and the former leaders are usually dispatched with violence.

"Don't pay any attention to the man behind the curtain!" said the glowering face in a fountain of fire (THE STATE/THE WILL OF THE PEOPLE), hoping that Dorothy and crew wouldn't notice who really is pulling the strings. But Toto (the beast) pulled aside the curtain. Now we might begin to see how Satanists factor in to this equation.

The Satanist should always be aware of who is really running the situation in which he finds himself. The clever know the ropes of the system in which they live and use that to their advantage. Satanists do not see themselves as being part of the herd and naturally resist any attempts to be forced to live under any regimes that would make them part of the controlled masses. However, Satanists might not care how the herd is being controlled, so long as they themselves aren't subject to being controlled along with them. If forced by circumstance to be part of such a governmental situation (and I caution the reader to examine how much he really knows about the machinations of his current nation of residence), the clever Satanist would either attempt to be the person who pulls the strings, or, more likely, his associate. Being the one behind a "leader" is generally a safer position, as the leader is always a target, while the advisors often survive changes in "top dogs." Let Machiavelli be your guide.

If one is not a member of the ruling class, but is actually part of a minority faction in a pluralistic society, then advocating that "everyone be treated equally under the law" may guarantee that you will have a maximum amount of personal freedom. Be aware of mitigating "power factors" at work—like wealth. Of course the amount of freedom depends upon the laws of the society in which one lives and we recognize that special interest groups often jostle to get more of the "pie" through handouts and privileges established via state mechanisms.

Satanists know that there are no natural rights as the concept of rights requires someone or something to be doling them out, and in the past this was usually considered to be some God. The only rights one has are those given by the laws of the governmental structure under which you live, and ultimately, even these devolve into what you may attain for yourself using whatever personal power you might have. That is why the rich get away with so much more, as their money gives them power and hence, more rights in a society ruled by lawyers and not justice.

However, if you belonged to the ruling class you might have a very different perspective. It is true that self-identified Satanists are currently a minority in a pluralistic society. But what if they achieved a position of being the ruling class? How would clever self-declared Satanists run a government? What would they advocate? How would they control the masses? This could be a fine question that could be dealt with in a novel of speculative fiction, as it is not likely to happen in reality. But, we do know that the people who really understand how to exercise power on the highest of human levels, regardless of whatever philosophy they proclaim as their cover, are actually maintaining their power by behaving in accordance with the true nature of the human species, and are thus *de facto* Satanists.

So, some Satanists who are "political idealists" might envision a fascistic future wherein Satanists are the "men behind the curtain" directing the herd to support their own personal indulgences—the herd sacrificing themselves to a ruling, but necessarily hidden, Satanic "elite." I see this as a political pipedream, a form of idealism incompatible with the essential pragmatism of Satanism. Running a state would leave little time for personal indulgences and enjoying one's life.

As you can see, in contemporary Western society, the only political factions likely to attempt create a fascistic system (as meant by the original meanings of the terms) are the right-wing fundamentalist fanatical Christians. The film, *The Handmaid's Tale* provides a chilling visualization of this possibility. They have the same moral self-righteousness as the Third Reich leaders and their kind has always found scapegoats to burn at the stake. I think it far more productive to advocate a system that guarantees freedom for the exercise of many points of view—so long as it doesn't require me to pay for wastrels who want a free ride.

We in the administration of the Church of Satan do not control the thoughts of our members, so if some of them want to toy with these political dreams, that is their prerogative, so long as they don't identify them with the aims of the Church of Satan, which are emphatically not political, nor are they idealistic.

The Church of Satan has never required anything of its members except that they hold the writings of Anton LaVey as their basis for membership in this organization. We do not try to force our members into some kind of lock-step unity in their personal choices for building upon LaVey's foundation. We thus celebrate an astonishing diversity. There are some perspectives that we hold in common. We champion merit and superior achievement in all spheres, and are the opponents of a society that is a rampant "mediocracy."

American Satanists tend to define the United States as the world's first Satanic Republic. Egalitarian types who reject that concept should note that the Founding Fathers did not grant freedom to everyone—it was thought to be a right only for those whom they deemed worthy and capable of intelligent ability to exercise such freedoms, originally excluding people such as slaves and women. Thus, they weren't giving everyone equality, but were advocating freedom for people whom they defined as equals in ability and capability, an important distinction that has been lost on many who want to interpret their wisely constructed governmental structure as being egalitarian and democratic. It was designed as a republic, which suggested that men of reason might need the ability to circumvent poor or repressive decisions that could arise if a "majoritarian" democracy was installed. That was considered "mob rule" which was just as intolerable as being controlled by hereditary monarchs, particularly since the Founding Fathers shared the same low opinion of the masses as that held by we Satanists.

So we come 'round at last to that question: "Is Satanism fascism?" The answer depends upon your definition of that term. If fascism is understood to be the totalitarian system of government enslaving its subjects to serve the state in drab conformity, then the answer is a resounding "NO!" However, if fascism is merely a loose epithet tossed at those who do uphold standards for excellence in human achievement in all arenas of endeavor, then we'll wear THAT as a badge of honor. We, who embrace Satan as our emblem, don't need no stinking good guy badges!

# Eugenics

EUGENICS—THE VERY WORD raises the hackles of the egalitarians, as it exposes fundamental fallacies that underlie their doctrines. Mankind is the only animal species which acts to circumvent the natural law of the survival of the strong and the weeding out of the weak. Acknowledging the non-equal, stratified status of humans, we Satanists see as one of our long-term societal goals the promotion of a higher percentage of creative and productive individuals, and a decrease in the numbers of simple believers and consumers, as well as the downright stupid. This could be advanced through the "forbidden" knowledge of eugenics. Simply put, it is a term applied to the scientific theories concerning the biological improvement of the human animal through the deliberate control of hereditary factors. This idea was pioneered by Sir Francis Galton. He thought that we could promote a progressive evolution in our species through increasing the proportion in our population of intelligent, healthy, and emotionally stable individuals via the strict control of human reproduction. We have used such techniques in agriculture and animal husbandry. Why not voluntarily apply such to ourselves?

Historically, a eugenic approach to species improvement was acceptable, and indeed was pursued with fervor in many countries, including the United States, up until the conflict called World War II, when this area of research was tainted by some of the grotesque excesses attributed to scientists in the Third Reich. With the widespread growth of egalitarianism and collectivist thinking in the mid-20th century, some social movements resented factual reports that did not support their aims at homogenization, and thus even serious researchers found that their funding was dropped and their data was suppressed. This censorship has continued through today.

Traditionally, eugenics has had two approaches: "negative" measures which reduce the frequency of inherited mental and physical defects through sterilization and birth control—particularly the prevention of reproduction among individuals bearing hereditary defects, such as lifelong mental patients and those with crippling diseases; "positive" measures that attempt to increase desirable hereditary mental and physical attributes by encouraging superior individuals to reproduce, and could include subsidies from governments or private foundations to aid such parents in this undertaking. We now have a "third side" approach, since researchers are coming to understand the human genome and techniques are being developed for manipulating the characteristics of the zygote. These may make it possible for parents to select the abilities that will be born into their offspring, presenting the option to amplify their strengths and eliminate their weaknesses.

Satanists have always explored areas forbidden to others, and we will not shy away from this topic so vital to the development of our species. We reject the flaccid maxims of universal equality and seek to ruthlessly reveal the truth about the human animal, so that we may move forward towards the proliferation of creative individuals. As champions of freedom of choice, we don't expect governments to enforce such programs on their citizenry.

However, we think this path should be a viable option for all who are concerned with increasing the numbers of the ranks of intelligent and creative people. There will always be many believers, consumers and parasites in human society. We do not advocate their destruction. However, their drain on the productive and capable inhabitants of this planet is debilitating to *us*. We wish the ranks of the "superiorly abled" to increase in number, before time runs out and we all perish under the crush of mediocrity.

# Iron Youth

IT IS THE 25ᵀᴴ YEAR of the existence of the Church of Satan. We Satanists are continually accused by the media and hysterical Christian fanatics of child recruitment. They tell grim tales of slavering Satanists lurking about playgrounds and schoolyards in search of apple-cheeked innocents who are to be kidnapped and then brainwashed into becoming servants of Satan. These feeble folk simply can't catch on to the fact that we find them, as well as the rotten fruit of their loins, to be unredeemably mediocre and not even worth pondering, let alone inviting into the Church of Satan. Such fantasies must stem from wishful thinking; these drones dearly hope that they will be considered important enough to get our attention. To such I say, "Dream on!" They also neglect our policy that only adults may join. The one exception to that rule is made for mature young adults whose parents are members in good standing.

The only youths that interest us are our own children, doubly blessed with fine genetic material as well as receiving the appropriate love, care, discipline and education to become part of the world's elite. As we move into the year XXVI A.S., we find that many of our members are in the process of raising a cherished second generation of Satanists. Our children do not take part in Satanic rituals save for a Satanic Baptism, should the parents so desire, which celebrates the glorious carnality that gave rise to these precious new lives. These young individuals are not forced into Satanism, but are reared to employ an open and questioning approach to all things, particularly religions and philosophies. If they have reached a stage of maturity wherein they do take an interest in their parents' religion, they will have it explained to them with candor and shall be permitted to read *The Satanic Bible*. So many of us discovered this book in our early teens and found it to have a beneficial impact.

We don't allow our progeny to participate in ritual workings until they have, of their own free will, gained a full understanding of Satanism as well as the principles involved in Greater Magic and can contribute to the actual process. Parents may mark the occasion of the young adults' stage of maturity, wherein they first take part in a ritual, through a Satanic Confirmation Rite welcoming the individual as a conscious magician and dedicated Satanist. This ritual should stress the nascent talents that the confirmee will work to develop through the application of Will, to become a true member of the elite. Satanic parents never pressure their offspring to adopt Satanism, particularly since so many of them recall being forced by their parents into participation in religious beliefs and rituals which they did not find satisfying.

Satanist parents are acutely aware of the great responsibility in their hands of giving their children the proper guidance to separate the diamonds from the dross in the overwhelming mass of information now available. They are careful to let their children know that they have few, if any, peers amongst the herd through which they must pass with utmost caution. They teach them to study all things, not to worship anything above themselves and those whom they value. They are taught to revel in their animal nature, and to study the nature of the human animal with great care, as

Mankind does exist as a society that must be comprehended in order to master the methods for achieving personal desires.

Above all, our children will be encouraged to discover and develop their unique aptitudes, to explore many alternatives and choose that which each loves best. We give them the freedom to become exactly whom they choose to be. These bright young sorcerers shall surely inherit the globe as well as the stars, living lives full of success and pleasure.

We Satanists are here to stay and our "iron youth," splendidly self-confident and disciplined, are the keys to the gateway into eternity. I have seen the glorious strength-through-joy radiating from the faces of our next generation and confidently predict that tomorrow, indeed, belongs to us.

# Founding Family: "Morality" versus Same-Sex Marriage

In these early years of the 21st Century, the issue of same-sex marriage is a hot topic in the United States. A groundswell of civil disobedience is afoot wherein couples of the same gender are being wed by various government officials as a test of existing laws. The Christian right considers this to be an abomination, and they continually attempt, on state and national levels, to legislate that marriage should be defined solely as a union between one male and one female partner. Politicians have used this as a dividing issue, some even painting supporters of legalized same-sex unions as agents of Satanic immorality. So, since we are a legally incorporated church, many have asked "Where do Satanists stand on this matter?"

The Church of Satan does not determine the politics of its membership. However, there are basic tenets shared by our adherents and so we Satanists generally agree on certain political points relating to the advancement of individual liberty. It is an intrinsic part of our philosophy as expressed in *The Satanic Bible* to accept a broad range of human sexual practice—so long as it is between consenting adults. The Church of Satan is the first organized religious group to fully accept members regardless of sexual orientation and thus our members advocate that any existing laws discriminating against homosexuality should be revoked.

It naturally follows that Satanists would support weddings or civil unions between adult partners whether they be of opposite or the same sex. So long as love is present and the partners wish to commit to a relationship, we endorse their desire for a legally recognized partnership, and the rights and privileges that come from such a union.

Currently the primary colloquial use of marriage is to form legally recognized "family" when partners formalize their bond of love. In the past, other religions have used marriage as a means for licensing approved forms of sexual activity—since fornication is generally considered "sinful" under their anti-human doctrines. The wedding was intended as an encouragement for propagation. Those who married and did not produce offspring were considered suspect, and infertility could be used as grounds to end the bond and free the bride and groom to seek more fertile spouses. Overall, the institution was held to be sacrosanct, serving to enforce Christian morality as the standard for behavior. Those days are over. Let's not go retro on this one.

Western society no longer views marriage solely as a licensed breeding program. Married heterosexual couples who cannot or choose not to reproduce are not stigmatized as being inferior in any way to their "fruitful competitors." Nor does our society find that marriage is required as a permit for sexual activity; that concept was shattered during the sexual revolution of the 1960s. If existing laws maintain outmoded religious moral codes that infringe on equal treatment for people subject to these dictates, then the time has come for legislators to purge these laws of religious dogma and bring them in line with the secular society that exists in the United States. And may the same be done in all nations that respect freedom and celebrate bonds formed by love.

Secularism was one of the goals of the American Founding Fathers and it generally remains sound, despite some successful theistic pollution. The changing of our national motto from the secular "E Pluribus Unum" ("out of many, one") to the religious "In God We Trust," and the addition of the religious reference "under God" to the Pledge of Allegiance are regrettable examples of aberrancy. Perhaps these anomalies need to be corrected as well? I suggest that it is time for Americans to stand up for the axiomatic principles of individual liberty and secularism upon which our nation was founded and thus prevent further incursions of Christian morality, meant to force non-believers into the straitjacket of their dogmatic belief system.

Allowing same-sex marriages does not mean that Christians and others who oppose such a practice will be forced into such unions. They may find it distasteful, but then, when a nation encourages the individual pursuit of happiness, there is no guarantee that everyone is going to like what everyone else is doing. That is a part of freedom—the tolerance of diversity. The idea of amending the U.S. Constitution to bring it in line with Christian dogma should be anathema to Americans who understand its conceptual basis. If they truly held allegiance to the principles upon which this nation was founded, they would be outraged by such flagrant attempts to blur the borders between church and state.

Over time, the resolution of this issue will serve as a barometer for gauging the tenor of a nation's basic character. It will reveal whether a government can be truly pluralistic, offering equal freedom to its diverse citizens or if it will instead allow its people to be shackled by antiquated values fostered by religious dogma.

# INTELLECTUAL BLACK HOLES

MANY ARE ATTRACTED to the Black Flame of Satanism yet not all of these individuals are truly Satanists by birth. Indeed, the death-centered folk who generally find "other-worldly" creeds most satisfying to their inclinations at times see Satanism as a challenge and temptation—a fruit to which they are irresistibly drawn, forbidden to them by their biological natures.

Anton Szandor LaVey identified "psychic vampires" as emotional energy-drainers who provide the vigorous with material goods as a means toward creating feelings of obligation. The Satanist recognizes this, accepts the offerings, and easily denies the need for reciprocity—he didn't ask for the goods so he owes nothing to the giver. No guilt will be accepted from this moocher.

Another type of vampire is one who, by dint of the existence of his "sovereign consciousness" feels that those who know more than he are thus obligated towards sharing their knowledge. These creatures spend their time in incessant "seeking" as their centers are yawning black holes of conceptual emptiness that can never be filled. They have no personal identity, and because of this lack are constantly in pursuit of those who do. They approach the Satanist as one who is "curious"—a beginner who "just wants to ask a few questions." Giving even one answer begins the endless spiral of your bright thoughts into the fathomless depths from which nothing will ever emerge. The Intellectual Black Hole does not seek information to use towards any creative or productive ends. These self-acknowledged armchair intellectuals produce nothing but questions with which to continually nettle their betters. They will never be satisfied, never use information towards synthesizing a new perspective, never bring anything of worth back to he who answers. Indeed, they will pick at the answers, tearing *any* sense into shreds so that they can then proclaim that "further explanation" is sorely needed, perpetuating the ever-taking relationship.

A frequent tactic is to require "personal attention" as they shrug off suggested reading and other avenues of research, claiming that your "human touch" is crucial for their understanding. They must speak to a living authority or representative; printed matter is never enough. That is a significant warning sign—they want your "warmth" of confidence, to drain it into their frigid depths of doubt and insecurity, never being satisfied to move on until they've accomplished the goal of reducing their victims to equal states of self-doubt. The secure Satanist may never be so diminished, leaving an extended period in which the Intellectual Black Hole will remain in orbit, wasting your precious time and vitality of thinking.

Once identified, such parasites can be marked and avoided. This type can frequently be found on the Internet—an environment particularly conducive to these thought-leeches. Just read from the myriad posts on a topic in a discussion forum and you'll soon spot these info-lampreys trying the suck the energy of anyone foolish enough to respond. They never limit their search to just one area and can be seen posting in various and sundry sites under numerous topics where this "constructive debating" can be sustained until the victims catch on. Their inquiries range from broad metaphysical issues all the way down to the nosiest personal details of situations that should never be the concern of any save those involved. Their advertised quest is for "meaningful dialogue" but the result for you is just a waste of breath or typing. Their motto is "All information should be available to all askers!"—though they never seem to have anything of worth to return. Their banner is the eternal question mark.

The cure? Simply refuse to acknowledge them. Don't answer. At most point them towards literature and say "farewell." Refusing to respond works like the proverbial garlic and holy water—they'll hiss and spit, "You never really did know anything, did you?"—a last ditch attempt to pull you into their gravity well. Silence works, an adamantine barrier they cannot penetrate. They'll kick up a fuss then disengage from you to continue to troll for further victims. You could also hold up the mirror to these creatures by not giving answers but simply asking questions in return. They'll demur that you are the authority to try and reverse the info-flow, but don't fall for it.

On line, in certain usenet forums, once spotted you can "killfile" their annoying hectoring and have a peaceful time, spending your energy as you see fit, browsing amongst topics of interest and passing by the copious amounts of gibbering idiocy that seem to multiply geometrically by the minute. Perhaps you might find a pearl or two, but you'll more likely be looking for the ponies who generated the manure. Cyberspace needs a clean-up squad—but oh what a high-tech Heracles is needed for that Augean stable.

# GREEN-EYED HAMSTERS

"Jealousy is the green-eyed monster"
- from common parlance.

JEALOUSY IS AN EMOTION often found in individuals whose estimation of their own worth exceeds their achievements. It can be conjured when they behold something in another person that they dearly want for themselves, but that they are unable to obtain or attain on their own. They deeply resent the person who can do what they cannot, and more specifically, they resent the recognition given to that successful individual by people in that master's field of endeavor. But beyond this garden variety of corrosive envy, there's a type whose lack of ability keeps them in a transparent (to them) cage of limitation. They are fiercely attracted to those whom they wish to emulate. These hamsters—meager in mind and talent—have lives fueled by jealousy of the people who can do what they cannot, and are incensed when they witness proclamations of admiration that they themselves cannot garner through their own works.

Here is the pattern. A Green-Eyed Hamster will encounter a work by a creative person, and they will love it so much that they wish to be able to produce something that might be loved to the same extent by other people. So, the hamster does what he can to imitate the creative work that he loves. Unfortunately, the hamster (unlike a developing creative individual) can only produce feeble imitations and poor regurgitations of the work he admires. The hamster then seeks out his role model, and while praising the master, the ultimate goal is to somehow be connected with him, so as to "get a rub" off of him—a classic case of coattail riding. Truly creative individuals in the developmental part of their career may imitate role models, but they are fiercely self-critical and would never even think to present their student efforts to the master. They wait until they have created something that is worthy of attention. The Green-Eyed Hamster will feel that anything he produces is somehow to be "bronzed" and celebrated, and more importantly, will eagerly point out to others that he is a personal associate of the creator, in hopes that this will gain him respect-by-association. And this tactic can work with many herd-folk. That convinces the GEH that he is not in that cage defined by his limitations.

The creative person who has become the focus (victim) of our hamster's obsession may find this admiration to be fine, up until the point when the hamster begins to submit his own meager efforts in hopes that peer recognition may be forthcoming. The polite creator will perhaps make some non-committal, but positive comments, suggesting that the hamster needs to put more work in to his products. Brutal honesty is often avoided. Creative people generally have an abundance of energy and a large outpouring of ideas. They have strong egos, and think that, perhaps with encouragement, the hamster might finally begin to produce something of worth, or may just move on and find something more suited his limited abilities as a means for occupying his time.

A creator might give the GEH something to do to as busywork. Let the hamster be an apprentice, or secretary. Once the hamster is set to running in his wheel, he does not have time to force his own paltry doings on his betters. But woe unto the creator and his associates if the hamster stops being thusly preoccupied! Previous positive comments will be brandished as warrants demanding that his weak products be granted status beyond their merits. The creator's politeness is turned against him.

Of course, another problem arises when the hamster encounters a person who uses merit as his standard—not a herdling. Such a diabolical individual might say, "Well, good for you for having been privileged to be with a proven creative person whom I admire, but now where might I find your great works?" The GEH then reaches into his drawer and pulls forth some sadly mediocre makings and presents them with a flourish to the questioner, emphasizing that the master has praised his efforts. The expectation is that he too will be lauded as a peer of the acknowledged master.

However, when the meritocrat's response does not present the level of praise so desperately sought and thought to be his due by the GEH, it is now time for the hamster to revile him, and claim he lacks taste or expertise. The meritocrat then begins to wonder if the master himself might have lacked judgment when having allowed the hamster to be an associate. Of course, the relationship with the master may never really have been all that the GEH claims it was, but the master is not privy to these hamsterly campaigns and thus cannot say to the meritocrat, with a wink and a nudge, that he was "only being nice."

In the Church of Satan we have a policy of rejecting the practice of *noblesse oblige* (literally "nobility obliges"). This is a medieval concept in which the upper classes (wealthy or highborn folks) were considered bound towards assisting the lower classes because of their elevated status. In the Church of Satan, our stratification is based on merit, hence our "nobles" are such because of the development of their creative skills. On my very first meeting with Dr. LaVey, he said to my wife and I that the Church did not support the idea that the talented creators were required to assist the weaker wannabes who were also members. This was because at the time a far less-talented member was trying to use the commonality of membership as a reason to gain my assistance in her own rather lack-luster musical projects. And so, pleased by such a rational and just policy, I politely disengaged myself from the clingy member, who then ran off to try and find other musical members to help realize her "vision."

If you are a creator, either a recognized master in your field or even a talented newcomer on the rise, beware of the Green-Eyed Hamsters. They seem like such little things, and you have such an abundance of ability that you'll think, "What can it hurt to be charitable to this talent-challenged person?" However, the time will come when the hamster demands more than he deserves, and you will be forced to disengage yourself with grace, but your gifts of mild praise will now be used against you. The GEH will cling with his nasty little teeth to your reputation, and those who admire you will perhaps even question your judgment for ever having been kind to the now vituperative hamster.

So, dear doers, recognize those Green-Eyed Hamsters. When these wannabes come-a-calling, either refuse to comment on their efforts, or be brutally honest. That's the best form of hamster repellent available. Otherwise you might find yourself with a disgruntled parasite out there who, since he has nothing better to do, will put all of his energy into besmirching your fine works.

No good deed goes unpunished.

# Satanic Aesthetics

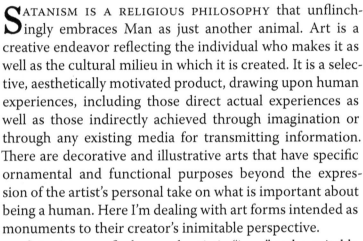

Satanism is a religious philosophy that unflinchingly embraces Man as just another animal. Art is a creative endeavor reflecting the individual who makes it as well as the cultural milieu in which it is created. It is a selective, aesthetically motivated product, drawing upon human experiences, including those direct actual experiences as well as those indirectly achieved through imagination or through any existing media for transmitting information. There are decorative and illustrative arts that have specific ornamental and functional purposes beyond the expression of the artist's personal take on what is important about being a human. Here I'm dealing with art forms intended as monuments to their creator's inimitable perspective.

Satanists can find several artistic "isms" to be suitable paths for a Satanic artist, and naturally these can be mixed according to the unique tastes of each creator. This is not an exhaustive survey, but merely intended to give pointers for further research to enhance your understanding of a broad range of possibilities.

**Realism**: Since our philosophy embraces an "unvarnished" look at the reality of our human existence, this form of expression in literature, narrative, and visual arts is obviously sound practice for any Satanist artist.

**Naturalism:** In so far as this is a means for exploring truths about nature, it is certainly a Satanic approach. The Naturalists in visual arts were influenced by Darwinian ideas and saw Nature as the dominant force. Literary proponents didn't flinch from what others might consider vulgarity. Scientific concepts supported aesthetic choices for artists in this school.

**Romanticism:** In art and literature, this is a means for creating highly personalized systems of symbols and subjective worlds of heightened emotions. Supernatural elements are often employed because of their emotional impact. The heroism of the individual is celebrated in this form that was influenced by concepts of freedom arising in the French Revolution.

**Expressionism:** Particularly in its application to horror films and *film noir*, this is a method for depicting a dark and hostile world, full of struggle. The earliest works were wildly unrealistic and meant to explore the psychology of madness through use of geometrically harsh sets and grotesque makeup. American crime films defined the world from a cynical, fatalistic perspective, with the outcome of the drama often being harsh, though at times the struggle for integrity might pay off, but only after sufficient angst is experienced.

**Idealism:** Satanists adopt a pragmatic view concerning their interactions with the world, hence "pie in the sky" idealism is unsuitable. The "best of all possible worlds" philosophy so diabolically mocked by Voltaire in his *Candide* is not one that is embraced by Satanists, who are anything but starry-eyed. However, Satanists know that, both socially and politically, the nations in which they exist are artificial constructs, just as are the justice systems which are in effect in them, so a Satanic artist would feel free to create artworks which depict the implementation of principles which he himself would prefer to see enacted in the actions of his fellow humans. This can be dramatized in an idealistic projection in which Satanic justice is carried out in ways not currently probable. An excellent way of exploring various idealistic depictions is through fantasy, both of the "science fiction" type, as well as in historical or fantastic re-imaginings of past societies. These can be projections of an Is-To-Be, and creations of this sort have magically become, in some instances, self-fulfilling prophecies.

**SURREALISM**: This school of artistic creation was meant initially as a way to explore dark regions of the human consciousness, juxtaposing seemingly incongruous images or concepts so that, through dynamic synthesis, a greater understanding could be reached of the psychology of the human animal. Since Satanism is concerned with ever-deepening its grasp of the functions of the mind and human behavior, this genre can provide a potent method for continuing to define the nature of the human beast.

Since Satanism cherishes individualism as one of its primary values, the aesthetically inclined Satanist would generally appreciate any artist's work that strongly captured the individual personality of that artist. That does not mean that this work is going to be selected to be amongst "favorite" or even "preferred" artistic experiences. Uniqueness and originality are but two standards for artistic evaluation. Satanists tend to define their true favorites as being created by unique artists who present a world-view which shares some congruity with that of the appreciator, or which so powerfully depict a world-view that is not congruent, but is deeply affecting on an emotional and or intellectual level to the Satanist experiencing that work. The Satanists I've known have always been very picky about whatever artistic creation on which they choose to spend their precious time. There's so much out there, both from past and present artists, one needs to discriminate with care. Hence the function of a wise critic is crucial. Finding a critical writer who shares your values can be vital. He'll filter out the crap and present the prizes on a silver platter so you can head right to them.

The Satanic artist has a broad range of expression open to him. I know that our creative members may take the above "isms" and synthesize new, refreshing modes for expressing their nonpareil visions. Our Infernal artists will provide through their darkly inspired creations a reflection of their own perspective on our kind, which will enrich the lives of those who choose to experience such works, and give them food for thought in their quest towards deeper understanding of our species.

# Diabolus In Musica

THE MUSIC I CHERISH, as well as the type that I write, can be categorized as bombastic music for the symphony orchestra. Historically, this type of composition using the orchestra for grand emotional expression as well as time scale began with Beethoven. I here present profiles of several major composers whose work I find to be deeply rewarding. They are worthy of your attention.

**LUDWIG VAN BEETHOVEN** (1770-1827): Musical Titan
Despite the prevailing cultural illiteracy, is there anyone out there who hasn't heard the name of the mighty Beethoven? And who is not familiar with the famous four-note motive—three shorts and a long—that begin his incomparable Fifth Symphony? (Who still recalls what that symbolized in Morse code during World War II?) Yet how many of you have taken the time to explore the works of one of the titans of music, whose compositions combine emotional heights and formal brilliance at a level that few have approached?

Beethoven was the prototype of the maverick composer, who told his patrons what he wanted to do, rather than vice versa (unlike Mozart, who enjoyed his life but was constantly having to do what his patrons wanted). The youthful Beethoven was hailed by Mozart as one who would make a stir in the world. Beethoven was thus accepted into aristocratic circles and was supported by wealthy music fanciers who tolerated his gruff manner and often unkempt appearance. In 1798 he became aware of a progressive loss of hearing and finally became completely deaf by 1819. Despite this tragic handicap, he continued to produce works that expanded western music to new heights of achievement and he maintained his love of existence through all of these, choosing to celebrate the forces of life in the face of his own tragedy. The dark current flowed through his being so strongly that he could continue despite the extinguishing of his sense to perceive the results of his efforts. The sound world that existed in his imagination went directly down on paper, for performers to later recreate so that we can share Beethoven's musical visions.

Beethoven turned his efforts to just about every genre of music that was extant in his time, transforming and expanding each of them, from chamber music and art songs to concerti, large scale vocal works and symphonies. The emotional hallmark to be found in all of these is a heroic sense of struggle and victory, the personal "I" making a direct assault on the universe and bending things to its will. Though Beethoven did write works on Christian texts, his *Missa Solemnis* being a prime example, he generally seemed to be more attracted to works by Schiller and Goethe for inspiration, as well as Greek mythological tales.

It is perhaps best to start one's exploration of Beethoven's music with his symphonies. His Third Symphony, subtitled *Eroica*, was originally dedicated to Napoleon. He failed to live up to Beethoven's concepts of what an enlightened leader should accomplish, so his name was removed from the dedication page. This symphony amazed audiences at the time for being about half again as long as any previous work in this genre. But Beethoven needed this enlarged time-scale to explore his concept of the hero, who is carried to the grave in the funeral march of the second movement.

His Fourth Symphony was on a smaller scale, but with Symphony #5 he achieved a masterpiece. It details in an amazingly compact way the struggle through to victory, and every movement, from the driven first through to the soaringly triumphant finale emerging from a shadowy transition, is based on the opening motto. Symphony #6, *Pastoral*, revels in a purely pagan appreciation of nature with Beethoven creating images of brooks, bird-calls, a rainstorm, and a peasant wedding, but really depicting the glorious emotions he felt by reflecting on the beauty of nature culminating in the final movement's hymn to nature. Symphony #7 intensely examines rhythm, concluding with a Dionysian dance. Symphony #8 is compact and full of wit and humor. The renowned Ninth Symphony is his largest. The first movement was unlike anything written before, being colossal in sound. The scherzo is fugal and developed in sonata fashion, and its movement is like the dancing of infernal flames. The lyrical adagio provides a soothing respite before the expanded finale. For the first time, this concluding movement included a chorus and vocal soloists in a celebration based on the never to be forgotten "Ode to Joy."

I suggest that you seek out the recordings by John Eliot Gardiner and the Orchestre Révolutionnaire et Romantic, as he uses Beethoven's tempo markings and the ensemble of original instruments preserves the proper orchestral balance making the detailed part-writing crystal clear. These pieces will repay repeated listening; they are to music what Shakespeare's plays are to literature. Start off with the Fifth Symphony and partake of a sound world embodying man the prideful hero. None of that Christian grovelling here. You'll be swept along in a current of upward motion, of evolution, of titanic battle and ultimate triumph. Here the dark force in nature has been given an aural existence. Hail Ludwig!

**ANTON BRUCKNER** (1824-1896): Naïve Sophisticate
He taught Mahler and is renowned as a Roman Catholic composer. Considered a social misfit and often viewed as a "country bumpkin," Bruckner became a sorcerer when improvising at the pipe organ or when composing his massive, contrapuntally complex symphonies. His focus was on the power he understood to be the source of the universe, not on Jesus as a savior. His symphonies are powerfully monumental, with prominent brass writing in organ-like sonority. The qualities most often felt in his work are nobility and majesty. Try Symphony #4 to start, called *The Romantic*. If you find it inspiring, go on to #5, #7, #8, and #9. Bruckner's style doesn't change, but his expertise and complexity increase over the course of his compositions. Herbert von Karajan is an excellent interpreter, but Kurt Eichhorn and Günter Wand also do splendidly.

**GUSTAV MAHLER** (1860-1911): Urbane Visionary
He composed one of the most dramatic and complex series of symphonies ever conceived—they are my favorites. Nine were completed, while the Tenth was unfinished at the time of his death but there are completions by musicologists and they are excellent. The song cycle symphony *Das Lied von der Erde* preceded his Ninth Symphony and Mahler himself saw it as an unnumbered symphony. As a student he was passionately interested in Nietzsche and adored Wagner, and his major life career was as one of the world's leading conductors, celebrated for his detailed interpretations of Wagner and Mozart.

His work grows progressively more complex over the course of his career, so it is often well to start with his Symphony #1. It evokes nature in the first movement, has an earthy peasant dance for a scherzo, a mocking funeral march for the slow movement and an apocalyptic/triumphant finale. His Symphony #2 is subtitled *Resurrection* but it isn't what one would expect from the Christian point of view. Mahler intended it to symbolize his own artistic triumph over negative critical response and it takes the paradigm of Beethoven's Ninth to even greater lengths and depths. His Third Symphony is his longest and it embodies Mahler's love of raw, pagan nature. The first movement is gigantic and pictures the awakening of Pan and the volcanic paroxysms of life's struggle. The following five movements take one on an evolutionary journey through several worlds, of plant life, of animals, of loneliness—a setting of a Nietzsche text, of naïve religion, and finally of deep human passion.

The middle group of purely orchestral symphonies is complex and exciting. The Fifth begins with a funeral march and finally ends in raucous triumph, based on a melody he wrote for a song that lampooned people with unsophisticated tastes. The tragic Sixth Symphony is one of the darkest pieces ever written, ending with a vast movement interrupted by actual sledgehammer blows, shattering the symbolic hero of the piece. The Seventh is sometimes called the "song of the night," and it evokes the night in many guises. His Eighth is another vast choral symphony, called at the premiere the *Symphony of a Thousand* because of the gigantic forces needed to perform it. Mahler goes back to Bach for contrapuntal thinking and sets a text invoking the creative spirit, and then moving on to a setting of the final scene of Goethe's *Faust*. His Ninth, written under the specter of declining health, is a sophisticated leave-taking, wrenchingly despairing, then finally resignedly detached. The unfinished Tenth goes even further in its despair, but finally concludes with a cherishing love of having lived.

Hyper-emotionalism is the rule in this music. If you like this then keep going with the rest of the symphonies in order, give them time and attention for it is repaid—get

THE SATANIC SCRIPTURES

Leonard Bernstein's recordings, either the old on Sony or the new on Deutsche Grammophon.

**RICHARD STRAUSS** (1864-1949): Celebrating Himself
Who could forget the thrilling opening music to Stanley Kubrick's film *2001: A Space Odyssey*? Who hasn't been moved by that sonic sunburst that Kubrick wisely used to herald the birth of conscious intelligence in Man's ancestors, and underscored the first use of tools—a weapon, I might add? That magnificent fanfare was penned by Richard Strauss as the opening for his tone poem *Thus Spake Zarathustra*, which was the composer's effort at creating an audio equivalent to Nietzsche's iconoclastic book.

Strauss was known in his youth as a radical modern, shocking the critics with his voluptuous music, whether it be purely symphonic or operatic. In his final years he was considered to be an aging reactionary, co-opted by the Nazis, and thus generally ignored by a world that had moved to embrace less human music, that had lost the ability to appreciate splendor and skill. To the modern listener, he appears as an artist that created works of great beauty overflowing with the joy and struggle of life.

Strauss actively rejected Christianity and its disgusting creed of self-sacrifice. He saw life as a heroic battle and himself as his own God. Thus, when he composed a tone poem called *A Hero's Life*, one should not be surprised that he Satanically made it a self-portrait. In this, he depicts himself as a mighty life-embracing warrior who enjoys a war against his critics—lampooned as the toads that they were, and who enjoyed his sensuous pleasures to the fullest.

He again celebrated himself and his family in the *Domestic Symphony*, a musical depiction of grandiose proportions that glorifies his home life with his wife and child. Though his detractors were always outraged at his self-glorification, they did not stand in the way of his fame, achieved at an early age as both a composer and conductor.

Strauss' mastery of orchestration was second to none, and he created soundscapes that astonished audiences with the verisimilitude of their tone-painting. Listen to his *Don Quixote*, where he uses woodwind and brass trills to sound like a noisy herd of sheep. The storm segment of his *An Alpine Symphony* is one of the most violent and realistic in all music literature, complete with both a wind machine and thunder sheet. We'll speak more of this piece.

As a young man, Strauss wrote *Death and Transfiguration* which depicts a man's recollections of his very full life while on his deathbed. Here he likened life to a series of ever more magnificent strivings after one's goals which are attained. Death is finally heralded by an ominous tam-tam stroke, yet the heroic spirit is not stopped, but soars on to self-glory. When he ultimately lay dying, Strauss claimed that it was just as he composed it years before.

His operas often caused scandals because Strauss was not afraid to embrace unbridled lust in *Salome* or poisonous vitriol in *Elektra* using surprising dissonance for the time to accompany lasciviousness and violence on stage. His later operas retreated into a more genteel but elaborately crafted style influenced by Mozartean grace, such as *The Knight of the Rose* and *Capriccio*.

This carnal philosophy of life permeated his work in all media, but it came most strongly to the fore in his mightiest tone poem, *An Alpine Symphony*. Ostensibly, this piece portrays a journey by a mountaineer, starting out in primal darkness, then greeted by another blazing sunrise, and continuing until he reaches the mountain's summit, experiences an apocalyptic storm, and then descends to the final darkness of night. Strauss said that the true intent of the piece was a representation of Man's appropriate ex-

THE SATANIC SCRIPTURES

istence. Here life is experienced as if it were a mountain to be conquered by dint of personal struggle, in heroic harmony with the magnificence of Nature. He clearly defined this as being in direct opposition to the Christian attitude towards life, and indeed the first title of this piece, which he later dropped, was *Antichrist*. You will find here an utterly Satanic embodiment of life. From out of the darkness, the rising theme of aspiration leads to a birth in triumph, a "yea saying" to the challenges before one. Next, life is launched with a vigorous assault on the universe that bears with it moments of astonishing beauty as well as bracing terror. In the end, death comes, but the ascending theme still struggles up out of the gathering darkness, expiring only in the final exhalation in a downward glissando into the night of non-existence, the Black Flame guttering out, but with the primal sounds of Nature still there to support the next hero to arise. No more Satanic a view of the human condition has been put into sound.

For the listener new to Strauss' works, I recommend that you seek out recordings conducted by Herbert von Karajan and Karl Böhm, as these are superbly realized with just the right touch of virtuosity and violence. First, listen to the tone poems that have been mentioned in this article and if you enjoy them move on to his other orchestral and operatic works. There is an exquisitely melancholy work for string orchestra, *Metamorphosen*, which is a lament for the shattered culture of Germany at the close of World War II, which may move you with its direct emotional expression. Strauss' music is rich and complex late romanticism which is decidedly passionate and totally Dionysian. Be prepared for the intricate textures, chromaticism, and detailed development of thematic material. At first, just let the sound sweep you along in its epic journey. Later, there is much more to appreciate structurally, if such is your inclination.

Try listening to the rest of *Thus Spake Zarathustra* beyond the famed sunrise and you will be amazed at how much more wonderful music it contains, fulfilling the promise of those first few minutes. Yes, Strauss did conquer death, for by hearing his works you will feel his essence moving within you. And you too will be transfigured.

**DMITRI SHOSTAKOVICH** (1906-1975): Honest Witness
Dmitri Shostakovich was the great atheist composer who suffered under the tyranny of Stalinist Russia, writing music that wryly commented on the totalitarian society in which he lived. He found a way to produce works that could pass for the vapid "socialist realist" paeans demanded by the government, yet still voiced opposition and mockery of the dominant authoritarianism. He did not flee this society, but remained to bear witness to the suffering and bravery of the millions who were prisoners to this grim nation.

You won't find much that is light in Shostakovich's work, for when it comes time to be humorous his laughter is often worked into a shriek. Triumph comes not from the forced public celebration, but from the intimate treasuring of the fragility of human tenderness, like a rare and ephemeral blossom clinging to a barren crag. He is one of the great symphonists, completing 15, directly inspired both in style and content by the mighty ten written by Gustav Mahler. He also wrote 15 string quartets, and these are as structurally dense as his symphonies and even more revealing in their exploration of Shostakovich's psychological states. There are as well film scores, operas, ballets, concerti, piano works and pieces written for specific occasions—a wealth of exquisite music that will take you years to fully explore.

His genius is to be starkly realistic in his exploration of the context of human consciousness in a universe that is fraught with danger created by other humans whose goal is control and suppression of individuality. Thus his work chronicles a struggle for freedom that is dear to the hearts of Satanists, who must often hide their true nature from the bigots who have the power to throttle their quest for the joys that life can offer.

Let us explore Shostakovich's powerful works from his series of symphonies. At the age of 19 his First Symphony made him an international star. It set the tone for what was to follow, wittily commenting on prior works by Tchaikovsky by using the biting satirical sense one finds in Mahler but in a uniquely Russian way. It was played the world over and put Dmitri in the spotlight. His next two symphonies written under the watchful eyes of the Soviet bosses are attempts to integrate modernist dissonant musical language with messages supporting the "Glorious Communist Experiment." These are oddly hollow pieces, perhaps that in itself being a personal commentary.

His massive Fourth Symphony, deeply indebted to Mahler, carried dissonant grotesquerie to new heights. Since Stalin had detested his opera *Lady Macbeth of Mtzensk* written in a similar style—and to displease this boss literally meant you would be dragged away in the middle of the night to be exiled to die in frozen Siberia—Shostakovich withdrew this symphony before its official premiere and produced another one far more conventionally tonal, the Fifth Symphony, and it too had the sort of success that the First had achieved. Listen to this work, with its almost Beethovenian first movement—stern and well-developed, the scherzo a Mahleresque peasant dance, the largo a darkly passionate lament, finished by a finale that works itself into a mighty peroration. Of course, those who understand this finale see it as a forced celebration, and conductors who knew the composer play this so that the triumph is more an agonized pounding than an actual victory.

His Sixth Symphony used three movements to make its point, starting with an adagio plumbing the depths of despair, influenced by the first movement of Mahler's unfinished Tenth Symphony. Its scherzo then continues in the cheeky vein so definitive of this composer, while the finale is a vigorous march, athletic and confident in tone. The Seventh, called *The Leningrad*, was written while Shostakovich was in Leningrad, under attack by the Nazis. He volunteered as a fireman to protect the city—a famous picture of him in a fire helmet was circulated for propagandistic purposes. The first movement of what is his longest symphony depicts Russia invaded by the mechanistic Nazis, who are portrayed by a simplistic march that proceeds through a series of pedantic variations, becoming more brutal as it goes along. This march is developed into battle music that finally vanquishes the invader. The moderato is a wood-wind-dominated scherzo movement with a harrowing climax and the adagio that follows has much poetry and passion. The finale movement brings back the battle, reaching a truly bombastic culmination with the return of the first movement's main theme. This work was supported by the Soviet government and was immediately played in the Western world as a symbol of the Soviet people's struggle against Hitler. Bartók was sick of hearing it on the radio, so he parodied the Nazi march in his own *Concerto for Orchestra*.

The five movement Eighth Symphony was also a wartime work, but it grimly explores the repressions of the communist regime, ending in a mode that is not shouting victory, but which is more an appreciation of having survived a nightmare—just barely. The government expected a triumphal choral Ninth, celebrating the end of the war. They got a sarcastic brief symphony that challenges the skills of the musicians and thumbs its nose at convention. Stalin finally died, and so the Tenth Symphony is a personal work, musically referencing one of Shostakovich's love interests and mocking Stalin with a fierce scherzo that ends with a scream.

His Eleventh Symphony is a vast tonal canvas often quoting Russian revolutionary songs, ostensibly depicting a Tsarist massacre during a protest. But of course it seems aimed at similar doings by the Soviet overlords. It is a long work, but very evocative, almost cinematic in effect. The Twelfth is much like an "agit-prop" film score, and it has a bombastic finale akin to the Seventh.

The Thirteenth Symphony is the one work by Shostakovich that should be heard if you explore no other. Based on five poems by Yevtushenko, it is scored for full orchestra, bass soloist and male choir. Here the sound of Russian Orthodox liturgical singing is absorbed and transformed into a secular "Greek Chorus," chanting texts damning totalitarian repression in many forms. The first movement is a frightening monument to the slaughter of thousands of Jews by the Nazis at Babi Yar. With its tolling deep bell and explosive outrage, there are hair-raising passages that will astonish. The second movement mordantly speaks about humor resisting all attempts to suppress it. The third movement sadly depicts the tenaciousness of the women in the Soviet Union who do their best with meager earnings to bring home food for survival, a heroism based on drudgery so foreign to most Western people. The Fourth gets even darker, telling of fears of all sorts, the worst being the fear to speak freely lest one be arrested and slaughtered by those who watch. Finally, the fifth movement begins with Galileo and then other creators finding "careers" that make them cursed for being truthful while "yes-men" lackeys often succeed over these iconoclasts by catering to society's rulers. The music here is wistful, delicate, ironic and warm, knowing the scarceness of such bravery in the face of the inertia of collective conformity. It is a masterpiece.

The Fourteenth Symphony was inspired by Mahler's *Das Lied von der Erde* and is for soprano and bass soloists, and string orchestra with percussion. It is based on collected poems confronting death in many forms, and is thus a secular meditation on the preciousness of life by examining the consequences of death. The final Fifteenth Symphony sums up Shostakovich's life with musical quotations of his own and other favored composer's works, with much parody, explosive lamentation, and finally a strange icy calm detachment, ending with a warm smile that fades Cheshire Cat-like into the air.

There is a set of the complete symphonies conducted by Rudolph Barshai, who premiered the Fourteenth Symphony, that are exquisitely played with all the beauty, terror, and mockery required. Other outstanding interpreters are Mravinsky, Rostropovich, Rozhdestvensky, Ashkenazy, and Haitink.

And so, fellow non-believers, you will find this music to be worth your while as it exhibits how an artist of wit and passion can resist dictatorship to speak his mind and poignantly capture what it meant to be a person of awareness in a society that destroyed so many who refused to conform.

**LEONARD BERNSTEIN** (1918-1990): Maestro of All Trades
On October 14, 1990 the world of music lost not only a star but an entire constellation with the death of Leonard Bernstein. Composer, conductor, teacher, showman, egoist, libertine—all were facets of this extraordinarily talented man who lived to suck the very marrow from the bones of life. He made his own way, developing his talents to the fullest and using his own mind as the arbiter of his direction, resisting those who would put him off his goals from his father who opposed Lenny's desire to be a musician to colleagues who wished for him to limit his scope to one facet of music.

He is an example of a *de facto* Satanist in his concentration on enjoying the present to its fullest. As a conductor, Bernstein was known as one of the most charismatic and Dionysian of podium personalities, having won his way to a status that had previously only been available to Europeans. I was fortunate enough to have witnessed several of his performances and can vouch for the pure ecstatic galvanism of the experience. He would completely identify with the composer of the work as he conducted, whipping the orchestra into a performance that would be filled with blood and fire, bringing the printed notes to life as if one were experiencing the music for the very first time. We are enriched by the legacy of recordings he made over the entire span of his conducting career. Indeed, everyone reading this will almost certainly have been introduced to some classical music via one or more of Bernstein's recordings. He excelled in works that gave reign to emotion on a grand scale, particularly the symphonies of Gustav Mahler.

As a conductor alone, Bernstein carved out a niche as one of the very greatest, but he also found time to compose original music as well, ranging from symphonic works to ballet scores and Broadway musicals. Again, I'm certain that all of you will have been touched by his compositions at some point in your lives. He gains immortality from *West Side Story*, an updated *Romeo and Juliet* set amidst rival gangs in Manhattan. This score is permeated with the interval of the augmented fourth, known as *diabolus in musica*. The milieu isn't that important, but the responsive melodies he crafted matched the words to perfection, and shall remain perhaps his greatest legacy.

For sheer Satanic satire, one can turn to *Candide*, which tears apart the "Best of all possible worlds" bunk by revealing the brutality of existence, the callous monstrousness of hierarchies, both religious and governmental, and in the end, the need to create your own meaning through what you yourself can do. The score sparkles with musical witticisms and the libretto is equally wry. Bernstein had a lifelong struggle against the idea of faith in external figures. He composed pieces that constantly turned the focus for meaning back to Man himself. His *Mass*, though dated with rock-influenced elements, was written as a condemnation of organized religion.

One of my favorite works is the Symphonic Suite derived from the score to the film *On The Waterfront*. Here we find a truly Satanic symphonic poem which captures the breadth of the struggle of life itself. It begins with a haunting, searching theme, then segues into an aural depiction of the violence and brutality of existence. Later we are embraced by a sweepingly romantic love theme. Throughout the work, these ideas are developed and combined in a way that signifies the struggle of existence, full of tragedy, but ultimately of triumph. The final peroration includes a combination of the opening searching theme with the love theme, passion united with purpose to achieve the chosen end. Life as a struggle, to stand above the herd and derive your own ends. Truly a masterpiece. Another noteworthy aspect of Bernstein's work is his depiction of New York City for its full range of majesty and terror. He even composed the famous, "New York, New York, a Hell of a Town," tune, certainly a Satanic gem.

In his personal life, Bernstein didn't stint on his enjoyment of anything. Known for having a mighty ego, and his talents certainly justified it, he also was reputed to be generous to his friends and lovers of either sex. His desire for success and the magical events that shaped his life prove that he knew where best to direct his energies.

Yes, he certainly had his flaws which included a certain vapidity concerning socio-political issues. Here he often followed the liberal herd. His infamous party for the Black Panthers was justly satirized by Tom Wolfe. But such things are minor when compared to the musical legacy that remains. He truly lived a Satanic existence, having flamed and tossed the fires about him, igniting passions in those whom he touched. He shall remain immortal in the brains

THE SATANIC SCRIPTURES

and sinews of those whose respect and admiration he has gained. Hail Leonard Bernstein! Bravissimo!

ORCHESTRAL WORKS:

Here follows a list of compositions beyond those mentioned above that are certain to stimulate. This is by no means exhaustive, but is intended as a beginner's guide for commencing the journey into this vast world of extraordinary sounds. I sometimes note particular conductors or recordings I consider to be outstanding.

**HECTOR BERLIOZ:** *Symphonie Fantastique.* A great iconoclastic symphonic depiction of an opium-induced fantasy ending with the "Dream of a Witch's Sabbath." John Elliott Gardiner and Colin Davis handle this best. Also worthwhile are his *The Damnation of Faust*, and *Symphonie Funèbre et Triomphale.*

**JOHANNES BRAHMS:** *Symphony #1* was the first substantial successor to Beethoven's symphonies. It is muscular and thoroughly well-developed with nobility and heroism in its expression. Listen to the other three as well. Herbert von Karajan and Bruno Walter do these great justice.

**BENJAMIN BRITTEN:** *Sinfonia da Requiem, Four Sea Interludes from Peter Grimes, Young Person's Guide to the Orchestra.* A 20th Century British composer who knew how to be dramatic and lyrical. Start with these and then try one of his operas, like the chilling psychological ghost tale *The Turn of the Screw.*

**AARON COPLAND:** Great American composer of tuneful ballets *Billy the Kid, Rodeo, Appalachian Spring*, and a powerful *Symphony #3* which incorporates his rhetorical *Fanfare for the Common Man*.

**PAUL DUKAS:** *The Sorcerer's Apprentice*. Disney's *Fantasia* added Mickey Mouse, but this doesn't need animation to present a perfect orchestral fable about meddling with forces beyond your control.

**ANTONÍN DVOŘÁK:** His Sixth through Ninth Symphonies are full-blooded works, influenced by Brahms and brimming with Czech elements. His tone poem *The Noonday Witch* and his two sets of *Slavonic Dances* are quite rewarding.

**EDVARD GRIEG:** *Peer Gynt Suite*, written for a play featuring a journey into the Mountain King's hall, deep beneath the earth. You'll know that episode when you hear it.

**GUSTAV HOLST:** *The Planets* is an evocative journey that has influenced countless film scores. Perhaps the best piece to begin your journey into orchestral music.

**ALAN HOVHANESS:** *Symphony #50* "Mt. St. Helens," has an explosive eruption section. *Symphony #22* "City of Light" is solemn and majestic.

**ARAM KHACHATURIAN:** *Symphony #2* has melodies imbued with Armenian folk music. Notable are its bold beginning and the potent climax of the funereal slow movement. It finishes with a vigorous dash, recalling themes from earlier in the piece.

**FRANZ LISZT:** One of the great innovators, *A Faust Symphony*, *Dante Symphony*, *The Mephisto Waltz*, and *Totentanz*, are must-hear pieces for the Satanist. Also worthy are his symphonic poems *Les Preludes* and *Hunnenschlacht*, and the two piano concerti. There's a wonderful recording by Alfred Brendel of the *Piano Sonata in B minor* along with *Funerrailles*. He is thought to have been the greatest keyboard virtuoso, and he lived a "rock star" lifestyle, with women, fame, wealth, and legions of fans. A *de facto* Satanist!

**FELIX MENDELSSOHN:** His music for Shakespeare's *A Midsummer Night's Dream* is full of nocturnal shimmering and contains the famed *Wedding March*. His Forth Symphony, the *Italian*, is energetic and tuneful with a furious *tarantella* finale. His overture *The Hebrides (Fingal's Cave)* is an excellent tone painting. Finally his romantic oratorio *The First Walpurgis Night* is based on Goethe's text describing Druidic rituals in the Harz Mountains in resistance to early Christians.

**OLIVIER MESSIAEN:** This mystical French composer created the brutally ritualistic *Et Exspecto Ressurectionem Mortuorum* as well as the more sensuous *Turangalîla Symphony*.

**MODEST MUSSORGSKY:** *Pictures at an Exhibition* in the Ravel orchestration and *Night on Bald Mountain* in Stokowski's version as seen in Disney's *Fantasia* are Satanic classics. These both rank with Holst's *The Planets* as perfect introductory works to bombastic orchestral music.

**CARL NIELSEN:** His *Symphony #5* depicts struggle against stasis leading finally to victory. The *Symphony #4*, called "The Inextinguishable" embodies the exuberance and inexorability of life.

**CARL ORFF:** *Carmina Burana* for chorus soloists and orchestra is rowdy and carnal and was used well in Boorman's film *Excalibur*. You'll recall it when you hear the opening "Oh, Fortuna" section.

**FRANCIS POULENC:** *Concerto for Organ, Tympani and Strings* often sounds as if it could have been a score for a horror film. I have fond memories of listening to this on the road while Dr. LaVey drove his black Jaguar.

**SERGEI PROKOFIEV:** The *Symphony #5* is very Russian in sound, ultimately triumphant, but sarcastic as well. The *Symphony #3* is very dark, dissonant and powerful. The *Romeo and Juliet* ballet is full of deep passion and violence. Try the suite compiled by Michael Tilson Thomas. The *Alexander Nevsky Cantata* is based on his film score. In particular, the galloping "Battle on the Ice" movement is a real roof-raiser!

**SERGEI RACHMANINOV:** *Symphony #1* was thought diabolical during its first performance after which it was temporarily lost, though there are many lyrical interludes. The Second and Third Symphonies are darkly expressive. His *Isle of the Dead* is a shadowy, surging tone poem inspired by the eponymous painting. His *Symphonic Dances, Rhapsody on a Theme of Paganini* and the piano concerti are all superb.

**MAURICE RAVEL:** Brilliantly orchestrated, *La Valse* captures European decadence through a disintegrating waltz and *Bolero* is a long processional of ever-rising passion.

**OTTORINO RESPIGHI:** *The Fountains of Rome, The Pines of Rome*, and *Roman Festivals* are colorful, exciting pieces, very much like film scores. Paul Tortellier conducts the

Philharmonia Orchestra on the Chandos label in a spectacular recording.

**NIKOLAI RIMSKY-KORSAKOV:** Known for smoothing out Mussorgsky's pieces, he was one of the pioneers of orchestration and his own works are based on fantastic exotic tales. Worthy compositions are the *Russian Easter Festival Overture, Capriccio Espagnol, Golden Cockerel Suite,* and *Scheherazade.*

**CAMILLE SAINT-SAENS:** His tone poem *Danse Macabre,* depicting death as a seductive violinist, has been oft-quoted by other composers—and Dr. LaVey did his own wonderful version on his synthesizers. His third symphony, the *Organ Symphony,* is splendidly dramatic.

**FRANZ SCHUBERT:** He followed Beethoven with works generated by melody, and his art songs are among the most expressive. The *Symphonies #8* and *#9* are potent constructs, and you'll note that the first movement of the Eighth, famous as the *Unfinished Symphony,* has been used in film scores from the 1930s onward, such as Ulmer's *The Black Cat.*

**ALEXANDER SCRIABIN:** A passionate and mystical composer whose interest spanned Nietzsche and Blavatsky. The *Poem of Ecstasy, Prometheus—Poem of Fire,* and his *Piano Sonata No. 9 (Black Mass)* are sure to delight.

**JEAN SIBELIUS:** His Second Symphony is stark with a finale full of grandeur while his tone poems deal with Scandinavian mythology, *Tapiola* being particularly foreboding. The rest of his seven symphonies are landmark works worthy of hearing.

**J. P. Sousa**: His marches are peerless and any collection of them will make you perk up. Instantly recognizable are the *The Stars and Stripes Forever* as well as *The Liberty Bell* which was used as theme music for *Monty Python's Flying Circus*.

**Johann Strauss**: The "Waltz King" wrote unforgettable life-affirming pieces such as *The Blue Danube, Tales From the Vienna Woods*, and *The Bat*.

**Igor Stravinsky**: He caused a riot with his pagan ballet score *The Rite of Spring* in which a virgin is danced to death. The fantasy ballet *The Firebird* (with the "Infernal Dance of King Kashchei") and circus-themed *Petrouchka* are colorful, powerful, and enduring. The suites from both of these ballets will do nicely.

**Bedřich Smetana:** *My Country* is a series of six symphonic poems describing Czech legends and landscapes. It includes *The Moldau* depicting a river and it truly gives one the sense of the ebb and flow of the water and the sites it passes.

**Pyotr Tchaikovsky:** Known for his ballets and symphonies, his unforgettable melodies and brooding compositions will be known as long as music is played. Of immediate interest: *Symphonies #4, #5*, and *#6, The Nutcracker* and *Swan Lake* ballets, the *Romeo & Juliet Overture Fantasy*, and the always thrilling *1812 Overture* with parts for actual cannons written into the score.

**Ralph Vaughan Williams**: His bracing *Symphony #4* is structured as a dissonant anti-Beethoven's Fifth. The *Symphony #7*, "The Antarctic," is based on his film score for *Scott of the Antarctic* and it uses very pictorial means to evoke the vast power of nature in that frozen wasteland, including wordless choirs and pipe organ. His *Symphony #6* begins in agony, has a pounding slow movement, a cynical scherzo with braying saxophones, and then finishes with what seems to be a quiet portrait of desolation. Kees Bakels recordings on the Naxos label are excellent.

**RICHARD WAGNER:** He transformed opera into what he called a "Gesamkunstwerk" meaning total theatre. Here all elements of the production from the music to the sets, costumes, and lighting design must be controlled for maximum dramatic impact. He made orchestral excerpts from these large scale music dramas to help popularize them and recordings of these as well as the overtures make a splendid introduction to his masterful music—Gerard Schwartz has recorded excellent compilations. Lorin Maazel's *The Ring Without Words* is a potent symphonic synthesis of highlights from all four operas in the Ring cycle. Nietzsche idolized Wagner and considered him the embodiment of Dionysianism, though he later became disillusioned.

FILM SCORES:

Here I list some favorite scores by each composer. If you enjoy these works, there are many more scores from most, so keep on listening.

**ELMER BERNSTEIN:** *The Ten Commandments, Robot Monster, The Great Escape, Animal House, The Black Cauldron.*

**WENDY CARLOS:** *A Clockwork Orange, Tron, The Shining.* Her albums of electronic music, *Beauty In The Beast, Tales of Heaven & Hell, Digital Moonscapes,* as well as the *Switched-On Bach* series, should not be missed.

**JOHN CORIGLIANO:** *Altered States.* His *Symphony #1* "Of Rage and Remembrance," mourning the deaths of many of his friends from AIDS, is a powerful work with one of the most frightening scherzos ever written.

**CLIFF EIDELMAN:** *Star Trek VI.*

**DANNY ELFMAN:** *Batman, Darkman, Nightbreed, Sleepy Hollow, Peewee's Big Adventure, Mars Attacks, The Nightmare Before Christmas.*

**ELLIOT GOLDENTHAL:** *Alien 3, Titus, Batman and Robin, Batman Forever, Cobb, Interview with the Vampire.*

**JERRY GOLDSMITH:** *The Omen Trilogy, Patton, Star Trek 1 & 5, Alien, The Blue Max, Planet of the Apes.*

**BERNARD HERRMANN:** *Psycho, Citizen Kane, The Day the Earth Stood Still, The 7th Voyage of Sinbad, Journey to the Center of the Earth, Vertigo.* My favorite film composer.

**JAMES HORNER:** *Aliens, Brainstorm, Krull, Glory, The Rocketeer, Star Trek 2 & 3*

**AKIRA IFUKUBE:** *Godzilla, Destroy All Monsters, Godzilla vs. Destroyer, Ghidorah the Three Headed Monster, King Kong Escapes.* Most of Toho Studio's classic monster films were graced with his scores.

**WOJCIECH KILAR:** *Bram Stoker's Dracula.* His *Symphony #3,* "September Symphony," in honor of the victims of 9/11 is a powerful work.

**ERICH WOLFGANG VON KORNGOLD:** *The Sea Wolf, The*

*Private Lives of Elizabeth and Essex, The Sea Hawk, Kings Row*. His only symphony is also a superb, post-Mahlerian work utilizing themes from some of his film scores.

**BASIL POLEDOURIS:** *Conan The Barbarian, Starship Troopers, Robocop, The Hunt for Red October.*

**LEONARD ROSENMAN:** *Beneath the Planet of the Apes, The Car, Star Trek IV.*

**MIKLOS ROSZA:** *El Cid, Ben Hur, King of Kings.*

**DAVIS SHIRE:** *A Return to Oz.*

**HOWARD SHORE:** *The Fly, Ed Wood, The Lord of the Rings* trilogy.

**ALAN SILVESTRI:** *Predator 1 & 2, The Abyss, Van Helsing.*

**DIMITRI TIOMKIN:** *The Fall of the Roman Empire, The Guns of Navarone, Land of the Pharaohs.*

**FRANZ WAXMAN:** *The Bride of Frankenstein, Sunset Boulevard, Taras Bulba.*

**JOHN WILLIAMS:** *Dracula, The Fury, Close Encounters of the Third Kind, 1941, Star Wars* (I-VI), *Superman.*

**CHRISTOPHER YOUNG:** *Hellraiser 1 & 2, The Fly 2.*

# Idol Pleasures

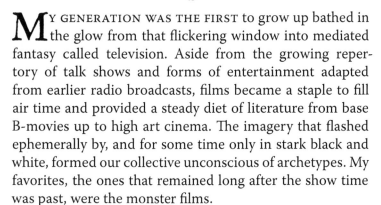

MY GENERATION WAS THE FIRST to grow up bathed in the glow from that flickering window into mediated fantasy called television. Aside from the growing repertory of talk shows and forms of entertainment adapted from earlier radio broadcasts, films became a staple to fill air time and provided a steady diet of literature from base B-movies up to high art cinema. The imagery that flashed ephemerally by, and for some time only in stark black and white, formed our collective unconscious of archetypes. My favorites, the ones that remained long after the show time was past, were the monster films.

In my youth, there was no ability to record these films on video, though I would record the sound on cassettes and could play the movie in my mind when listening later. Nor was there any way to purchase and see a complete film that you might have read about. There were brief super-8 excerpts if you had the proper projector. You had to wait upon the mercies of the programmers for your local channels, which were few in number. Television reception was obtained through positioning an antenna on the roof—no cable—and at times I had to climb onto the roof to reposition the antenna in hopes of catching a signal from a more remote broadcasting station that might be showing a particularly fascinating film listed in the essential *TV*

*Guide*, usually in the early morning hours. That magazine was our missal, and I'd get a copy every week and circle the entries of the new and old favorite creature features listed therein. Of course, the best monster films populated "The Late Show" beginning at 11:30 pm, or "The Late, Late Show" past the "witching hour" of midnight at about 1:00 am. As a youth I would at times need to sneak out of my bedroom in the middle of the night and plant myself in front of that TV set, volume on low, to catch the broadcast of some forbidden work of horror. It was a truly magical experience, and the heights of anticipation whetted my excitement so that often films that weren't particularly outstanding—like *The Mermaids of Tiburon* or *The Screaming Skull*—might have just a scene or two which made the vigil worthwhile.

So many monster movies were celebrated in Forrest J. Ackerman's magazine *Famous Monsters of Filmland* that it became the sacred scriptures for aficionados of the macabre. When the clock struck the proper hour, I would thrill to seeing the wonders that had previously only been blurry, but infinitely suggestive, stills from *FM*'s pages. At times, even with antenna adjustment, I often only got a snowy image, but I'd watch anyway, just to have some knowledge of the film. Since school was mandatory, I'd often go to sleep and set the alarm so that I could rise, like my cherished vampires, to view that late, late, late show.

The creatures in these films were my kin. I readily identified with the "mad scientist" who sought forbidden knowledge which, in a sense I was doing just by being up at these truly ungodly hours to watch the films. I "knew" that if I had half the chance in the same situation, I wouldn't come to the bad end as did the tragic failures depicted, but would actually break through to really new Understanding of the secrets of the Universe.

I identified particularly with the monsters—with the

Lovecraftian Creature from the Black Lagoon, who swam so gracefully beneath Julie Adams' sexy scientist and reached out with lust and curiosity towards her lithe body. And I felt frustrated along with him when he was put in captivity in the second film, and even worse in the third when he was horribly burned and lost his ability to remain in his natural environment, only to finally drown as he sought his home. I identified with the various vampires, the Draculas portrayed by Lugosi, Lederer and Lee (and began to lust after those full-figured beauties which Hammer trademarked); the black and white Mexican vampires who moved through fog-shrouded vistas into ornate mansions that were often constructed of adobe, even the cowboy vampire who at his undead birth resembled Zorro, only to become an invulnerable gunslinger—until felled by a fragment of the "true cross" fired as a bullet by a preacher.

I also identified with the giant monsters, loosed by man's tampering with forces beyond his comprehension, bringing Nature's justice home to roost: *The Beast From 20,000 Fathoms*, *Gorgo*, *The Giant Behemoth*, *The Black Scorpion*, and most powerful of all—*Godzilla*. These hulking gargantuas embodied an immemorial potency that shattered the plans of the parvenu masters of the globe.

These films provided archetypal imagery that surged through the imaginations of all we young fans. And since we couldn't see these films again unless we were lucky, we sought out toys that were made as remembrances of the film. There weren't many of these, and they could be crudely rendered. The well-crafted Universal monster models put out by Aurora were major icons, lovingly built with airplane glue and carefully painted to be as evocative as possible. Other toys were manufactured for television series, and if there weren't toys, I'd draw images of my favorite icons, working to perfect them, and I would also script further adventures.

These toys served as idols of our archetypal divinities. They were power sources for conjuring—sigils that caused atavistic surges of our emotional responses to the movies. We revered them with the same fervor that people in past cultures used for the fetishes and statuary of tutelary divinities that populated home shrines. The models in particular made a prominent impact on my internal psychological landscape, since they had to be constructed, with parts sanded to remove imperfections. Then I used Testor's paints, as aromatic as any sacred incense, to paint the uni-colored styrene and thus bring the monsters to vivid life. Painting Frankenstein's monster and working multiple layers to texture the green skin brought on the same ecstasy I supposed was experienced by that brilliant scientist when he harnessed the lightning to resurrect the dead tissues of his creation.

These avatars of the outré were our ensigns of our outsider status. By embracing these monsters, seeing them as parts of ourselves, they provided a bulwark against the staid, dull normalcy of so many of the other kids around us who had more mundane interests. And our passionate devotion to our dark heroes was not a passing phase, but became a creed that provided a perspective used in dealing with the world around us. We were never apostates to our night brethren.

If you enter my lair, you'll note the many figures of my patron divinity, the giant radioactive reptile who has always been closest to my heart. Here the "King of the Monsters" remains supreme, and now through the techno-wizardry of audio chips many of my totems even give voice to a throaty *skreeeeeonk!* Hail Gojira!

Today, my generation is creating the movies, and making certain that toys are issued for all major efforts. This is why there are so many remakes—we look back and some feel that the magic is somewhat diminished (oh they of little imagination!). So they remake films with contemporary technological wizardry in an attempt to re-create the wonder felt as a child, now that standards for illusions are much higher and belief in the magic is less powerful.

And the toys, the fabulous toys! These are now wrought with an exquisiteness only dreamed about by us as children. We now can go to Toys "Я" Us and buy, often for small amounts of money, intricate and imaginative demonic creations that would do Bosch proud if they appeared in one of his Hell scenes. So we now have a ready-made pantheon of dark deities and grotesque demons that we can use to conjure forth the deep feelings that for many have lain dormant since their youth. These are potent talismans, real idols that can evoke dark and shuddersome responses. They are indeed *daimones*, for these figures made of plastic inspire us. They are reservoirs of power that many of my generation seek, even if they do not understand why they are compelled to do so.

But we Satanic magicians, we DO understand, and haunt the aisles of regular toy shops as well as those exotic stores that carry Japanese imports, an experience like visiting the temples of another religion. Many have become ecstatic converts. So seek out those gnarled beasties that take you back in time, to the ECI of your emergence from innocence to understanding. They are deeply magical tools that can be used to create rituals of astonishing potency.

# HELL OF A TOWN

## THE GREAT DARK OF 2003

T HERE WAS MUCH POETRY in the shadows last night.
The mighty light-bringer wrought by Edison and
Tesla closed its eyes at 4:10 pm EST. The people of New
York were startled, but soon gained their bearings as traffic lights went out on the avenues, and those on the side-
streets insisted "green" for a while. As the radio broadcasts
confirmed that the lack of power was not caused by terrorists and then began singing "Blame Canada" for the grid
failure, people started to head towards their homes by bus,
cab, or on foot. Stores did a brisk business selling food and
drink and batteries. There was some urgency as the sun
drew closer to the western horizon, enflaming New Jersey
with its crimson glory.

Peggy and I went out amongst the shuffling throng and
brought home some food. We enjoyed a pleasant repast,
and then took Contessa Bella Lugosi, our black Chow pup,
out for a stroll before the dusk turned to full darkness.
Our neighborhood streets were filled with people passing
through. Many locals had set up grills on the sidewalks and
the smell of cooking meat wafted through the air, accompanied by competing musics launched by battery powered
boom-boxes. A guitarist was on the stoop of the building

where Comedy Central produces *The Daily Show*. Our culture has bred an unending thirst for entertainment.

As the darkness enveloped Manhattan, flickering candlelight proliferated in windows. Several nearby telecommunications structures had generators, so their windows streamed brightness and stood as beacons in the dimmed canyons through which people were still wending their way, some with flashlights in hand. There was an air of a street festival, yet it seemed that this bravado was fending off the primal fear of the dying light that most of the herd holds in their hearts. It was, for we children of the night, a time of great beauty. Moonlight bathed the black concrete towers while random spelunkers made their way past their bases. The pinprick glimmers of guttering candles died one by one as the night pressed for victory. Ursa Major was clear to the naked eye for the first time since 1977 above these now quieted, mean streets.

While traffic lessened and the headlight beams grew scarce, we experienced what this vast urban sprawl had been like before the impact of the night had been fended off via artificial luciferism. That was a time when anyone, or perhaps any*thing*, might be awaiting prey in the ink-black interstices of the sleeping city. The spell of the classic monsters, both human and supernatural, could again be cast on those who now sweated and dreamed in their apartments—victim to long-buried terrors. It was heady and invigorating to we who eternally embrace the ebon majesty. The great dark reached forth in conquest, and we patriots of its empire celebrated its hegemony.

Hours later, as night was banished by a pearlescent dawn, the masses stirred and rose with the returning Aton. We wistfully observed the profound quiet that still reigned, as radio oracles predicted that soon the slumbering giant would again send its pulse to animate the silent great machines. Bathing and breakfasting in the gray light was a pleasure, yet the modern world abruptly intruded as our refrigerator trembled into activity at precisely 7:45.

And so the poetic caress of the age-old night has once again been banished from our metropolitan sprawl. But its magic, as always, beats in the hearts of Satanists, for we are kin and the living priesthood of its eternal mysteries.

15 August, XXXVIII A.S.

---

## ALAS, BABYLON

EVER SINCE MY YOUTH, I visited New York City and have always been impressed on a very deep level with how it encompasses the entire range of capabilities of the human animal. When I moved here to Hell's Kitchen twenty-five years ago, it was the fulfillment of a long ambition. As a Satanist, I savor the stratification of our kind. I enjoy the rich creations of rare individuals and am fascinated by the depths of depravity of others. I attempt to avoid the majority of people as they are generally mediocrities and not worth any time or attention. What was refreshing about The City at that time, as opposed to upstate New York from whence I came, was the lack of moderation, with little of the dull middle ground to muddy the stark black and white scenery.

In my experience it has always seemed to be the "world city," the capital and pivotal exemplar of what it means to be "homo urbanus." All extremes of human types can be found here: sub-moron, genius, the sophisticates, the naïve. Times Square used to be the most potent vista for viewing this entire spectrum in one glance. If one stood on Broadway and 42nd Street, simply by looking around you could see human passions embodied: base sexuality in the venues for all facets of pornography, the restless mind hungry for information in the endless electronic crawl of headlines and in the publications cramming the newsstands. Our need for fantasy was served by the many theaters showing every level of film being produced and a similar range of live performance from the splendid to the sordid. There were shops that sold exotic weaponry and tacky souvenirs.

The cuisine ranged from street vendors of dubious cleanliness and the quintessentially American Howard Johnson's to the second floor exotica of The Chinese Republic—one of the oldest Chinese restaurants in midtown. During its final years, a visit required one to elbow aside pimps and hookers to get through the street-level door and then climb up through the dingy, graffiti-covered stairwell to reach the red-lined lounge with its faded light-boxed photos of Chinese locations. Times Square was such a heady place to visit; it functioned in the way symbols do, allowing so much information to be in conscious focus in one intuitive flash. Sadly, most of this is gone, replaced by invading franchised businesses catering to the bland needs of tasteless drones. Neither belong here.

I mourn the homogenization of this area that has been in effect in recent years, as it has slapped a sanitized mask on the true face of our Babylon, inviting hordes of consumer zombies to wander the sidewalks in fulfillment of Romero's "Dawn" vision. Each year Coney Island, longtime avatar of dreams just beyond one's grasp, loses more of its resonance as the archaeological remnants of people's desperate search for diversion and fulfillment are swept clean. New York City has been attracting more of the marching morons of the herd, who now linger rather than pass through, and in that way it becomes a more accurate reflection of our whole species. I am lately missing the purity of the old perspective.

Our Hades-on-the-Hudson seems to have had its sharp edges blunted, made child-safe and tepid.

But I take heart, as I know that "no human ideal standeth sure." While the renovations and new construction currently shunt aside the more Plutonian elements, they have not disappeared, been ameliorated, or cured. Our town always works to "renew" itself, but the squeaky-clean results are short-lived. The hungry darkness still lurks on the fringes and will return to center stage in time, as the lodestone at these world crossroads is a powerful lure. Like the urban Hellscape in *Blade Runner*, the glittering techno-orgasmic displays create even deeper shadows that will again be filled with those who always call them home. Yes, our once and future Babylon is still Satanic, and those of us who know it intimately can still find the stimulating extremes, sidestepping the alien throng of mall cultists. Their moment is now, but I suspect that it shall be fleeting. The mask will slip, and when the true visage is glimpsed, it will send them scurrying back to the imagined normality of their prosaic suburbs and "heartland" states.

The current forces of sterilization are different from previous attempts to bowdlerize The City because of their premeditation and financial power, and it may be that the areas blighted by them may remain under their sway for some time. So long as there is a profitable market for a "Manhattanland" experience amongst visitors who think that visiting safe simulacra is preferable to something more spicy, these spots will remain "improved" and resistant to the surroundings which haven't yet been "redeemed." I cannot say for sure what may turn that tide, but in their greed, as soon as the income begins to decrease, the maintenance will lessen and things will become seedy, and again havens for what they view as the less savory. Unless the entire isle of Manhattan is turned to the "Light Side," the remaining adjacent crepuscular areas will be poised to ooze back when the opportunity presents itself. I am not enough of a prophet to risk prediction of time frames.

So many precious and bizarre things have vanished without proper replacements, such as Herman Slater's "The Magickal Childe," which was truly a pluralistic palace of religious diversity. We need those fringe blocks with spaces with low enough rent to present opportunities for entrepreneurs of the bizarre. There was always enough business to support such niche providers—New York was the place that embraced the types who cherished the unorthodox, and I hope that these don't end up only as virtual emporiums in cyber-space. This city still interests me, as there is enough remaining eccentricity, with peculiar folk plying trades in manners long forgotten elsewhere. But you have to look harder for them these days. So long as they can afford to remain in business, and so long as kindred outsiders with unique visions and the drive to try and make it here brave the pilgrimage and put down roots, the heart of this dark carnival will continue to beat.

17 May, XL A.S.

# ANTON SZANDOR LAVEY:
# A TRIBUTE FOR
# THE CLOVEN HOOF

HIS NAME RINGS OUT—a clarion call to those who recognize their true nature, the human animals who are proud to call themselves Satanists. He was a man who looked, and saw, and acted upon that knowledge. His great genius was to weave together seemingly disparate threads from many cultures and times, as he recognized them as emanating from a single, caliginous source. His powerful intellect and fleshly intuitions guided him to create that dark tapestry, shot through with flaming highlights and silver lightning bolts, whose substance comes from the very Lord of the Inferno Himself. Thus Anton Szandor LaVey formed the first church in Western history to be consecrated in the name of Satan, and thereby he shouted proudly to the world that the Left-Hand Path was his course, and he would take it further than had any of those who came before him.

He made it possible for us, his kin—for Satanists are born and not made—to know and embrace our legacy, that of the great men and women in history who were inspired to pioneer new realms of understanding. They used the great key of doubt to ask the questions left unasked, to travel to the lands, both physical and conceptual, which had remained previously unexplored, and thus forbidden to all but the bold.

Anton LaVey was one of these bold animals, complete in

ANTON SZANDOR LAVEY AND PETER H. GILMORE AT THE BLACK HOUSE

his understanding and brave enough to stand before his fellows and challenge the hide-bound platitudes that bind the complacent masses. His wisdom was not meant for all, as many are not born burning with the ardor of the Black Flame within. He knew that such will always seek after the false spiritual realms in an effort to fill that emptiness which knaws them from within. He warned his fellows to beware, for we are few and they are many, so we must walk with care amongst these living dead.

LaVey saw one of the fulcrum points upon which the conceptual weight of the world finds balance, and he knew how to push, altering the course of perceptions in a way that will have repercussions for millennia. He was truly a titan among men, and though we are the poorer for no longer being graced by his personal presence, his burning ideas have a life of their own that is crystallized in those who know that it is their Will to continue along the trail which he blazed with such brilliance.

He was gifted beyond what is normally considered a standard for excellence, being able to turn his hand to many arts with a deftness often only attained by dedication to but one muse. He left a creative legacy that enriches us, and he lived his life as the true exemplar of all that he extolled—pursuing his pleasures without stinting, while producing works only attained through the most vigorous self-discipline.

Anton Szandor LaVey touched many of us, and most particularly those who had the great privilege of being welcomed into his personal circle. But he will continue to touch many, even generations yet to be conceived, for he captured parts of himself in his writings, his music, and his videos, that will galvanize all true Satanists to stand forth with might and Understanding, dual weapons which cannot fail to bring victory.

We owe him our gratitude for opening the adamantine gates of Hell itself, giving form and structure to a philosophy that names us as the Gods that we are. His ultimate blasphemy against the puling sheep was to shatter their idolized dictum that all men are equal. His comrades, living as true Devils, would thus exercise their faculties to judge and be judged in all that they do. He dethroned the external saviors and championed responsibility for all consequences, perhaps the most frightening principle in a world wherein none are held accountable for their actions.

The Church of Satan is a tenebrous cabal of those who work to continue human society's momentum along the vector set by Anton LaVey. And it shall remain the treasured domain of the imperious few, the mighty-minded who live by their own blood and brains—who sail the ebon river into the bourne of darkness which welcomes only those who bear the blazonry of almighty Satan upon their very souls.

Anton Szandor LaVey, we salute you! Upon our faces we bear the smile of privileged information, the outward ensign of our tribal bond with thee, who wore this ironic standard so very well. You are forever in our hearts and minds.

Hail Anton Szandor LaVey!

Hail Satan!

# Farewell, Dark Fane

O<small>N</small> O<small>CTOBER</small> 16, XXXVI A.S., the infamous Black House—Dr. LaVey's residence for many years and the birthplace of the Church of Satan, was demolished.

For the past several years, the Black House at 6114 California Street sat empty and brooding, the quintessential "shunned house." Like the San Francisco lair of Dr. LaVey's mentor, Cecil Nixon, it was not meant to survive the death of the unique owner who had given it preternatural life.

It was the real-world equivalent of fictional "haunted houses" belonging to charming outsiders, like the Addams Family domicile of both cartoons and video. With Dr. LaVey as its *genius loci*, it became a nexus point for those who shared his Satanic sensibilities. It was truly an "unholy of unholies" for the select group of sinister individuals who were fortunate enough to be invited to cross its threshold and pass through the stygian pall of the entry hallway. Those of us who enjoyed many hours in its tenebrous embrace will never forget its charm—and its mysteries.

With its passing, it gains greater power as it moves into the realm of legend. Now it continues to exist as the archetype for lairs belonging to many of the members of the Church of Satan. And in the years to come it shall continue to serve as an inspiration for those infernal souls who have the will to construct their own dark sanctuaries.

# On Elaboration
# and Justice

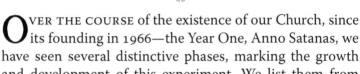

OVER THE COURSE of the existence of our Church, since its founding in 1966—the Year One, Anno Satanas, we have seen several distinctive phases, marking the growth and development of this experiment. We list them from our first decade retrospective written by Anton LaVey, and printed in *The Cloven Hoof*, Volume VIII, #2.

**THE FIRST PHASE**, Emergence, crystallized the zeitgeist into reality—let loose the knowledge of a Satanic body politic into a ready but dumbfounded social climate.

**THE SECOND PHASE**, Development, saw an organizational and institutional expansion as a result of carefully stimulated exploitation attracting a variety of human types from which to distill a Satanic "ideal."

**THE THIRD PHASE**, Qualification, provided sufficient elucidation to establish the tenets of contemporary Satanism, contrary to prior or current misinterpretation. *The Satanic Bible*, *The Satanic Rituals*, and *The Satanic Witch* might have been conveniently overlooked, but were readily obtainable to any who chose to gain knowledge of our doctrine and methodology. An aura of respectability prevailed—often to a point of overcompensation—to counterbalance inaccurate presumptions by the outside world.

**THE FOURTH PHASE**, Control, encouraged dispersion and the "Peter Principle" as a means of isolating the "ideal" evaluated from Phase Two. De-institutionalization separated the builders from the dwellers, thus filtering and stratifying what began as an initiatory organization—or persuasion—into a definite social structure.

**THE FIFTH PHASE**, Application, establishes tangible fruition—the beginning of a harvest, so to speak. Techniques, having been developed, can be employed. The Myths of the Twentieth Century are recognizable and exploitable as essential stimuli. Human foibles may be viewed with an understanding towards radical embellishment.

**THE SIXTH PHASE**, the development and production of Artificial Human Companions, has become part of our Pentagonal Revisionism statement.

We have seen some fascinating strides in the evolution of this Sixth Phase, particularly in the work of the Real Doll company. But overall, the general lack of discrimination that characterizes the herd has led them to be content with something less concrete for their sense of self-satisfaction. Indeed, the spread of the personal computer has provided the outlet wherein the masses' fantasies of adequacy, both sexual and social, are fulfilled. We "misanthropologists" have observed that it now takes place in chat rooms, via instant messaging, and in the fantasy world of web sites, all played out on the screen of a cathode ray tube—the computer monitor as messianic son of the television God worshipped in the homes of all herd peoples. It is only for the pioneering few to reject the touch of the keyboard, and pursue actual flesh-like textures produced by the artificers of contemporary androids. In their secret laboratories, they carry on in this Rotwangian endeavor, and currently we may look to Japan for the latest technological advances in the emergent art of robotics.

We are now, nearing our fortieth year of existence, in the midst of a *Seventh Phase*, that of **Elaboration**, wherein the results obtained from the continued application of our basic theories are examined and then crafted into ever more effective practice. Our productive members are now refining the materials which we began to reap in the harvest of the Fifth Phase, and combining them in ways ever more subtle and complex, which influence society in the directions of our Will. Based on our understanding of the myths of the Twentieth Century, some of us may work towards the formation of the mythology of the Twenty First Century. From the shattering of sacred icons we move towards secular icon building, generating new archetypes that will join the current pantheon of essential imagery. We are on the threshold of what may be a long period during which the innovators in our movement formulate symbols and characters that embody the quintessence of our values—self-determination, discrimination, and pride in accomplishment. In time, these may become broadly accepted sigils of what is truly Satanic—as we define Satanism.

Culturally our philosophy promotes the idea that a diverse range of choices should be open to the aware individual. The availability of such options will always threaten tyrants who wish to force "infidels," often on pain of death, towards conversion to their "One True Way." It doesn't matter which deity is pictured benignly spreading his or her arms for the forced followers. Satanists see this embrace as that offered by the "Virgin of Nuremberg," and we refuse it. And the time may come when our fellow travelers, who enjoy the benefits of our global secular society, do likewise. Let those who fear us continue to do so for the precise reason: that our way of life, if widely embraced, will limit the repressive reign of spiritual fanaticism.

As our ideas gain acceptance in new areas of the globe, we may see a swift progression through some of our earlier phases in various previously isolated locales. Wherever members of our "tribe" may be found, they shall use Satanic philosophy as a pragmatic means for attaining the fullest satisfaction in their lives. As a movement, Satanism may find it wise, wherever possible, to promote the proliferation of social structures that champion individualism as a value, and advocate maximum personal liberty for those who have the proper strengths required to wield this privilege with absolute responsibility.

***

**Indulgence** was the watchword chosen by Anton LaVey when he founded the Church of Satan in 1966. I think a case may certainly be made that this concept has in the interim made a lasting impact on human society. As we look through the landscape of what is currently offered, we see that Dr. LaVey's vision has had broad cultural effect, as the amount of freedom for personal pleasure has abundantly increased on all levels of social strata.

Dr. LaVey also noted that a prime danger was that the old concept of finding a scapegoat to blame for one's actions is becoming part of the weft and weave of our society. The escape clause that some "Devil made me do it" is behind the current victim-culture of political correctness that has seen full fruition in the extant laws of many nations.

Criminals who commit reprehensible acts are often deemed blameless, while nebulous currents in society itself are given the mantle of responsibility for demented, irresponsible behavior. We see our judiciary tacitly accepting the idea that people are automatons, who must of necessity be programmed from without by societal influences. This absolves criminals from blame when they do what is consensus "evil," and seeks to put the responsibility anywhere but upon the heads of the perpetrators. Hence, we witness the widely practiced twisted theory of injustice, which mandates that "blameless" criminals must be offered mercy and forgiveness.

Satanists now call for a halt to this grotesquery. We do this through the advocacy of our current watchword: **Justice**. Our means for its implementation is *Lex Talionis*—that punishment must fit in kind and degree the crime. Such a dictum has been cherished in ancient cultures and is overdue for a full-scale rebirth. The doom that should be over every person is: "Let it be upon your own head." Only you can take credit for your successes, and only you must be at fault for your failures. It is high time to put an end to the perpetual whining, finger pointing, and begging for special dispensations. And the current of general opinion is now flowing towards our desired direction.

The recent terrorist attacks on the United States evoked a worldwide fervor that just retribution be meted out for these criminal acts. Mercy is being discarded in favor of a true Satanic passion for justice. We have reached a historical fulcrum point wherein the mass of widely embraced values may now be leveraged in our desired direction. The time is now for Satanists, and others who cherish individual liberty, to expose the madness of religious fanaticism, wherever it may arise, and show the world-at-large that our freedom is threatened by those willing to die for their immaterial deities. We may see a continued societal transformation, if the understanding of the nature of the current situation is kept in sharp focus. The former days of forgiveness will be ended as aroused nations visit their wrath upon those who are enemies to the freedoms offered by secular civilization.

I stress that our organization and philosophy are both organic, ever evolving, for they are predicated on the continued deepening of our understanding of the beast called Man. Such knowledge may be utilized to broaden the horizons of freedom and responsibility—but this practice demands virtuosity. Anton LaVey established an insightful foundation which stands us in good stead as we further explore the implications of his ideas while we elaborate the applications of Satanism in our current cultural milieu, setting the stage for future permutations. He sounded the fundamental tone, and we now compose exquisite symphonies from the resultant overtones, provoking sympathetic vibrations in those of like nature. We shall never become hidebound, as the natural progression of evolution and revolution are axiomatic to our philosophy. Satanism's essence is to flow with Nature—ever forward!

So, my Epicurean comrades, we are in exciting times. Indulge, innovate, and celebrate the unique life that is your precious treasure, as well as the lives of those dear to you, who enrich your days by their very existence. The world is ours, so go forth and fill your experience with satisfaction. As you flow with the eternal now, may it be in exquisite pleasure.

# Natural Hierarchy: As Above, So Below

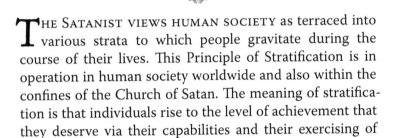

The Satanist views human society as terraced into various strata to which people gravitate during the course of their lives. This Principle of Stratification is in operation in human society worldwide and also within the confines of the Church of Satan. The meaning of stratification is that individuals rise to the level of achievement that they deserve via their capabilities and their exercising of them. This is an example of justice in action, another important principle for Satanic practice.

Each person is naturally endowed with a different level of raw talent. However, to Satanists, the cultivation of these abilities determines an individual's worth. *This must not be confused with a person's self-evaluation.* You alone can determine how you are fulfilling your chosen life goals, and this must be by your own standards. Judging yourself by others' standards is for the rabble. Your own satisfaction should be paramount.

It is also natural to wish to be esteemed by those who have won your respect. That many people desire to be judged according to our standards is evidenced by the many letters received asking "How can I advance in the Church of Satan?" Well, here's the answer: We judge our members with ruthless candor, equating their achievements *in the real world* to their worth. Thus, to advance in the Church of Satan, you must be applying your talents toward measurable achievements in your chosen fields of endeavor. After all, Satanism is an elitist religion, so if you desire recognition, you must prove to us that you are a being who excels at something notable.

It is not our intention to encourage members to seek position in our organization. Ambitious new members should look to advancing their own lives, for by so doing they will be living proof of the superiority of Satanists to the general masses. This is primarily how you can help the Church of Satan. By demonstrating that you can live a joy-filled and productive life through the Satanic philosophy you will help to spread our ideas to the worthy few whom you will contact in your day-to-day life. Let those who respect your achievements know that you are a Satanist and you will be advancing the public reputation of the Church of Satan. In turn, such successful members who keep us apprised of their doings will be granted recognition, which is a fringe benefit, not an end in itself.

We've seen over the years that those who come to us eager for titles are generally persons who have failed in meeting the demands of the real world, having no significant achievements, now seeking some form of ego bolstering to make up for this lack. They do not meet our criteria for advancement. When not given unearned laurels, they depart in a huff, and that is as it should be.

We do not require our first level of Registered Members to prove anything to us. The desire to join indicates that you stand out from the herd enough to want to call yourself a Satanist, which is no small step. But this does *not* mean that you are automatically the top of the heap. All kinds of individuals join our organization for their own reasons. Some demonstrate that they have only a rudimentary grasp of the philosophy of Satanism. So long as membership pleases them, that is wonderful, but we won't be putting them forward as paragons. Others come to us after having made names for themselves that are quite impressive. That prowess is deeply appreciated and will be acknowledged. To be successful *as a Satanist*, one must live one's life in a manner that fulfills one's values. If your life is joyful, you have achieved an important goal. However, if a member of the Church of Satan wishes to be elevated, he must measure up to very high standards to take a place amongst a cadre of superior individuals.

New Registered Members receive an application for Active Membership—our way of getting a picture of you as an individual, or at least of what image you wish to portray of yourself. We do not initially know what is accurate or exaggeration from our first reading. After submitting this, we might wait for the member to prove certain claims by submitting evidence of his abilities. At times we will request a sample of something that you have mentioned that seems of interest. We also wait to see whether you are working to move on with your life towards your stated goals, because static people are not material for advancement in our organization. If this application is accepted, you are deemed an Active Member, which is our acceptance of you as a Satanist in our terms. You receive by mail a certificate of acceptance to "Satanist, First Degree." All degrees beyond this first level are by invitation only.

Anton LaVey formulated our system of degrees during the early years of the Church of Satan, as such was a general practice in many prior social and esoteric organizations. He mandated that the standards for elevation in our Church were based not on mysticism or occultism, but on knowledge of practical subjects beyond Satanism, and even more than that, on the application of such wisdom towards measurable ends. Dr. LaVey experimented by designating the specific colors for medallions that could be worn by each member according to degree. And, for a time, written exams were given to assess a member's readiness for a particular level.

In the mid 1970s, it became clear that many members had become obsessed with "jockeying for position"—being overly concerned with their place in the organization rather than working towards advancement in the world "outside." This was contrary to our carnal philosophy's emphasis on tangible personal progress and so, after that point, the existence of the degrees was de-emphasized in church literature and formulaic methods for recognition were jettisoned.

Our church is unique as a loose cabal of individualists and our protocol for member interaction is based on the paradigm of a "mutual admiration society." We do not expect all of our highly individualistic members to like each other, but we **do** require that they behave as ladies and gentlemen when mingling in all situations and forums, online and face-to-face. Interaction is never required, and in the case of extreme disagreement wherein civility apparently cannot be maintained, we expect involved members to cease confrontation with each other. Violation of this standard can be grounds for expulsion.

Today, we maintain our traditional degrees, but these should not be seen as "initiatory steps" which are expected of our members. The Church of Satan is **not** an initiatory organization. It is our position that, for those with awareness, by living fully you will have plenty of authentic initiatory experiences through the many avenues you explore, hence there is no need for such artificial posturing in our church. No member is required to move beyond Registered Membership. The First Degree denoting Active Membership is for members who seek more involvement with the organization and other local members. The remaining degrees (from the Second through the Fifth) are **not** open to application or to request. The administration watches the progress of qualified members, and may choose to grant recognition to outstanding individuals based on demonstrated excellence in the understanding and communication of Satanic Theory, coupled with significant potent practices which have produced superior achievements in the arena of the human endeavors. People naturally and quite organically rise to particular levels, and we may take note at our discretion. This is meritocracy at work.

Here are the levels of our hierarchy, with the feminine form preceding:

> **Registered Member** (no degree)
> **Active Member—Satanist** (First Degree)
> **Witch/Warlock** (Second Degree)
> **Priestess/Priest** (Third Degree)
> **Magistra/Magister** (Fourth Degree)
> **Maga/Magus** (Fifth Degree)

We also have people who perform tasks for the organization and so they have descriptive titles such as "Administrator," "Agent," and "Grotto Master." These responsibilities can be assumed by members with different degrees. "High Priest" and "High Priestess" are the top administrative titles, and can be held only by Fourth or Fifth Degree members.

An individual who demonstrates a thorough grasp of the philosophy of the Church of Satan, skills in being able to communicate it, and would like to be a contact for local media and other interested parties may be chosen to serve as an Agent for the Church of Satan. Those who are appointed as Agents must demonstrate that they have already been successfully making efforts to publicly clear up misconceptions regarding our philosophy. You will have seen many of our spokespersons in various media, so they may inspire you to follow their lead.

The first advanced level one can attain is that of Witch for the ladies and Warlock for the gentlemen, our Second Degree. This is a position of esteem we offer to our members who have shown impeccable taste in self-presentation, rising to various occasions with exquisite aplomb. Naturally, these diabolists understand and apply the principles of Satanic Theory we all hold dear, moving through the world in such a way as to be exemplars of Satanism in action. They are accomplished in some chosen field and have garnered the respect of their peers. Their lifestyles are directed towards reduced contact with the human herd. In short, our Witches and Warlocks are up-and-coming achievers with personal panache.

Those who hold the Third through Fifth degrees are all members of the Priesthood of Mendes and individuals with these titles may be called "Reverend." These are the individuals who act as spokespersons for the philosophy of the Church of Satan. Members of the Priesthood make up the **Council of Nine**, which is the ruling body of the organization, appointed by and responsible to the High Priest or Priestess. The **Order of the Trapezoid** consists of the individuals who assist in the administration of the Church of Satan. Members of our Priesthood are people of distinguished accomplishment in the real world—they have mastered skills and have won peer acclaim, which is how they have attained their position—"as above, so below." They are movers and shakers who are the core of our movement. While expected to be experts in communicating our philosophy, they are not required to speak on our behalf and they may even choose to keep their affiliation and rank secret, in order to better serve their personal goals, as well as those of our organization. You may encounter members of our Priesthood and never know it. The Fourth Degree denotes consummate mastery of our theory and practice, and the Fifth degree of Satanic Master is someone who has advanced the standing of Satanism itself.

Why join? That depends upon what being a member means to you personally. The basic reason is to show allegiance to the organization that embodies the philosophy that has galvanized your life, serving to clearly represent these concepts to our society as a darkly blazing beacon to all born Satanists. Additionally, avenues may be provided for deeper involvement with members, as a means of working on projects of mutual interest. The Church of Satan is emphatically not intended as a means for socializing. We expect our members to have the skills needed to fill those needs on their own. You can't be a master of Lesser Magic if you are a closet case.

Ultimately, there are two perspectives which we address: your self-image as to how successful you are living as a Satanist measured by your degree of satisfaction with your life, and our evaluation of you as an exemplar of Satanism which determines your degree level measured by our exacting standards. If you choose to live as a Satanist, learn to satisfy yourself. We demand no other obligation. That alone is a challenge few conquer. If you want to be recognized by the Church of Satan as role model, you must then satisfy our criteria. Those are in constant evolution and based on the context from which an individual arises to make himself known. The trend is for them to grow ever more stringent, forcing a higher quality from people who work towards elevation.

There is no need for members to put themselves up for our judgment. You are all free to determine your own paths and standards of achievement. Self-satisfaction is an admirable goal in itself. However, if it is your desire to gain our recognition, you must prove your accomplishments to us. Let us know how you are doing, particularly since we are proud when meaningful goals are attained. There are misguided people who wish to establish membership in our elite group based on pretension and puffery. Satanism provides that "leaky inner-tube test" to puncture those who inflate their egos with hot air instead of demonstrable deeds. If you are an outstanding individual, and so many who enter are dark portals are, then you will take your rightful place in a circle of your peers. We will appreciate you for your triumphs. For some it *is* worth the effort.

# Masterful Slaves

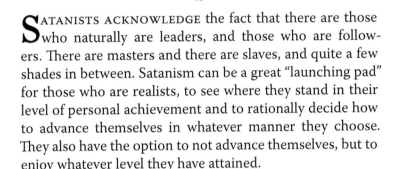

$S$ATANISTS ACKNOWLEDGE the fact that there are those who naturally are leaders, and those who are followers. There are masters and there are slaves, and quite a few shades in between. Satanism can be a great "launching pad" for those who are realists, to see where they stand in their level of personal achievement and to rationally decide how to advance themselves in whatever manner they choose. They also have the option to not advance themselves, but to enjoy whatever level they have attained.

The old saw about a group being "all chiefs and no Indians" is certainly one that has found a new lease amongst "nouveau Satanists." They are simply not being honest in their self-evaluation—a practice that all but guarantees their failure to work magic of both Greater and Lesser varieties. The self-aware individual evaluates his position with ruthless accuracy, and if he has the desire to attain a higher level, then he makes the efforts to do so by exercising his talents. The observation of the development of how an individual sees *himself* is a strong indicator for marking his true journey along the Left Hand Path.

What many fail to grasp is that there is no requirement that one must move to a higher echelon. As long as one has contentment and is enjoying one's life, we Satanists place no moral value on the stratum to which one belongs.

Being what you really are and procuring pleasure is the goal that Satanism helps one sustain. There is no obligation to push yourself in a direction that does not come naturally, and true Satanists don't "lord it over" others whom they perceive to be of a lower rank. It is a fact, when one considers the vast population on this globe, that there is a strong likelihood that someone will come along who is brighter, more learned, more talented, more accomplished, and in some way may have "bested" you in an area that you have as a personal pursuit. Screaming that one is always "top dog" is a sure sign of insecurity as well as ignorance of actual Satanism. Competition with one's own prior achievements is a healthy stimulus for self-evolution, but the final goal is to be the best you can be, and not have unrealistic images of what one "should" become. Self-satisfaction is the desired result, not constant internal strife.

Similarly, many neophytes read about the LaVey Personality Synthesizer in *The Satanic Witch* and then make moral judgments concerning where they should stand on that symbolic clock, often misjudging their actual position and thus ignoring that there is no ethical verdict placed on any clock position. Satanists come in a remarkable variety—not all are "great innovators" or "fearless leaders," or dominant individuals. In fact, it takes a real Satanist to appreciate the few who do have those abilities to create and lead, and to enjoy what these people have to offer without feeling any need to try and outdo them if such is not natural to himself. To think that "activity/dominance" is "good" and that "passivity/submission" is "bad" means one has fallen into the false dichotomy of dualist thinking. Satanists see the need for polarity, the necessity of opposites that provide the tension that leads to the flowing of the current inherent in all things. Both are part of existence and neither is preferable.

Amongst Satanists it is natural to find some who embrace the principles of this philosophy and do not feel that they have the capabilities to "make their own horizons," as Nietzsche defined a characteristic of his "superior humans." These honest individuals have the choice to personally (and wisely) select their masters, and thus to guarantee that they will get the beneficial guidance they desire. Unlike unwilling slaves, they are also free to switch masters should they so choose. Few are honest enough about themselves to make such a decision.

All authentic Satanists exhibit genuine confidence and "personal power," using it to determine the courses of their lives to whatever extent is possible in the society in which they live. They explore and ascertain their strengths and weaknesses, and do not flinch from adapting to best meet their needs.

There are times when masochistic individuals, oblivious to their own natures, are attracted to Satanists, antagonizing them in an attempt to goad them into exercising this real, not postured, power. Each Satanist, as LaVey explained, is an Epicurean Sadist, and when such masochists approach, the Satanist often says "No!" to the symbolic requests for a "beating," thus turning the masochist's sought-after *eustress* into distress. But the Satanist's option to say "Yes!" also exists, and he can then provide the masochist with the requested "beating," but only if it also gives the Satanist satisfaction.

These are subtleties, and the misdirected masochist should preferably find a loving master willing to dispense the desired disciplinary actions in the degree that will gratify the masochist's needs. An enlightened Satanic masochist will find a Satanic sadist, and each can engage in the tango of mutual satisfaction, wherein the one asking for fulfilling pain controls how much is administered by the figure that outsiders would mistake to be the controlling party.

The truly self-aware Satanic individual will earn the attention of mentor masters who can give the needed directions if they are the types who treasure being in that position of power and responsibility. The polarity here is natural, elegant, and fulfilling, and no "bottom" need feel lesser than the "top," for the flow of gratification cannot continue if both sides of the equation are not present. The student fulfills the teacher's need to instruct. In time, the student may become a professor and have his own pupils. Flux is natural. The slave can actually dominate the master, and such is well known in the sexual subculture of Bondage and Dominance. But the sagacious Satanist knows that these principles apply far beyond the bounds of lust, and so will be truly free from placing a value on such a label. He will grasp that to be Satanic is to be beyond such conventional judgments and naïve assessments. He is satisfied with himself, and honest in appraisal, and will seek out those of equal wisdom and sovereignty. Under the aegis of Satanism, the masterful slaves and the enslaved masters will meet and continue their eternal dance.

# THE MYTH OF THE "SATANIC COMMUNITY" AND OTHER VIRTUAL DELUSIONS

THE INTERNET, that ultimate means for the spread of mediocrity, spans the entire globe, and it has, for good or ill, a "Satanic presence." It is time to address some tendencies that, while previously hampered by snail-mail low technology, have now been set loose to undercut our movement by turning it into a circus, with particularly poorly-trained clowns taking the center ring.

The use of the adjective "Satanic" with the noun "community" is oxymoronic. Why? The process of creating a "community" implies that its members come out into the open and become quantifiable, defining and exposing themselves. This technique is almost always used by an assemblage of people who want to claim some form of victim status, who want to whine that they are oppressed, and thus agitate for some form of "special dispensations" for their members. This idea is anathema to Satanists and contrary to Satanic principles. Recall Anton LaVey's dictum that the Church of Satan must remain "a custard that can't be nailed to the wall"? While our philosophy is made abundantly clear through publicly available literature, the organization itself remains largely hidden. There is power in mystery. And it serves us well, should some form of organized anti-Satanism actually gain political or social power. So here is a simple fact: there is no "Satanic Community" nor should one ever exist. Please re-read the previous line until it begins to sink in.

Satanism is a unique philosophy that has spawned an even more unusual movement and an organization, the Church of Satan, which has found a means for facilitating the interaction of a membership comprised of radical individualists. It is, in an apparent paradox that is a "third-side synthesis," an organization for non-joiners. The structural basis for the Church of Satan is the cabal concept. It is maintained, for the most part, as an underground cell-system of individuals who share the basis of the philosophy created by Anton Szandor LaVey, but who find very unique ways of applying this philosophy towards their own personal goals. Above the surface, you might see some spokespersons and some discussion forums that have a public presence. But, like an iceberg, most of our membership remains hidden in the murky depths. Some new members mistakenly want to publish membership lists, as they fail to grasp this concept behind the structure of the organization. They still haven't shaken off pre-conceptions absorbed from herd culture. If, after explanations, they don't begin to grasp that they are still thinking in a non-Satanic paradigm and thus they are working to counter our intentional structure, they may be asked to leave the organization.

Many members have chosen to affiliate but do not want to find others with whom to associate. Their reason for membership is to affirm their allegiance to the organization that publicly represents the philosophy that they hold dear, which gave a name to who they really are. These members do *not* interact with other members; they don't seek out fellow Satanists. They remain underground and pursue personal goals. We support these valued members who are non-joiners and their commitment remains strictly confidential. Other members may find through our organization a means for locating others who share particular passions, not just an interest in Satanism *per se*. Our Special Interest Groups admirably serve to kindle new projects among participating members. This last assembly, it should be noted, is not the majority of the total organization. Due to the present ease for finding other like-minded individuals provided by current communications technology, the intelligent Satanist has every means at his disposal to exercise on his own any social prerogatives he might have.

Over the past 35 years, we have learned a striking truth: Satanists are amazingly diverse individuals and they may share very little in common beyond the fact that their approach to living leads them all to adopt the label "Satanist." This is the reason why we generally do not have large gatherings of Church of Satan members, nor do we have conventions, as this group of individuals would not get along with one another *en masse*. Look at the evidence for this in the ghetto of online Satanism, which is a very small subset of people who call themselves Satanists. This bunch is the most contentious and cantankerous collection of curmudgeons ever seen in one place. So the very idea that these people could ever work together as a community is completely naïve—misguided idealism, rather than Satanic pragmatism. Satanists by nature follow their own tastes in such areas as politics and aesthetics; they have uniquely personal hierarchical systems of values that are not necessarily congruent with those of other Satanists. I have met and corresponded with thousands of Satanists. I know this to be a fact. There are certainly some common threads, which can be deduced by considering the principles that under-gird *The Satanic Bible*. Love of and respect for animals, a desire for swift justice, and an aesthetic sense that demands that things rise above the mediocre are some of these. When interests other than a mutual embracing of the philosophy created by Anton LaVey do match, then

Satanists can develop very deep friendships and amazingly potent partnerships for attaining mutual goals. But just because two people call themselves "Satanist" does not mean that there will necessarily be such common denominators.

To attempt to make this very loose and shadowy assemblage into something resembling other existing communities would mean disregarding the core principles of Satanism as a philosophy. Satanism as a movement would then become just another typical social device for human herding. Anton LaVey expressed his contempt for people who demonstrated the "huddling" instinct, explaining that it is a certain indication that they weren't Satanists at all, just "sheep" who want to pretend to be "goats."

He was right. And we are constantly treated to displays of Satanic wannabes parading around with websites and "organizations," using our symbols and literature as a means for attempting to gain attention for themselves, while ostensibly claiming to want to be helping Satanism as a movement. Well, we say "Thanks, but no thanks." We don't need amateur help, particularly when this "help" demonstrates that the amateurs don't grasp these very basic principles.

Let's look at a typical example. Here's Joe (it could just as easily be Jane) Schitz, a general loser whose age is between 15 and 29. He's heard about Satanism from his favorite "let's freak out the parents" rock star, and since he's too lazy to go to the library to do research and too cheap to buy a book, he turns to the Internet. He surfs the web and is confronted by hundreds of sites claiming to be giving valid information about Satanism. Since his image of Satanism includes (like his musical hero's stage persona) public acclaim, wealth, sex, and notoriety, he is ill equipped to deal with all this material, lacking any measure to discriminate the valid from the invalid. If he purchased and read *The Satanic Bible* or carefully read the essays and interviews on the Church of

Satan's official site, he'd begin to see what Satanism is really about. But that would be too much like work. Some of what he sees in this morass—imagery that might prove shocking to others, he likes. He thinks he's found the passport to a position in the limelight. He compares his own humdrum existence with his perception of Satanism and suddenly wants to be a part of it. So, first off, he changes his name to some less-than-euphonious moniker like, Damien Anton Manson Dragon Azathoth the 23rd.

> *A brief aside:* What is it with these people who feel the need to adopt these "spooky" names? If they really hate the name with which they have been gifted by their parents, why not change it to something more effective as many Hollywood actors and other showbiz types have done? Something simple and catchy, easy to remember, but impressive. Names like John Wayne, Marilyn Monroe, Jayne Mansfield. Or they might even look to character names from pulp fiction or classic literature to find an appellation more suitable to their personalities. However, names that sound like they should be listed on a membership card for a Count Chocula fan club should be avoided like the plague, yet they abound in the ranks of Satanic *poseurs*. Stop looking through lists of demon names—especially if they are from role-playing or video games. Here's a challenge: don't change your name at all. If you've looked at history, most of the great names are simply known because the people who had them achieved memorable things. People remember names like Mozart, Einstein, Edison, and Galileo, not because these names had any prior "resonance," but because of what these individuals created. So, do you have what it takes to stick with your own name and, through your own creativity, make it a name that future generations will use as a synonym with fame or notoriety?

Back to our newbie. He might then start dressing in bizarre outfits, inspired by his favorite musician's stage show, forgetting the fact that he isn't a rock star and he isn't on stage. He might wear black lipstick or nail-polish, or even go so far as to get a piercing or a tattoo (what a maverick!). He's now received the negative attention of family and friends, but since he wants to be a rebel, he feels this is a good beginning. Now to expand his horizons as there's a whole world out there waiting to be annoyed! So, he gets on his parents' computer and signs up for a free website—an easy process that has predictably lead to the ever-expanding Internet dreck festival. Time to grab some content. He again looks up Satanism online so as to find his own kind, now that he thinks he's a Satanist. What does he find? A plethora of others like himself! Must mean there's a "community," and he's dying to be a big cheese in it. He's his own God, isn't he? He's just got to show everyone else out there that he's better than they are. So, he immediately begins to lift graphics from the sites he encounters, as well as any essays he thinks sound scary enough to enhance his reputation—only writings by the most famous names in Satanism will do. The very idea of copyrighted material and creators' rights never enters his mind, particularly as he feels—by putting these graphics and texts on his site—that he is helping to support Satanism. Any who'd tell him otherwise must just be old fuddy-duddies who just want to rain on his parade—so screw them!

He is now determined to be the "Great Black Hope" of Satanism. He wants to evangelize people concerning his new-found identity. Just because he's unaware of the vast amount of representation that's been done over the last 40 years by Church of Satan spokespersons must mean it just wasn't very good—it couldn't possibly mean he didn't know how to do research. He also hasn't learned that proselytizing is not a part of Satanism.

Eventually, he runs across the official website of the

Church of Satan. He finds it to be a goldmine of material to pilfer. That he **is** stealing and thus violating the Satanic concept of "responsibility to the responsible" would never come to focus in what passes for his "thinking."

Next, he decides that he'll start a Satanic organization. Since he's a God, how can he not be a leader? He'd never think of "following" someone with more intelligence and experience. That would make him seem "weak," to admit that he doesn't instantly know everything. Naturally he's got to be the High Priest (move over Anton LaVey). Anyone who emails him and compliments his site becomes a member and if they kiss ass particularly well, they receive an instant Priesthood. After he's been at this for a few weeks (if he's patient), he finally decides that he's going to approach the Church of Satan and propose an alliance, as he thinks he's really become the leading force for keeping Satanism alive in the world. The poor old Church of Satan just better recognize this, lest it be left in his dust. So he sends an email full of bluster and bravado, claiming he's got a huge international organization, and a website (Satan save us!). He signs this portentous missive with his grand new name, appended to which are numerous titles such as "High Priest of the Universal Elite Legions." One of our representatives reads this, and a dozen like it which came in that week, and then dutifully checks out the site, discovering—once its interminable download is over as it is chock full of crappy animations and sound files—that it is also full of stolen Church of Satan material, both copyrighted texts and graphics. Our representative then sends a formal email pointing out these blatant copyright violations and asks "High Priest Azathoth" to remove them, or else we'll have to approach his service provider. This naturally enrages the impotentate. How *dare* the Church of Satan stop him from becoming the world's greatest Satanic leader? So he writes back, his response full of profanity and indignation—after all, his "Satanic Genius" has not been recognized. Our Church of Satan representative must then go through the tedious task of contacting HPA's Internet service provider, quoting the guidelines for service of which HPA is in violation, and then monitoring the situation until that page has either removed all copyrighted materials, or is simply cancelled by the provider (the usual outcome).

Now, disgruntled Damien, thwarted in his bid to rule the world of Satanism, must start a campaign to re-assert himself in the "Satanic Community," with the Church of Satan as his target. He thinks, "What gall they have to protect their material when I know how to use it better!" He'll email his cronies and they will try to invade message boards frequented by real Satanists, doing their best to prevent pleasurable discussions from taking place. That the moderators for these boards kick and ban them only serves as a stimulant. They could make their own message boards in which they would be free to gather and discuss how rotten the Church of Satan is, but that usually does not suffice. They desperately want recognition by real Satanists, and they'll get it by being annoying, rather than trying to earn respect for any tangible achievements or simply engaging in intelligent discussion.

Of course, our would-be High Priest may eventually find something else to hold his interest. He might actually go out on a date, or find that he does have some kind of skill that he needs to practice, aside from being a royal asshole—the one skill which he's perfected by now. But he may prolong his tenure in the "Satanic Community" if he stumbles into another kind of online group—a collection of like-small-minded losers, who have washed up on the shoals of the Internet, after their website-vessels have been sunk by the torpedoes of the mean old Church of Satan. Here is the haven wherein he'll find fellow self-proclaimed "High Priests." They are usually collected under the direction of a new "Magus" who is even more pretentious and pompous then they are, hence he's top of that shit heap. Here they will huddle together, fueled by their hatred for the fact that they couldn't conquer the Satanic Universe as embodied in the Church of Satan and united in their envy of those who have earned positions therein. Now they have a peanut gallery to cheer them on, as they spew their illiterate vitriol (of particularly dilute vintage) against the real Satanists whom they might encounter. They will clutter Usenet as well as message boards with their pointless, moronic postings. Of course, when the time comes to sort out the pecking order amongst these "High Priests," then the fur will fly and schisms will abound as they scratch out each other's eyes fighting over ever-sillier titles. Eventually they will just leave Satanism behind altogether. If only this would happen with greater speed.

Does any of this sound familiar? Does this example hold up a mirror to *you*? If so, please take a good long look and think about what you are projecting to those real Satanists whom you might encounter.

You may well ask, "So what is it that the eager individual, new to Satanism, might do to help the Satanic movement?" (Not the "Satanic Community.") The answer is simple. Satanism is about centering the world on yourself, which means knowing yourself as fully as possible. What are your consuming interests (aside from Satanism) and what are your talents? Once you have an answer to this question, then you should set out to achieve something in these arenas. Sounds easy, doesn't it? But it is a tall order for many, who must buy a ready-made identity and then bludgeon other people with it in order to be noticed. Lately, too many of them have the mistaken idea that they are Satanists. And they have access to computers.

The person who has a talent for baking and figures

out how to make some damn fine chocolate chip cookies, and then shares this secret with friends thereby enriching their world with delicious cookies or makes an empire out of selling these to other people, is someone who is using a Satanic principle to further their lives. If this person becomes a world famous cookie magnate, or just the neighborhood's most revered baker, and THEN lets people know that his philosophy is Satanism, then THAT is a deed which forwards the movement. Our baker will have demonstrated that a Satanist is a person with the capability to do something exemplary. Dressing up weirdly, making shabby websites, and screaming to the world that you are a Satanist only impresses utter fools, and does nothing to help our movement.

Want recognition from other Satanists? Deliver the goods. Don't make hollow promises, pretentious claims, and over-blown pontifications. Just do something and do it well. Are you a musician, artist, mathematician, publisher, athlete, scientist, engineer, designer, scholar, architect, writer or craftsperson? Show us that you understand the Magic of Mastery. I guarantee that the real Satanists will take notice.

Founding your own Satanic organization is a detriment to our movement. First off, why reinvent the wheel? We already have an international organization, the Church of Satan, which is the fountainhead of the movement, and it is one that is exceedingly flexible in accommodating qualified members' desires to flex their leadership muscles. Just ask us. We have plenty of members who have founded special interest projects requiring someone with intelligence and organizational skills to head them. If you agree with our philosophy, then there is a place for you with us. A proliferation of organizations fragments the movement, particularly as they offer nothing new. It is like putting a poor imitation of a fine wine in a bottle with a label that is very much like that of the original fine wine. There is no differentiation or enrichment, just half-assed knock-offs. Seen those fake Rolex watches? It is the same principle. People may be very sincere in this imitation, but they should understand that the effect is ultimately negative to our movement.

Additionally, these far-too-numerous website-based "organizations" give our movement the appearance of a gaggle of squabbling children, all stamping their feet and crying for attention. We do not support any other organizations calling themselves Satanic. We can't possibly know what their standards are, nor if their members even grasp and practice Satanism as defined by Anton Szandor LaVey, which is our basis for authenticity. So if you have thought to imitate the Church of Satan rather than joining it, we cannot endorse your efforts.

If instead you want to create your own group whose purpose is some creative endeavor, like a consortium creating art or publishing a magazine or producing music rather than simply an attempt to be yet another Satanic organization, then that *does* have validity. If you want to start an online pen-pal site with message boards, then by all means do so. You can have whatever standards you choose concerning those who may participate, but don't claim that it is a Satanic Church and hand out titles. If it becomes successful and productive, instead of a haven for drooling malcontents, we might give it notice. Just be honest about what it really is. Remember "Satanic Sin #2"?

Also, if you really have a take on Satanism which is *not* congruent with that put forth in Anton LaVey's writings— which means, it *is* something different, then you should try to start your own group. See if others might share your vision. Just don't claim it is the Church of Satan and don't steal the Church of Satan's symbols and literature. And don't waste everyone's time by being a member of our organization.

If you do agree with Satanism as formulated by Anton LaVey and you have a website promoting your personal creative efforts, just put up a link to the official Church of Satan site (www.churchofsatan.com). You don't have to be a member to link to us. Let your own site be a reflection of yourself, an exploration of things that you enjoy and admire, things about which you are so passionate that you are becoming an expert in them (other than Satanism). Then you might discuss how Satanism is a natural outgrowth of your individuality, and how it has helped you in your pursuits. Finally, send your audience on over to our site to get all the basic material. Isn't that easy?

We have been at this task of representing Satanism to the international media for a long time now. The people currently running our organization have been at it for about two decades, and we were assisting Anton LaVey himself when he was alive. So we continue the practice of screening our representatives with great care. Some might fear that they won't measure up, or their eagerness makes them impatient to "get out there." But they need to realize that we are the caretakers of a worldwide movement, and it is our job to make certain that those who are authorized to represent us can do so at every level and with consummate skill and lucidity. Our members around the globe, and even Satanists who have embraced the principles of *The Satanic Bible*, may stand up for the ideas they hold dear, but only if they understand them fully and can articulate them with finesse in whatever situation arises. Nothing is more saddening to us than a well-meaning but verbally unskilled individual attempting to explain Dr. LaVey's concepts and thus garbling them completely, or allowing an interviewer to lead him into a distortion that is damaging to our public visage. Then, our chosen Agents must do double-duty to clarify the misinformation inadvertently spread, and with today's electronic media such brushfires can rapidly become widespread conflagrations.

If you really think you might have talents in this area, then you should be able to prove that to us. It is relatively easy for members to become Agents, and part of the journey towards that official responsibility is to already be working to clarify errors you might find about Satanism and showing us how well you did. Since our religion is a very controversial one, we cannot afford to make mistakes, so we will not allow people to represent us unless we are convinced that they will always present our ideas with great precision.

One of the dangers of Satanic philosophy is that it "puffs-up" some people, giving them over-inflated illusions of their own value to others. The current appallingly-democratic notion that everyone's opinion must be given equal validity is carried over into Satanism when these folks all take the notion that "You are your own God" and then assume that they are everyone else's God as well. And they forget, once entering into a pantheon of self-proclaimed deities, that all Gods are not of equal stature. Stratification, once again, always comes into play. This principle is another that is frequently ignored or misunderstood by those new to Satanism.

As far as I can tell, the rest of the world's religions and philosophies don't have this problem, and this is generally because they preach submission. When someone reads *The Holy Bible*, he doesn't immediately go out, make a web-site-Vatican emblazoned with the Papal Seal, claim he is a Cardinal or Pope, and ordain his correspondents as Priests, Bishops, and Arch-Bishops. Satanism's championing of self-empowerment is used against Satanism itself when over-zealous amateurs decide they have a mission to represent Satanism. Our answer: "Live Satanism. Leave the representation of it to those who have been carefully trained in that area." If you really want to be among those people, then take the time to practice and study and show us the results of these efforts. Remember, "Satanism demands study, not worship!" But that study is an in-depth one of the human animal. It includes such topics as philosophy, history, religious beliefs, anthropology, sociology, psychology, and the hard sciences. The members of the Priesthood of Mendes, who represent us publicly, understand much in these areas. But there's more.

They have their Priesthoods not only because they have this knowledge, but because they have also *applied* it to honing their talents and using them to make a mark on the world itself, outside of the subject of Satanism. This is a great deal to ask of people, but we require no less for entry into that distinguished company. The Priesthoods of other religions require years of study and apprenticeship, so it shouldn't come as a surprise that we also have exacting standards. We are a worldwide religious and philosophical movement, and we will not lower our standards to accommodate over-eager neophytes.

Anyone who sets up a website and proclaims himself and his friends priests, or other pompous titles, demonstrates a lack of security and an inability to understand that meaningful titles must be earned from people who have attained concrete achievements. Otherwise, such titles are a pretentious joke, and those who hand them out make organized Satanism seem like a goofy Satan fan club in which practically everybody who joins is a priest. This does not help the stature of the movement, for reasons that should be obvious.

> *Another aside:* Here's a diabolical thought. If someone really started an actual, honest-to-Satan "Anton LaVey Fan Club," and had the guts to call it that, they just might gain

our respect. Fan clubs are associations of people who band together in their admiration for something that they had no hand in creating. These groups often focus on films—particularly those that create their own fictional universe, actors, musicians, or other publicly prominent personages. The fans didn't make the film, nor did they create the stage persona of the actor or assist in the growth of his talent, nor did they organize the band. They just encountered these things and developed a fervid interest in them. These fans do not claim to represent "that which they admire" since the objects of admiration naturally have professional representation. They just share their interest with each other. The object of their admiration might even license them the right (for a small percentage) to produce authorized souvenirs or in the case of films, the studios make their own merchandise to sell to the fans. This is generally a light-hearted means for people to interact, though bitter disputes have been known to erupt in such groups. We see no relevant reason for those who agree with Anton LaVey's philosophy not to join the Church of Satan. However, thinking that Anton LaVey was "cool" does not mean that you are necessarily a Satanist. Some who might find our philosophy and standards too challenging, but who admire Dr. LaVey, could band together and create a fan club, without the pretensions at being a Satanic organization or towards representing Satanism, Anton LaVey, or the Church of Satan. Will anyone online be so bold and honest?

So, if you really want to assist us in promoting Satanism, then the door is wide open. Know yourself, master your abilities, and win the respect of people whose respect is worth gaining—and it is up to you to select them. They will then become part of your life, and mutual enrichment will follow. We who administer the Church of Satan can then add you to the list, when we proudly point out our amazingly talented and creative members. You'll be an exemplar of whom we are proud when you stand forth and show your mantle of Darkness, for you will impress the world by the quality of your deeds, not simply by professing to be a Satanist. Then those who look in on Satanism from the outside will be awed at the richness to be found. Clear away this flea circus of pseudo-Satanic websites and online pretend organizations and instead promote Satanism by living life to the fullest. Retain the mystery, explore your obsessions, confound and confuse 'til the stars be numbered. That is the future of our movement. We're still looking for a few outstanding individuals—care to join us?

THE MYTH OF THE "SATANIC COMMUNITY"

# REBELS WITHOUT CAUSE

**W**E ARE OCCASIONALLY APPROACHED regarding membership by those who have beliefs incongruent with Satanism yet claim the title "Satanist." They desperately cling to this moniker and want to join our organization. We refuse entry. Some argue against our rejection, trying to obfuscate the concepts of "freedom" and "individuality," along with their desire for "rebellion" as a means to justify demands for fundamental alterations to our philosophy. Their desire to purloin our designation does not change the fact that Satanism has been defined. It does not allow for distortions such as belief in cosmic entities, animal sacrifice, or claims that one is a "demon incarnate" amongst other theistic delusions. Our Church has no room for people who do not fully understand our philosophy.

Additionally, the tapestry of Satanism cannot be stretched to promote criminal behavior and mindless hedonism. These ideas are at odds with the logical and life-celebrating demeanor of the skeptical Epicurean atheism that is our axiomatic philosophy. The selection by these postulants of disjointed phrases taken out of context does not pass for an understanding of Satanism nor the accurate advocacy thereof.

Some of these "Satan-fans" propose that Satanists should rebel against Satanism or its organizational exemplar, the Church of Satan, to prove their individuality and thus be considered "more Satanic." They misperceive our championing of freedom and individualism to mean support of a disregard for personal responsibility. They are wrong. "Responsibility to the responsible" is one of our mottos.

Some newcomers to our philosophy do not grasp its axioms and tear at Satanism as if it were some kind of straitjacket. Others hope to wield it as an "anything goes" card rather than the key to accountable liberty that it is. They observe our list of "sins" and "rules" and don't grasp that such terms are used with tongue firmly planted in cheek, while simultaneously missing the point that there is an ethical structure to our philosophy—our "third side" which is so elusive to those limited to dualist thinking. These lists are guidelines and tools based on keen observation of human social behavior, not arbitrary regulations or "shalt nots" handed down from on high or belched forth from down below. Each Satanist is welcome to take 'em out for a test drive and see how they work. Most of us find them to be both accurate and useful. That's why we adopt "Satanist" as a proper label for ourselves—Anton LaVey's philosophy is completely coincident with our personal approach to living.

What self-styled "Satanists" fail to realize when they find themselves disagreeing with the principles established in the literature of the Church of Satan is that it isn't Satanism that must change to accommodate their disagreement. They themselves must abandon their improper self-definition. Satanism is codified—a rational and coherent construct. It is not an amorphous ragbag of loose concepts up for grabs to anyone who wants to call himself a Satanist. Yet some wish it were so, and invoke the word "freedom" as an escape clause from culpability. Anton LaVey's entire purpose for founding the Church of Satan was to create a rational philosophy defining Satanism for the very first time in Western history as an aboveground, coherent movement.

He succeeded in his efforts to do so, demonstrated by the health of his Church and the expanding presence of his writings 40 years later. And we who worked at his side intend to preserve and build upon his legacy, which we see as a durable foundation in no need of amendment. If we found it otherwise, we would not be Satanists, and would have sought other labels and thought structures to define ourselves. We invite wannabe external reformers to just keep on moving. We aren't going to change to suit your particular wishes. Find some fellow daffy devil-worshippers and make your own party.

Anton LaVey directly addressed the issue of those rare Church of Satan members who reach a point where they feel that they must try to appoint themselves as the "saviors of Satanism." To most Satanists, these sowers of discord appear ignorant since one of our fundamental principles is that we are each our OWN saviors. We have never welcomed people who suffer from a messianic martyrdom complex, and members of the Church of Satan are expected to know this.

From his essay, "The World's Most Powerful Religion":

Satanism is the only religion which serves to encourage and enhance one's individual preferences, so long as there is admission of those needs. Thus, one's personal and indelible religion (the picture) is integrated into a perfect frame. It's a celebration of individuality without hypocrisy, of solidarity without mindlessness, of objective subjectivity. There need be no deviation from these principles. They should summarily negate internecine strife and bickering. Any attempts at Satanic 'reformation' should be seen for what they are: creating problems where none exist. There should be no place in any religion for reformers whose very religion is the fetish of reformation. There is even a place and title for compulsive dissidents, and if they can wear the mantle, they are welcome. They would delude themselves to be revolutionaries. In our camp, they are called "House Masochists."

LaVey vividly described the antics of these types as "shitting on the carpet and throwing themselves out the window." That sort of "performance" leaves the reluctant audience to clean up the excreta and puts the perpetrator outside the cabal he had formerly treated with respect. The good Doktor said that he was not inclined to open the door, allowing such desperate "emancipators" back inside when they can't be trusted to refrain from an encore. He saw this happen again and again, and would shake his head at such infantile conduct. Inevitably, we've been witness to a number of shows by newer additions to "The House Masochist Players" since our founder's demise.

In past years our members were isolated from one another and being a lone iconoclast making your way amongst the dull rabble was a powerful means of self-definition for a Satanist. Today, with so many lives played out publicly online in blogs and via those vilely egalitarian personal networking sites, the solitary outsider has a greater opportunity to encounter more of his kind, as well as the *poseurs*. In the Church of Satan one quickly finds that the orthodoxy is being unorthodox. The robust member of our "association of the alienated" will be delighted to discover fellow tribe members. However, some who have weaker egos might feel stifled, that their uniqueness is compromised when they aren't the primary nonconformist in the bunch, but must take their place amongst comparably outrageous oddballs. Or they might discover that their personal aesthetic choices aren't equally embraced by all of their diabolical *compadres*.

At that point, if they decide that they must find a means to distance themselves from their fellow cultural renegades, then the only place they can go is back to their isolated outpost amongst the shuffling zombies. Unfortunately, they might treat us to a farewell exhibition before they exit—stage right.

These agitators may have issues caused by self-aggrandizing tunnel vision, missing the big picture that our organization supports many unusual individuals and their singular preferences. Instead of rationally discussing personal dissatisfactions, the House Masochist "acts out" in a manner disrespectful to the company he supposedly holds in regard. He may have lost the ability to command attention and respect from his peers through creativity, and so now must throw a tantrum to gain notice. Ironically, he casts himself in the role of "outsider to the outsiders" which places him back in with the various classes (prole, middle, upper) of herd-types. Thus he is exiling himself from the "X Class"—a self-created, aristocracy of the bright and talented, which includes all genuine Satanists (see Paul Fussell's book *Class*). So, following the practice of our founder, these self-proclaimed turds in the punch bowl are welcomed to flush themselves, unless they are content to receive the scorn and derision their masochistic behavior has merited. Some seem surprised that they've "asked for it." There's nothing more pathetic, or less Satanic, than a masochist lacking self-awareness.

LaVey emphasized that his paradigm for deportment within the Church of Satan was for our members to treat each other as ladies and gentlemen. There is enough strife outside of our organization to satisfy those with a fetish for conflict. He never required that all Satanists like each other. Since we've never been about fellowship, we don't require that all of our members work with each other, either. Here is the basic house rule: When members have conflicting values, they are to go their own ways, not wasting energy and time sniping at the members who have selected different methods of applying Satanism to reach personal satisfaction. Quite a simple guideline, we think. However, this is too much to expect from some, usually the ones who never got Satanic Rule of the Earth number 1: "Do not give opinions or advice unless you are asked."

If you encounter a would-be mutineer to Satanism, you should ask the question "What are you rebelling against?" If the reply is that "Satanism is conformist" you might look around at the varied collection of interesting folk and wonder what blinders he's been wearing. If you hear that "Satanism is too restrictive," then you need to follow-up and find precisely what this person thinks is being forbidden by Satanic philosophy. Chances are it will be some act currently deemed to be against local laws. Satanism can't stop people from criminal behavior. It does counsel them to be aware of laws and to advocate their reform when proper, but meanwhile to be prepared to accept the results if disobedience leads to prosecution and incarceration. If the answer is simply "What have you got?" that reply indicates the responder is simply a directionless malcontent, with no self-definition and no grasp of the fundamental principles which go to order the hierarchies inherent in the human species. Freedom always requires responsibility, and that responsibility includes an honest and accurate evaluation of the facts at hand as well as wise decisions based on that knowledge. To simply think that being "anti-everything" and utterly without restraint is a definition of Satanism is to entirely miss our discriminating foundation—our roots in Epicureanism.

Satanists always remain in control of their exploration of pleasure. "Indulgence—NOT compulsion" is our founder's dictum that moves us out of hedonism, which by definition is unbridled and thus compelled. Epicureanism—the balanced seeking of physical and mental self-satisfaction—embraces a wider range of gratification. It is refined, selective, and embodies our concept of Indulgence. We are gourmets in the banquet of existence. Hedonism is limited to base carnal pursuits. Epicureans aren't prudes, nor are we slaves to any of our desires; rather these are motivators toward seeking all manner of fulfilling experiences. The hedonist blindly sates his lusts for sex, sustenance, and soma—consequences be damned! That is a self-destructive course inappropriate for Satanists.

The Satanist does what he wishes, taking full responsibility for all consequences to his actions. We live in human society and must be aware that there are legal repercussions that vary in each locale. If you choose to ignore this factor and wind up in prison, you've become powerless and will waste your precious days under the dominion of others. Not the Satanic position of choice. If you live the life of a petty criminal and consider your jail time to be a badge of "outrageousness and iconoclasm," you'll win only scorn from true Satanists. We see that penal institutions are full of skells of a similar ilk and are not favorably impressed. Satanism does not deny pleasure or deep and varied pursuit of it, but it counsels that wisdom and sensibility must be employed in search of fulfilling Indulgence. Pragmatism is axiomatic to our system; we are realists. So the idealism of "just do whatever feels good" is exposed by Satanists as a childish recipe for personal disaster.

Satanists understand that "good" and "evil" are purely subjective values, hence we oppose that which affects us negatively. That is a personal judgment based on what we determine to be of value. We are not automatic contrarians, simply countering whatever is in widespread social fashion or might be prevalent in our vicinity. This latter approach brings to mind the Monty Python sketch in which a fellow seeks an argument, but simply gets an opponent who automatically gainsays whatever statements are presented. Being guided solely by "whatever it is, I'm against it," means that you are enslaved to the people whom you oppose, as they determine what your reactions will be. The Satanist, who naturally sees himself as his own God, does not generally care what other people think about him. His monumental sense of self worth leaves no possibility for him to be touched by critiques from the unworthy, but he does examine the reactions of the individuals whom he has come to cherish and respect. Thus the discriminating iconoclast and true rebel dissents out of reason and passion, and possible options, not knee-jerk reactivity.

Definitions are crucial for establishing human communication. If the meanings of words were whatever one felt they should be according to whim (remember Lewis Carroll's Queen of Hearts?), only confusion would result. We therefore defend the clear and concise definition of Satanism created by Anton LaVey, and do not permit it to be adulterated by outside pseudo-Satanists and insiders who lose track of the elegant architecture of Dr. LaVey's principles. Satanism will continue to take into account the evolution of human society, based on an unflinching evaluation of the nature of the human beast. Such adaptability is "built-in." It is a system without frozen dogma, being inherently flexible. But there are the basics in *The Satanic Bible* which will always remain constant, providing meaningful differentiation from other religions and philosophies. We also know that freedom, in practical application, means that one has a choice between actually available alternatives. It does not mean that the world will suddenly alter itself simply because someone decides they wish it were otherwise.

The universe is not chaotic. There is most definitely

structure and order, and much of it is based on very complex levels of stratification and interaction. This is not a limitation. Nature to be commanded must be obeyed. In understanding the mechanisms that move the universe we become empowered to comprehend what is mutable and what must remain immutable. This is the essence of the Magic of Mastery, and the key to success in all undertakings. It is the hallmark of the true Satanist.

So, we do not accord the honorific of "Satanist" to rebels without cause acting the part of misguided mavericks in a shallow attempt to one-up the true "alien elite." It is reserved for the noble few who by their nature are drawn to their own reflection in the integrally sound philosophy of the Church of Satan. House Masochists should realize that we have no interest in witnessing their threadbare theatrics. Those *meshuga* messiahs should look elsewhere for appreciation, to people who use self-sacrifice as THEIR guiding image, not from Satanists. We stand sure and proud as the captains of our own destiny, plotted with all of our faculties sharply enabled towards the task of maintaining triumphant joy. Know that the authentic Satanist, like our founder before us, is fully self-aware, hypercritical of himself above all, cognizant of his allies and—as it suits his purposes—he employs reasoned dissidence as a means for inspiring meaningful, evolutionary revolution.

# THE MAGIC OF MASTERY

**B**EING A SATANIST, one is often mistaken for being a purveyor of mystic claptrap like so many "occultists" when in truth we are masters of reality, striving to understand and utilize the universe for our personal indulgence. One of the surest outward signs of the Satanist is not the sporting of all-black clothing or the prominent display of the Baphomet sigil—granting that these could be dead giveaways, but the projection of the self-confidence and success which springs from the mastery of a field. Satanists can DO things and do them quite well! This is why they have chosen to embrace Satanism, the only religion to revere the talented few who stand above the dim and barren hordes.

There is true magic in the mastering of skills. Most members of the herd will look with awe upon a talented and accomplished practitioner. To them, the producing of quality results with the effortless-seeming ease of mastery will appear to be pure wizardry. Just think of how similar to occult practices are many fields when one becomes an "initiate." There is the inevitable jargon that serves as an "arcane" language. Computer programming has such mystic tongues as COBOL, Pascal, and Fortran. Painting has many "exotic" terms such as medium, ground, umber, cerulean and uses such esoteric items as aromatic oils, varnishes and athamé-like pallet knives. Cooking has many abstruse practices such as maceration, basting and sautéing and we know how effective a tool of Lesser Magic it is. Let's not forget mastery of mechanical and electronic devices, as those who know nothing about their vehicles and machines always look at mechanics and repairmen as a priesthood privy to obscure and forbidden techniques. Music is a wonderful practice in that it has weird symbols that are incomprehensible to most people these days, while the result of virtuosity is the ability to communicate directly with people's emotions. Remember that such past masters as Paganini and Liszt were thought to have made pacts with the Devil for their skills.

In truth, anyone who excels in a material field *has* made a pact with Satan, as they have embraced the belief that success in the here and now is of the greatest importance. This is why Satanists are wonderful people to be around for they are brimming with honed talents to be experienced.

So to be a master of magic, toss out those musty grimoires, unless they're printed by Chilton. Pick some field and become an advanced practitioner. Be a writer, pastry chef, seamstress, flower arranger, plumber, sculptor, carpenter, photographer, upholsterer, electrician, pilot, beautician, steelworker, medic, whatever you have an affinity for. You'll amaze those around you, gain their respect and envy, achieve material success and you won't even have to say "Shemhamforash" in public. The better you are, the more Satanic you'll be, a member of the true elite of the able. The sheep will be so dazzled that they won't even notice the Baphomet around your neck—if you choose to wear it. But when they do, they'll certainly think there's something to it because of your position of achievement in the mundane world. We not only rejoice in the fleshy life, we are masters of it. That is Satanic magic.

# Every Man and Woman is a Star...

...Yet each is of a unique type and magnitude. But, how many have the wisdom to honestly recognize their particular role in the cosmos?

Each individual consciousness may be likened to a black hole, a form of gravity lens. But this lens is not one that focuses and pulls in the existing components of our material Universe; it is one that pulls in and focuses time. The present is an "event horizon," the eternal moment in which we live. It is the domain of our awareness. That which is whirling into the hole is the yet-to-be-realized future, the events that might happen. Amongst this nebular cloud of possibility (which is finite, with greater particles being more likely probabilities) are the Is-To-Be's that will become reality once they reach the present. These are the consciously desired future events established by the magical Will of a Satanic Sorcerer. Once these things pass through the Now, they fall into place in the linear progression that is the past of each individual. Motile possibility becomes actuality and is frozen as the past. History is thus made.

Most people's consciousness is continually focused upon their past—the events of which are like a row of tableaux on a foggy plain, receding into the distance and becoming less clear as the present moves further away. People are thus walking *backwards* into their future, each step a second in time. One second per second. They are thus rather blind to the events that will soon come into their Now and then be locked into their history as past experiences.

The Satanic Magician attempts to turn around, to be hyper-aware, so he is walking *forward* into the future, and before him is that swirling smoking mirror of the possibilities that his Will attempts to make actuality when they pass through the eternal Now. The Satanic Magician projects his visions for his Is-To-Be's upon this nebula, and they coalesce, begin to take form and definition of ever greater clarity as they move through the whirlpool and come closer to the event horizon. The important point is that the Satanic Magician's Is-To-Be's do not only go through his own event horizon, but through those of certain other individuals as well, to strengthen the reality his vision creates. This is a metaphorical perspective for viewing the mechanisms of Greater Magic.

Time travel is an attempt to look backward and bring those things that have passed and are distant in memory/time into sharper focus—to leapfrog over interim experiences and experience chosen past moments afresh. Some of these events have a tie to the eternal Now of consciousness, which allows that consciousness to jump immediately to these past tableaux, skipping all other less significant events in one's linear past. The cable that binds the consciousness to these ever-visible mountain peaks is emotion. Emotion apparently comes from the "oldest" part of the brain (that which was earliest to evolve), and is an instantaneous instinctual deep evaluation of a situation that is being experienced in the Now. It adds what could be viewed as a "color" or tonality to that situation, so that it is eternally marked in the consciousness and is thus hierarchically ordered in the past.

A Satanic Magician can thus attempt consciously to emotionally "tint" or harmonize events from the linear past of others (which collectively is referred to as history). By making a "time travel journey" to them he may absorb them into his own past through the "virtual reality" experience which a rite of time travel can bring to this past event.

The gateway which one must open in order to toss his Is-To-Be's into another's gravity well is that oldest "reptile" part of the brain that can only be accessed via very strong emotion. In essence, the Greater Magic described by Dr. LaVey is a process wherein one creates these coalescences taken from possible future events and focuses them into the one you want to happen. You must feel the *need* for it to happen with the deepest emotions of which you are capable, and it is by giving vent to this need in the ritual chamber that you open that trap door and throw these Is-To-Be's out there into the future possibilities of other consciousnesses, to become a need that will fall into the gravity wells of individuals who have a bearing on the matter, who thus will feel compelled to move *their* purview according to *your* Will.

Of course, Lesser Magic is simply the day-to-day charm and glamour the Satanic Magician uses to manipulate people into doing what is wanted. In order to be successful at this, first he must be consummately skilled at reading people, to be able to determine what it is that they are seeking. But then, the Satanic Magician must be willing to role-play, to be a chameleon and an actor of exquisite skill to be able to push those buttons and throw the switches in that target individual to make him do as you desire.

Some jejune people balk at that, saying, "I want people to know the real me!" But they fail to realize that most people are far too crass to actually "see" them and too narcissistic to even care. They only see what they solipsistically project on others. The Satanist chooses to be protean, a person of mystery, and only those whom he really cherishes ever get to look behind the myriad masks to see the substance of the individual who sports them. Each Satanic Magician naturally adopts a general persona that is often reflective of chosen elements of his essence. He is satisfied with his knowledge of his personal nature and so has no fear in adopting different guises. He is emotionally secure enough not to care that many people will know him only as the selectively projected façade. And really, why should he care, if these folk have done as is required by his Will?

So my fellow sorcerers, let the rabble observe your passage through their constellations, noting your magnificent gravity and superior stellar magnitude while being dazzled into following the orbits you have plotted for them. The successful Satanic Magician has a presence that can sweep galaxies of lesser celestial objects in his wake. With his highly attuned awareness, he controls his own destiny by consciously selecting his desired future, motivating many satellites into roles supportive of his sublime vision of self-deification.

# Time Travel—
# Cheap and Easy

IN THE LATE 20ᵀᴴ CENTURY we are enmeshed in a society that has cast off subtlety with a vengeance and has increased the pace of daily existence far beyond the norm of biological cycles. The Hopi word "koyaanisqatsi" (life out of balance) is precisely *apropos* (and do see the film—a very magical amalgam of images and music with Satanic insights). We Satanists find this constant barrage to be particularly aggravating since we cultivate *sensitivity* as a value important for all who would be magicians of any sort. Thus we retreat from the clangor and clamor to our dark retreats wherein we may contemplate and experience choice items culled with care from the dross offered by mass production and enforced homogenization. That is the nature of a "Satanic bunker."

"Nuance" should be a working term in every Satanist's vocabulary. If you wish to gain expertise in both Lesser and Greater Magic, then you *must* be hyper-aware of subtle shadings in all of the aspects of your endeavors. The insensate herd has been battered into a benumbed state that makes them even less perceptive than their limited intellectual and emotional capabilities would allow—even at their greatest level of development. The Satanist who cultivates his sensitivity becomes the one-eyed man in the kingdom of the blind. As you advance your magical skills, you then open both eyes—and as you attain Mastery, you augment these natural, though often undeveloped, perceptions with the magical equivalents of telescopes and microscopes.

Time travel is a wonderful exercise to stretch your magical muscles and sharpen your perceptivity. The methods I am about to discuss were surprisingly crystallized in Richard Matheson's romantic novel *Bid Time Return*. In this magical book, a writer wishes to travel to a past era to meet a woman with whom he has become obsessed. He reads J. B. Priestly's *Man and Time* (a book recommended by Dr. LaVey) and immerses himself in a total environment embodying the era he wishes to visit. With the help of a recording of the final movement of Mahler's Ninth Symphony, he actually accomplishes the physical transportation. I strongly suggest that you seek out both Matheson's novel and Priestly's book. Forget the novel's rather weak film adaptation starring Christopher Reeve where passion was depicted as mere sentimentality.

While I cannot guarantee your actual physical transport to another epoch, with a bit of effort you can make an interior journey that should have an equal emotional weight. In fact, it is quite a "real" experience in your Subjective Universe. For starters, I suggest that you attempt to return to the time and place of your gestation and birth. Since that is recent history, there is much material upon which you can draw to base your re-creative contemplation. First of all, select music from that period from whatever type ranging from popular to serious with which you can find an affinity. With greater experience you might choose period music of a style for which you don't have an immediate connection as this can broaden your sensibility and thus the comprehension of that time. Select films that date from this period, which should be easy from the many filmographies and databases extant. Go to a library and seek out synchronous periodicals for further images. Advertisements serve well. Having the physical items in hand is more vivid than just seeing scans. You can recreate an awareness of what might have been general concerns. Ask yourself, what did the world's denizens worry about at that time? Now, here comes the fine detail: use older relatives' memory to uncover personal data concerning your parent's emotional tenor at that time. Add to this knowledge of local happenings, events, and personages to give depth and uniqueness to this evocation. Get pictures out of the family album. If you can include appropriate scents, or food and drink, so much the better.

In the course of my experiments I have identified a **Principle of Resonance** that is of supreme importance. Music is a particular range of energy vibrations that we perceive as sound, given structure and thus meaning by a human agent. It follows by analogy that vibrations on a "higher" level will perhaps behave in similar fashion to the lower vibrations with variations germane to that vibrational frequency. Resonance is defined as a state wherein sound oscillations are reinforced, and thus sustained, because the natural frequency of the resonating body is the same as that of the sound source. Magically speaking, you must assemble your evocative devices for this targeted time period so that they *reinforce* and *sustain* each other's vibrations, actually magnifying the result so that the sum is far greater than the components. These "time travel talismans" must be *consonant* with each other—in the same key, so to speak. This is more complex than simply matching frequencies, for chords that derive from a key organize the many frequencies of possible tones and their resultants into *functional* relationships that establish a progression. You are creating, in effect, a symphony of sympathetic vibrations whose structure will serve as the vehicle for your excursion while it is playing in the reverberant hall of your consciousness. It is the ubiquitous *dissonance* that characterizes today's culture that causes a general malaise, softening the audience (victims) so that they are far more pliable to being programmed.

When you have completed your research and assembled your materials, close yourself into a proper chamber wherein you can be completely undisturbed by the outside world. Now bring this past epoch into sharp focus. For ritual garb, use clothing from that era's styles. Let your senses be stimulated by your talismans and take your psyche for a ride. Perhaps enact a scenario using your various props. A chamber made into a total environmental replica of a room from the target time is an excellent means for "setting the stage." If you do your work well, you will find yourself transported via your meditations to another era. Savor this period, let yourself breathe the air, think and feel as a denizen of the period, fully engaging both your emotions and your intellect. If your working is strong, this will "set" in your memory as an interior landscape to which you can return with greater ease the next time. When you have experienced complete saturation, and thus emotional and physical exhaustion, consciously pull yourself back to the present. This can be cued by having some object concealed in the chamber that is quite evidently NOT of the time period of your journey. By then exposing it to your perception, you will be jolted from your reverie in that past era. You can control the time of this fantasy journey by having chosen music play for the desired duration, then an anachronistic piece of music can be introduced and this will have the same effect as a dissonant object, shattering the immersion in that vanished period. For a smoother transition you can have recordings of music play in succession that will ease you from the past into the present. You will probably regain full temporal awareness during this accelerated forward motion before the sequence has fully elapsed.

At first, practice traveling to time periods for which you can find media documentation. As your skills advance, you will find yourself able to make the journey with far less an assemblage of "talismans." This is crucial, for when you attempt to experience eras more distant in time you will find that there is far less material available for your use.

History is generally a chronicle of the individuals, activities, and events of a past period that are most memorable to the succeeding generations who create and maintain the records. Such documentation is thus highly subjective and should not be construed as an objective portrait of "what happened." The most difficult information to obtain concerns the details of the day-to-day existence of most inhabitants of these past periods. With this area on the map of history being generally blank, it thus becomes difficult to enter into the consciousness of the people who existed then, particularly when you are dealing with cultures that are remote in time and geography and people who spoke languages that formed particular shadings of perception that are now truly alien to our current cultural milieu.

When you have mastered this art, you will find trips to museums and to sites of ancient architecture to be even more highly rewarding experiences than previously. The mere contemplation of a single artifact will fill you with a sensibility of its creators, while being enclosed in the total environment of a complete archaic structure will constitute an epiphany of major significance.

The ultimate purpose of this "time travel" experimentation is to develop a sense of perspective, so that you rise above the conceptual confines of the two-dimensional plane of contemporary existence and grasp its cultural, political, sociological, and anthropological processes from a third dimension. From this vantage point you will have won the wisdom of Clarity—a very rare prize.

TIME TRAVEL—CHEAP AND EASY

You will never again let past orthodoxies be forgotten and you will be far better equipped to deal with the tribulations of making your way in the current harried environment. You will also be contributing to your future, for you will be able to embody and advance the best elements selected from the past for synthesis into a more Satanic society around you, one that is invigorating and stimulating, rather than exhausting and frenetic—life IN balance. From out of our darkened, intimate chambers shall dawn a new order to sweep the globe that can proudly be called, without exaggeration or apology, a "civilization."

# What, the Devil?

SATANISM IS NOT DEVIL WORSHIP. That comes as a shock to many who haven't explored our philosophy and it is the prime misconception outsiders have regarding the Church of Satan. Our founder Anton Szandor LaVey asserted this stance from the beginning. Over the years, individuals with the need to feel embraced by a deity have claimed that Dr. LaVey somehow came to believe in a literal Satan. If we examine his work, it is clear that he never changed his mind about this, nor was belief in the Devil ever some secret "inner circle" practice of the Church of Satan.

We Satanists understand that both truth and fantasy are needed by the human animal. It is a step towards wisdom when one knows with certainty which is which. Man relies on symbolism and metaphor when building a personal conceptual framework for understanding the universe in which he lives. He has always invented his own gods using his carnal brain. From *The Satanic Bible*: "Man has always created his gods, rather than his gods creating him." However, this act of creation is usually denied. History shows that the founders of religions claimed personal contact with the deity fabricated through their imaginations, and legions of followers bolstered that fiction. There is nothing wrong with fantasy, so long as an individual knows he is using this controlled self-delusion as a tool for dealing with existence. For we skeptical, pragmatic Satanists, it is wielded in the ritual chamber. Reliance on fantastic constructs becomes dangerous when the believers in spiritual religions dogmatically insist that their personal or collective fantasies are real in the world at large, that they are the only absolute truth, and then wait for the myth to guide them or try to force others to share this delusion. That has been the source for countless wars, as any student of history can see.

Dr. LaVey's seminal book, *The Satanic Bible* published in 1969 lays out some basic principles:

> The Satanist realizes that man, and the action and reaction of the universe, is responsible for everything, and doesn't mislead himself into thinking that someone cares.

> Is it not more sensible to worship a god that he, himself, has created, in accordance with his own emotional needs—one that best represents the very carnal and physical being that has the idea-power to invent a god in the first place?

From a 1986 interview with Walter Harrington of *The Washington Post*:

> "Satan is a symbol, nothing more," LaVey says. "Satan signifies our love of the worldly and our rejection of the pallid, ineffectual image of Christ on the cross."

Accepting the axiomatic premise that no gods exist as independent supernatural entities means that Satanists are *de facto* atheists. We know that the objective universe is indifferent to us. Since our philosophy is self-centered, each Satanist sees himself as the most important person in his life. Each individual thus generates his own hierarchy of values and judges everything based on his own standards. Therefore, we Satanists appoint ourselves as the "Gods" in our subjective universes. That doesn't mean we think we have the powers of a mythological deity, but it does mean that we revere the creative capacity in our species. So to distinguish ourselves from the atheists who simply reject God as non-existent, we call ourselves "I-theists," with our own healthy ego as the center of our perspective. This is truly a blasphemous concept that flies in the face of just about every other religion, and it is why Satan serves us well as a symbol. He was described as the prideful one, refusing to bow to Jehovah. He is the one who questions authority, seeking liberty beyond the stultifying realm of Heaven. He is the figure championed by the likes of Mark Twain, Milton, and Byron as the independent critic who heroically stands on his own.

Dr. LaVey made his most detailed presentation of his concept for how Satan functions in his philosophy in the following monologue that appeared in Jack Fritscher's book *Popular Witchcraft*, published in 1973.

> I don't feel that raising the devil in an anthropomorphic sense is quite as feasible as theologians or metaphysicians would like to think. I have felt His presence but only as an exteriorized extension of my own potential, as an alter-ego or evolved concept that I have been able to exteriorize. With a full awareness, I can communicate with this semblance, this creature, this demon, this personification that I see in the eyes of the symbol of Satan—the goat of Mendes—as I commune with it before the altar. None of these is anything more than a mirror image of that potential I perceive in myself.

I have this awareness that the objectification is in accord with my own ego. I'm not deluding myself that I'm calling something that is disassociated or exteriorized from myself the godhead. This Force is not a controlling factor that I have no control over. The Satanic principle is that man willfully controls his destiny; if he doesn't, some other man—a lot smarter than he is—will. Satan is, therefore, an extension of one's psyche or volitional essence, so that that extension can sometimes converse and give directives through the self in a way that thinking of the self as a single unit cannot. In this way it does help to depict in an externalized way the Devil per se. The purpose is to have something of an idolatrous, objective nature to commune with. However, man has connection, contact, control. This notion of an exteriorized God-Satan is not new.

The approach outlined here, of consciously creating an exteriorization of the self with which one communes solely *in ritual*, is a revolutionary religious concept of LaVey's Satanism, and it is a "third side" approach which proves elusive to many to whom it does not come naturally. It is a psychological sleight-of-mind, not a form of faith. It establishes that to the Satanist in ritual, he *is* Satan.

To be fair, people attending workings of LaVey's bombastic and theatrical rites might not be able to separate the shouting of "Hail Satan!" while in the ritual chamber with the disbelief in any external gods outside of the chamber. But then, Satanism isn't meant for everybody. When asked if there is an upcoming volume *Satanism for Dummies*, we reply: "Satanism is NOT intended for dummies." As he said in *The Satanic Bible* and often in interviews: "Satanism demands study—NOT worship." The capacity to *think* is expected of Satanists. So LaVey expected those who embraced his philosophy to understand where to draw the line between the fantastic and the real. He proclaimed that he was a showman, and felt that his Satanists would not be rubes, mistaking the mummery for reality. As a carnie, he knew how to entertain, to draw attention so that he could then present more serious ideas. Some might sneer at his methodology, dismissing his deeper cogitations because of the circus-like elements. However, I believe a case can be made that all religions are in the "show business," but the Church of Satan is the only one honest enough to admit it.

In an interview released on an LP called *The Occult Explosion* from 1973, Dr. LaVey explained how the Church of Satan deals with different concepts of Satan:

> "Satan" is, to us, a symbol rather than an anthropomorphic being, although many members of the Church of Satan who are mystically inclined would prefer to think of Satan in a very real, anthropomorphic way. Of course, we do not discourage this, because we realize that to many individuals a picture, a well-wrought picture of their mentor or their tutelary divinity is very important for them to conceptualize ritualistically. However, Satan symbolically is the teacher: the informer of the whys and the wherefores of the world. And in answer to those who would label us "Devil worshippers" or be very quick to assume us to be Satan worshippers, I must say that Satan demands study, not worship, in its truest symbology.

> We do not grovel; we do not get down on our knees, genuflect, and worship Satan. We do not plead, we do not implore that Satan give us what we wish. We feel that anyone who is going to be blessed by any god of his choice is going to have to show that god that he is capable of taking care of the blessings that are received.

Thus he advocates creating a god-symbol based on one's own needs and aesthetic choices. Creative fantasy is employed for emotional fulfillment, experienced in the context of the ritual chamber. Satanists see Satan as their proper symbol to fulfill those needs, a magnification of the best within each of us.

Additionally, LaVey speculated on the idea that when attempting Greater Magic, it may be that the operator is tapping into a force that is part of nature to magnify his "Will." This force is hidden, unknown, and thus "dark." But LaVey did not view the force as a supernatural entity. In *The Satanic Bible* he originally explained "the Satanist simply accepts the definition (of God) which suits him best." He closely follows that with the definition he uses:

> To the Satanist "God"—by what-ever name he is called, or by no name at all—is seen as the balancing factor in nature, and not as being concerned with suffering. This powerful force which permeates and balances the universe is far too impersonal to care about the happiness or misery of flesh-and-blood creatures on this ball of dirt upon which we live.

LaVey clearly posits a disinterested, remote force—not a personality or entity—that balances the universe. He sees it as indifferent to life forms, much as any other force such as gravity would be. It is a mechanism, not a personage. It does not merit obeisance, appeasement, or worship. It can be named or not. It operates without awareness of conscious beings. He spoke of this to Burton Wolfe who wrote in the introduction to *The Satanic Bible*:

> Of course LaVey pointed out to anyone who would listen that the Devil to him and his followers was not

the stereotyped fellow cloaked in red garb, with horns, tail and pitchfork, but rather the dark forces in nature that human beings are just beginning to fathom. How did LaVey square that explanation with his own appearance at times in black cowl with horns? He replied: "People need ritual, with symbols such as those you find in baseball games or church services or wars, as vehicles for expending emotions they can't release or even understand on their own."

So LaVey accepted that there may be currently unexplained elements of the universe that are part of its fabric, but these are not supernatural. He suggests that Man's inquiring mind may eventually come to understand how they function. The implications of these ideas offer great freedom. Since there is no actual deity watching over or mandating the behavior of our species, men are free to imagine whatever sort of God they choose to satisfy their own needs, however they should not forget that such fantasies are only that—nothing more.

In that same passage, he also addressed the prime reason for engaging in ritual, which he defined as Greater Magic: it serves as a means for releasing pent-up emotions that people may not even fully understand. Hence ritual has a *psychological* purpose; it is clearly not meant as a means for worship of some supernatural entity. Ritual is demonstrably part of human culture. LaVey knew that it served a value for people over the millennia, even if it was done for reasons that didn't square with reality. It made people feel better than they did beforehand. So, as he continued in *The Satanic Bible* when addressing the search for a proper religion: "If he accepts himself, but recognizes that ritual and ceremony are the important devices that his invented religions have utilized to sustain his faith in a lie, then it is the SAME FORM OF RITUAL that will sustain his faith in the truth—the primitive pageantry that will give his awareness of his own majestic being added substance." Thus the device of ritual, which he explained as "controlled self delusion," can be of practical use for the well being of one's state of mind. The truth referred to above is that all gods are an invention of the creative beast called Man.

To summarize a typical individual's journey from observing reality to declaring himself a Satanist, let us list several assertions:

Nature encompasses all that exists. There is nothing supernatural in Nature.

The spiritual is an illusion. I am utterly carnal.

Reason is my tool for cognition making faith anathema. I question all things. I am a skeptic.

I do not accept false dichotomies, finding instead the "third side" which brings me closest to understanding the mysteries of existence.

The universe is neither benevolent nor malevolent; it is indifferent.

There are no Gods. I am an atheist.

There is no intrinsic purpose to life beyond biological imperatives. I thus determine my own life's meaning.

I decide what is of value. I am my own highest value therefore I am my own God.

I am an I-theist.

Good is that which benefits me and promotes that which I hold in esteem.

Evil is that which harms me and hinders that which I cherish.

I live to maximize the Good for myself and those I value. At all times I remain in control of my pursuit of pleasure. I am an Epicurean.

Merit determines my criteria for the judgment of myself and others. I judge and am prepared to be judged.

I seek a just outcome in my exchanges with those around me. I thus will do unto others as I would prefer they do unto me. However, if they treat me poorly, I shall return that behavior in like degree.

I grasp the human need for symbols as a means for distillation of complex thought structures.

The symbol that best exemplifies my nature as an aware beast is Satan, the avatar of carnality, justice, and self-determination.

I see myself reflected in the philosophy created by Anton Szandor LaVey.

I am proud to call myself a Satanist.

These ideas fundamental to Satanists serve as an earthy foundation that we find deeply liberating and a welcome acceptance of ourselves as human animals. For the type of person who feels the need for an external supernatural parental figure, the responsibility for self-determination explicit in this path would be terrifying. For the Satanist, belief in any actual God or Devil to which one would be beholden is repugnant and stultifying. We "agree to disagree" with those who are spiritually oriented concerning our different approaches to living, hence our advocacy of pluralism in society. We Satanists know that our way is not for everyone. We simply ask that others follow their own path and allow us to be as we are.

But please, all of you believers, understand that we are not simply your "flip side." We are not Devil-worshippers. We are simply carnal self-worshippers looking to enjoy our lives to the fullest. May you find bliss in your serving of your chosen deity. We certainly will!

# Walpurgisnacht LI A.S.

**50** YEARS AGO THIS EVENING, Anton Szandor LaVey opened the adamantine gates as he founded the Church of Satan—a social experiment in blasphemy, liberty, and individualism. Once he and his intrepid cohorts stepped within, they found not a sanctuary, nor a fortress, but instead a road, for Satanism is not a place or position where one cowers and stagnates, but is instead the journey each one of us takes over the course of our vital lives. He did not establish a place of comfort, for the Church of Satan is not a clubhouse offering readily demanded and easily earned group hugs. He gave us an arena, wherein we challenge ourselves to be the best we can possibly be, standing alongside brave individuals who do the same, an Amphitheatrum Satanicum of earned glory where we are each the heroes of our own existence. We are the gods of this Colosseum, who win our victories by our own efforts, without requiring the approval of the plebs who can but look on with awe and terror. Our accolades arise from our self- satisfaction and the admiration of our fellow gladiators whose achievements have won our esteem. We boldly seize the crowns of laurel and place them upon our own brows, damp with the sweat and blood of our fierce struggles. Hear the sounding of horns and trumpets, echoing the pride bursting forth from our hearts, as we stand amongst our kind, warriors who will not tolerate any who would obstruct the goals we seek. Barriers are smashed to flinders, whether they are placed before us by adversaries or are aspects of self that must be overcome. We do not shrink from any challenge.

Our kind is not complacent, something Magus LaVey discovered when true colleagues answered his call to fellow aficionados of disciplined carnality. Society then witnessed they who wallow in collective guilt band together in slovenly brotherhood. He despised those who touted mediocrity, rejecting their enforced group therapy meant to tear all down to the lowest level of shared banality. Instead, he proposed iconoclasm, and saw the few who answered his summons also led lives wherein they flamed and tossed the fires about them. They understood that existence is bounded by time and must be lived to the fullest amongst fellow mavericks, unhampered by the surrounding shuffling hordes.

Over the years, his message reached 'round the globe, finding resonant response in the minds of kindred free-thinkers who would not accept the chains of dull convention constraining the masses in the societies in which they happened to have come into being. The "alien elite" saw in his thinking the definition of their true natures and thrilled at the approbation he gave to those who seized that mantle of indomitable pride encoded in the honorific title "Satanist." And as his life progressed, Doktor LaVey was delighted to welcome those of us whom he could call colleagues and friends—his allies by choice and nature who shared his vision. He relished these comrades who dared to shape their lives, molding personal worlds to suit unique obsessions, for their pursuits energized him in their fascinating diversity. He envisioned a cabal of erudite, civilized ladies and gentlemen who would treat one another with the gentility of true nobility arising from ability, but who also could rouse savage opposition when confronted by foes whose intent was to thwart freedom and enforce conformity.

Over the passing of fifty years, this road has taken us

through bizarre landscapes. One was of widespread fear directed our way by Christians whipping up a "Satanic Panic." We mounted our steeds of reason and donned the armor of fact, to joust against the terror-mongers who would have had us declared outlaws fit for prosecution, as it had been in times when "Satanism" was an insult condemning heretics to torture and execution. We survived, and afterwards our founder ended his reign, departing life as an emperor whose triumphs could be counted as both magnificent and abundant. We, his co-conspirators, have kept his vision intact and brought this Church of Satan forward into the 21st Century, for his perceptive philosophy is ever-adaptable to the evolving world that confronts us.

Yet on this leg of the journey it now seems that the countryside is again ominously familiar. We look about as we move forward on our chosen courses and on the left side we note the crowds of the timorous, rejecting challenges. They grovel in fear of "trigger words" and shrink from ideas that could shatter their puny paradigms. Their idea of justice is enforced vapidity, with banners of forced equality serving as shrouds for any who rise above their tepid cowardice. On the right side are a gaggle of squabbling theists pressing for forced submission to their mythical deities. They claim it is their freedom to wield bigotry against our kind, and given opportunity would kill those who resist the unnatural doctrines of their deity dictators.

Never has it been more important for us to keep the Black Flame burning. We Satanists see a possible future of widespread secularism—abetted by knowledge and technology—through this current thorny thicket of religiously fostered irrationalism and xenophobia. We perceive the possibility of limitless human vistas, beyond the charnel stockades of enforced obeisance and unreason meant to maintain narrow minds and miniscule spirits. The stakes are high for all of us. We might attain a world wherein we are at liberty to proclaim who we are and have that be widely understood, or one in which those who are not like most must wear masks so as to manipulate the hostile rabble from the shadows.

Regardless of the outcome, we Satanists will survive and prosper, for that is our will and vital existence is a treasure that each and every one of us will wrest from our surroundings, which we will never cease to fashion in favor of our self-deification.

As I look upon all gathered here tonight, I know that the Is-To-Be cast by our founder, Magus Anton Szandor LaVey has been realized. You are those potent ladies and gentlemen whose honor has been won upon the sands of the Ludus Maximus of life, which bears witness to your triumphs. He knew you'd come forth, for by calling upon the Infernal Names of myth, he summoned each and every one of you for you are the actuality of such legends. In celebration of the man who inspired us all, we include him in the roster of dread demons and deities, for those in millennia to come might look back and see his smiling diabolical countenance as archetype, rather than the reality that some of us were fortunate to experience. As he would wish, in saluting him, we hail ourselves, for he was the champion of our individual godhood, and he would have us put no one before our sovereign selves.

Hail Anton Szandor LaVey!
Hail Ourselves!
Hail Satan!

**Magus Peter H. Gilmore**
30 April, LI A.S.
Poughkeepsie, New York.

DECLAIMED BEFORE THE ASSEMBLED MEMBERS OF
THE CHURCH OF SATAN CELEBRATING THE
50TH ANNIVERSARY OF ITS FOUNDING.

# THE RITUALS

# Satanic Ritual

I N *THE SATANIC BIBLE* Anton LaVey presented a format for performing the basic Satanic Ritual that has become a tradition over the forty years of the existence of the Church of Satan. He explained quite carefully that "Greater Magic" is the use of ritual, and that this is meant as a theatrical and emotional experience. It is not a time for intellectualizing. He felt that three basic types of rite could be used to cover most basic human desires: Compassion, Lust, and Destruction. However, if your needs went beyond these three, you were to feel free to adapt them to fill your unique requirements.

Satanic Ritual is a technique of self-transformative psychodrama. It is a tool for releasing emotions that are pent-up and thus hindering you from the pursuit of Indulgence in your daily life. There is no guarantee that ritual can do anything more than serve as a cathartic experience for the ones performing it. That is why we do not perform rituals for other people; if they are not performing it, they will not benefit from the experience. Performing Greater Magic for hire is not endorsed by Satanism.

Outsiders are always fascinated by the symbols, imagery, and litanies used in Satanic Ritual, and journalists unfortunately want to focus almost solely on this aspect of our religion. It may come as a surprise to these people that the use of ritual is not required of Satanists. It is an entirely optional tool, and many of our members tend to find that their personal acts of creativity are cathartic enough so that the formal practice of ritual would be redundant or pointless. Ritual, when used, is done as needed—there aren't compulsory weekly services.

Our rituals are not thought of as "spells" which guarantee that some actual change will occur in the real world. Satanism rejects faith as a tool of cognition, and so Satanists who practice ritual must gather evidence that satisfies their standards of truth if they suspect that their rituals are having results outside of the chamber. Since we are skeptical atheists, we do not believe in anything supernatural. However, there are many aspects of the human experience, some of which have been investigated under the label of being paranormal, which may have validity. A theory advanced by Ingo Swann in his *Natural ESP* suggests that there may be a gateway through the most primitive part of the brain by which thoughts and imagery might be in some way "broadcast" to other minds when fueled by extreme emotional experiences. We Satanists see this as a possible means for Greater Magic to impact the world outside of the ritual chamber.

Biologist Rupert Sheldrake has documented phenomena of the "extended mind" such as people's pets sensing from a distance the time their owners are deciding to return home, as well as the "feeling" that you are being stared at by someone else, even when you don't see the person doing the staring. These could be supernormal abilities for which talent at either sending or receiving would be required, so results most probably would not be the same for every person. Like the ability to understand music or mathematics, perhaps only a small percentage of our population has these intuitive capabilities, and they might also require practice to be successfully developed and deployed.

Thus we leave this as an open question that each Satanist who chooses to use ritual must answer for himself—does it do more than simply give emotional relief? Only you can answer it, based on your personally chosen criteria for validity. You might find yourself surprised.

The format for our traditional ritual was created as a guideline that may be amended by Satanists to suit their own aesthetics and emotional needs. Thus, Satanic Ritual is not presented as dogma, but as a standard that has been found to be quite effective by thousands of Satanists from many different cultural backgrounds. You may celebrate the rites precisely as presented in the works of Dr. LaVey and in the following pages, since they are effectively dramatic in structure and content. However, you may find elements that detract from your deepest emotional arousal and so these may be altered to serve you best.

Here at the Central Office for the Church of Satan, we're often asked by interested parties if they must use black candles, or absolutely must have all of the devices for ritual described in *The Satanic Bible*. Some ask if they have to have a dedicated room to serve as a ritual chamber. The answer is that you really don't need any of the suggested implements, since the most important tool for ritual is your own imagination. A Satanist who does not have a fancy chamber, sonorous gong, ornate chalice, or elaborate sword, may close his eyes and picture all of these devices and he should have the ability to raise his emotions to their highest levels. If you do decide to gather the tools, they should be personalized and each have some meaning that is most stimulating to you. The idea of having an "instant ritual kit" sold to order is anathema. You should obtain within your means whatever sort of the described tools that will evoke your strongest aesthetic response. You may even have multiple versions to be used for differing ritual intent. The choice is yours.

In *The Satanic Bible* the original prescribed practice was to use at least one black candle on the left and one white candle on the right of your altar. That was dropped fairly quickly in rituals performed at Central Grotto, with two black candles lighting the altar and a white candle on top of a human skull used when cursing sessions were in order. The concept evolved that Satanism should be positively celebrated and that the white candle representing the sterility of spiritual religions need only be employed when Destruction was invoked. Ultimately, any color candles will do, so long as they "feel proper" to you. As is said these days, it is "all about *you!*"

The texts themselves can also be altered to suit your particular sense of rhythm and imagery, and of course memorizing them is worthwhile as it allows you to concentrate more intensely on their meaning. However, if this is too difficult or leads to the fear that you'll "forget your lines," you may read the printed words. Many Satanists have found that printing the specific texts in a format that is easy to read in candlelight is worthwhile. Retyping or hand-copying the texts, putting them in a pleasing font, printing them on beautiful paper and binding them in a large book or even keeping them in a ring-binder with a plain or decorated cover are effective methods. Your self-created "Black Ritual Book" can grow over time, and be a unique accouterment and record of your ritual practice.

Since ritual is about unashamed releasing of emotion and single-mindedness of intent, it is often far better to engage in ritual by oneself rather than have any additional people in the chamber who distract from your central motivation. Solitude can be best. The person leading the ritual always takes the role of Celebrant, but this isn't meant for the ritual to be a theatre piece making you the "star" for a captive, passive audience that has other issues on their minds. Satanism is self-centered, so you as your own God take the prime position, thus you should only have additional participants if they are truly "in synch" with your purpose and can be utterly and actively supportive of you as Celebrant.

When Satanists new to ritual ask about when they should ritualize, I explain that whatever time suits them best is perfect, whether it's dictated by the need for privacy and quiet or by coordinating the schedules of like-minded fellows who wish to join in the particular working. Dr. LaVey presented theories for properly timing rituals in his books, so do explore his suggestions. If the dark hours are most suitable for your rites, and that is traditional, many Satanists have enjoyed using the night of the new moon as the chosen occasion, as this is the time of the month when the sky is black, suiting the symbolism of Satanism's embrace of Darkness as a positive image.

Our standard ritual takes note of the very ancient idea of the four compass directions having a correspondence with what were once considered the four basic elements that comprised all that existed. In the standard Satanic Ritual, Anton LaVey linked these with the four crown princes of Hell found in grimoires such as *The Book of the Sacred Magic of Abramelin the Mage*: Satan—the south—fire, Lucifer—the east—air, Belial—the north—earth, and Leviathan—the west—water. Additionally, since Christian churches often had their altars set in the east to identify their mythical Christ's rising with that of the rising sun, Dr. LaVey suggested the preferred direction for the Satanic altar be the west, blasphemously opposing the Christian mode. However, this is not obligatory and any direction may be utilized by the Satanist. You might even try focusing your ritual in different directions, should that bring enhanced stimulation.

Since Satanism is a religion that embraces the Earth and views ourselves as being part of nature, we don't have the same thinking that other religions do about the need to "purify" our ritual tools. We are carnal, profane people, with an "un-religion." The consecration of implements was not addressed by Anton LaVey in *The Satanic Bible*, so you may simply obtain your devices and use them directly. In Western magical practice, and in neo-pagan religions that have evolved from roots in ceremonial magic, the idea of dedicating ritual tools is persistent. So, even though there is no need to take this step with your ritual tools, the Satanist might decide that it would be pleasurable to dedicate, rather than purify, a ceremonial object before using it. This is an enrichment of ritual practice, but is not in any way mandatory. If you choose to dedicate your ritual tools I present the following method.

## A SATANIC RITE OF DEDICATION

This is a solitary rite, since you are personally recognizing an object as being raised as significant to you, an "elite" tool to be your companion in your workings of Greater Magic. To honor your newly acquired tool, in addition to the standard devices listed you will need incense. Granular incense burned on coals held by a fire-safe thurible is best, but you may alternately use cone or stick incense, placed in a proper holder for safe burning. You will also need a bowl containing water and a smaller receptacle containing salt.

Perform the first seven steps for the Satanic Ritual from *The Satanic Bible*. The eighth step, meant for blessing the congregation, becomes the point where you dedicate the object. Here we use incense (fire and air—Satan, Lucifer) and salted water (earth and water—Belial, Leviathan).

CELEBRANT SPRINKLES INCENSE ON COALS
(OR IGNITES CONE OR STICK INCENSE) SAYING:

Behold the amalgam of the blazing inferno and tempestuous storm.

HE PICKS UP THE OBJECT TO BE DEDICATED AND HOLDS IT OVER
THE RISING INCENSE (OR SWINGS THE THURIBLE AROUND AN
OBJECT TOO LARGE TO HOLD OVER IT) SAYING:

In the name of Satan, Lord of Fire, and Lucifer, Lord of Air, I dedicate this [*name of tool*] of the Black Art. You shall serve me well.

THE TOOL MAY BE MOVED IN THE PATTERN OF A PENTAGRAM
OVER THE THURIBLE, BEGINNING WITH THE UPPER LEFT HAND
POINT. ALTERNATELY THE THURIBLE MAY BE SWUNG IN THAT
PATTERN OVER A LARGER OBJECT. AS THE SMOKE CURLS AROUND
THE OBJECT ENVISION THE ESSENCE OF BLAZING SATAN AND
RADIANT LUCIFER BEING INFUSED INTO IT, ENERGIZING IT.
SET DOWN THE OBJECT (OR THURIBLE) WHEN YOU FEEL
IT IS FULLY "CHARGED."

CELEBRANT NOW PICKS UP SALT WITH THE LEFT HAND AND
SPRINKLES IT INTO THE BOWL OF WATER SAYING:

Behold the amalgam of the fertile earth and raging sea.

HE PICKS UP THE OBJECT TO BE DEDICATED AND WITH THE LEFT
HAND, DIPS FINGERS INTO THE BOWL AND SLOWLY DRAWS UPON
THE OBJECT AN INVERSE PENTAGRAM STARTING WITH
THE UPPER LEFT POINT SAYING:

In the name of Belial, Lord of the Earth,
and Leviathan, Lord of the Sea, I dedicate
this [*name of tool*] of the Black Art.
You shall serve me well.

THE CELEBRANT SHOULD ENVISION THE WATER GLOWING
WITH THE FECUND ESSENCE OF BELIAL AND THE POTENCY OF
LEVIATHAN. SET DOWN THE OBJECT WHEN YOU
FEEL IT IS FULLY "CHARGED."

CELEBRANT RAISES HANDS OVER THE OBJECT
IN THE MUDRA OF FLAME AND SAYS:

Shemhamforash! Hail Satan!

HE STRIKES GONG.

THE CELEBRANT NOW READS THE SIXTH ENOCHIAN KEY
FROM *THE SATANIC BIBLE*.

THIS IS FOLLOWED BY THE THIRTEENTH STEP—RINGING OF THE
BELL AS POLLUTIONARY AND PRONOUNCING THE TRADITIONAL
CLOSING PHRASE,

So it is done.

YOU MAY SET YOUR DEDICATED TOOL IN ITS PROPER PLACE
TO AWAIT ITS USE IN YOUR NEXT RITUAL.

The tool is now pledged to its new identity, and is an extension of your Will. Some Satanists choose to preserve this "charging" by keeping the tool hidden until a ritual is about to be performed. A lockable cupboard works well, particularly if your chamber is a room that must serve other purposes and might have visitors not sympathetic to your proclivities. If you celebrate your infernal rites at night, it can be worthwhile to not open the cupboard until the room is lit by candles, the proper atmosphere being conjured for the practice of the Black Arts. If you have a chamber that may remain locked, only entered by yourself and those of your diabolical cohorts with whom you wish to share the intimacy of ritual, then you may display the object in an honored location in your chamber.

Once you have gathered your tools and mastered the techniques presented in *The Satanic Bible*, you may find the rites that follow to be suitable works to enhance your ritual practice, particularly for marking significant experiences in your rich and vital life.

Ultimately, the use of ritual is entirely a personal decision for each Satanist. If you do decide to employ this exquisite tool, may it serve you well to celebrate your own Infernal Godhood.

# A SATANIC WEDDING

IN THE EARLY DAYS of the Church of Satan, one of the events that attracted high publicity was a wedding rite with press attendance. The public already had their senses benumbed from the social upheavals of the sixties, yet they were shocked to witness a couple making vows in the name of Satan before a nude female altar, being joined in unholy matrimony. Weddings are widely accepted as the domain of established religions and this is why people were alarmed—they saw how an alternative religion could usurp a practice they felt belonged only to them. How dare we! Of course, most religions snub secular civil weddings as just a poor man's alternative to their "superior" product, endorsed by their deity of choice. Finding a church dedicated to championing Satan and using the Devil's name to hallow a bond was truly revolutionary. As far as most religions were concerned, Satan was the one who inspired rampant lust which lead to the dissolution of the unions they were trying so hard to cement! At most, they might have thought, the Prince of Darkness would cajole people to elope for one of those wacky Las Vegas ceremonies. Being joined by a pseudo-Elvis was certainly diabolical—remember how he used to lasciviously swivel those hips?

Since we Satanists are dedicated to enjoying our lives to the fullest, we embrace the full range of human emotions and that goes from the extremes of darkest hate through deepest love—both of which are rare in our lives' experience. In *The Satanic Bible*, Anton LaVey provided a means for throwing curses to purge the destructive urges arising when one is unjustly wronged. He also celebrated the profound love that members had for each other by performing wedding rites. The text below is inspired by a fragmentary ceremony from the early days of the Church of Satan that was then used as a basic format which could be amended at will depending upon the circumstances of the union. The rite presented here has been newly revised, yet has much in common with my original version that had been performed by members of our Priesthood of Mendes for many years.

In Satanism, the basis for a couple forming a union is the loving relationship they have created. It does not matter if the couple is of the same or opposite sexes. This bond requires no sanction from the state, nor any blessings by deities of any sort. It is formed by the partners, will be sustained by them, and may dissolve when they evolve beyond whatever factors caused their love to flourish. Since we Satanists are generally solitary folk, we've never felt the need to have overt displays of our feelings to the public at large. When we form deep relationships, they are between the individuals involved, and not subject to external social contracts. But the Church of Satan does not ignore the history of human behavior, and so we understand that a loving couple may wish to demonstrate their exultant pride in the relationship they've formed by having a ceremony and inviting people who have meaning in their lives. We celebrate our joy and share it with those we cherish.

Pragmatically, in most nations, married couples achieve legal benefits and privileges that cannot be duplicated via civil unions or other alternative modes of lawful bonding, thus the state of marriage remains singular as the pinnacle of means for uniting the lives of the partners. Most institutions, such as hospitals, recognize this bond as being beyond blood relationship, and so it holds a potency as yet unmatched. Therefore, it is a powerful institution that we Satanists use for the advantages it can provide. I hereby present a truly unholy rite of matrimony to assist you prideful lovers to glorify that dark Satanic love which galvanizes you to find the world in each other. May your passions be unparalleled!

# PRELIMINARY:

In section III, if incense is not used, proceed directly to the blessing of the chalice. Sections VI and VII are optional, meant for a more formal Satanic Wedding Mass, and can be omitted without any loss to the ritual. In Section II, I've presented Infernal Names which are diabolical figures related to lust and sexuality. Of course the couple may select names suiting their own tastes. Naturally, the couple to be married may personalize their vows, and the ones presented here should provide inspiration. If there are texts dear to the couple that they'd like to have read by family or friends, these may be added wherever dramatically appropriate.

This ritual is to be performed by members of our Priesthood only if the couple has already been legally married by the local secular authorities, or if the officiating Celebrant has been authorized by the local authorities to perform legal wedding ceremonies. Laws vary greatly, so the need for licenses and other documents legitimizing such a union must be explored thoroughly before this rite is employed. Of course, partners may celebrate this rite themselves without state sanction simply to mark their personal bond without it having any legal ramifications or obligations.

The ceremony can be used for same sex couples, or even polyamorous unions, with the proper amendment of wording, again noting the laws of the place where the partners reside if governmental legitimization and privileges are desired.

All words are spoken by the Celebrant unless otherwise noted. Participants dress for ceremony. Devices standard to satanic ritual are assembled as required. A copy of *The Satanic Bible* must be present for the "Invocation to Satan," passages from the "Book of Satan," and the "Enochian Key" detailed in the liturgy. In addition, a pillow, paten, or tray with two rings is also placed upon the altar.

External light sources are shut out. Congregation is seated (they may stand throughout if they wish). Lights are extinguished; decompression music is begun. Celebrant and assistants enter with lit black candles, they proceed to the altar and light altar candles. Bride and Groom then enter to processional music and sit front and center, closest to Celebrant (they may stand throughout if they wish).

A SATANIC WEDDING

# I. PURIFICATION OF THE AIR

RING BELL 9 TIMES, DIRECTING TOLLING TO THE FOUR CARDINAL
COMPASS POINTS WHILE TURNING COUNTER-CLOCKWISE. THE
"HYMN TO SATAN" (OR OTHER APPROPRIATE MUSIC) IS PLAYED
SIMULTANEOUSLY.


# II. INVOCATION TO SATAN

INVOCATION FROM *THE SATANIC BIBLE*,
IS INTONED BY CELEBRANT.

THE INFERNAL NAMES:

Baphomet, Moloch, Ishtar, Bast, Asmodeus, Mammon,
Kali, Lilith, Amon, Pan, Ashtaroth, Naamah, Melek Taus.

CONGREGATION REPEATS EACH NAME AFTER CELEBRANT.

CELEBRANT: Arise oh Gods of the Abyss and manifest
thy presence through the blessing of this
union!

# III. RITE OF THE CHALICE

CELEBRANT: As our incense ascends to thee,
Infernal Lord, so shall your blessings
descend upon us.

*CENSE CHALICE THRICE, BOW. CENSE BAPHOMET THRICE, BOW. CIRCUMAMBULATE CHAMBER COUNTERCLOCKWISE AND DIRECT INCENSE TO THE CARDINAL POINTS.*

*BLESS CHALICE WITH MUDRA OF FLAME.*

Lord Satan, Imperator of Fire, Hell and
Earth are filled with your glory.
Hosanna in profundis!

*CELEBRANT ELEVATES CHALICE. GONG IS STRUCK.*

Behold the chalice of ecstasy filled with the
elixir of life. As kindred to the undefiled
beasts, I drink and celebrate the Black
Flame within.

*CELEBRANT DRINKS.*

Satan, thy strength is mine!

*CELEBRANT TURNS TO OFFER CHALICE TO GROOM AND BRIDE.*

Drink and honor the bliss you both share.

THEY TAKE THE CHALICE TOGETHER AND EACH OFFERS IT TO THE
OTHER. EACH DRINKS AND REPLIES, WHILE LOOKING INTO EACH
OTHER'S EYES:

**GROOM & BRIDE:** My joy is thine, forever!

COUPLE RETURNS THE CHALICE TO THE CELEBRANT.
HE FACES ALTAR, ELEVATES CHALICE A FINAL TIME
THEN REPLACES IT ON ALTAR.

# IV. SUMMONING THE PRINCES OF HELL

Celebrant takes sword and points toward the domain
of the Prince to be called.

CELEBRANT: From the south I summon thee almighty
Satan. Come forth oh Lord of the Inferno,
I bid thee welcome!

From the east I summon thee great Lucifer.
Come forth oh Bearer of Light,
I bid thee welcome!

From the north I summon thee fearsome
Belial. Come forth oh King of the Earth,
I bid thee welcome!

From the west I summon thee dread
Leviathan. Come forth oh Dragon of the
Abyss, I bid thee welcome!

Shemhamforash!

CONGREG. (*responds*): Shemhamforash!

CELEBRANT: Hail Satan!

CONGREG. (*responds*): Hail Satan!

GONG IS STRUCK.

CELEBRANT REPLACES SWORD ON ALTAR.

# V. BENEDICTION

CELEBRANT ELEVATES PHALLUS.

CELEBRANT: For thou art a mighty Lord, oh Satan, and from thee arises all potency, justice, and dominion. Let our visions become reality and our creations endure, for we are your kindred, demon brethren, scions of carnal joy.

CELEBRANT SHAKES PHALLUS TOWARDS
APPROPRIATE COMPASS POINTS SAYING:

CELEBRANT: Satan, give to us thy blessing.
Lucifer, grant to us thy favor.
Belial, confer upon us thy benisons.
Leviathan, bestow to us thy treasures.

CELEBRANT REPLACES PHALLUS ON THE ALTAR.


# VI. THE READING

CELEBRANT: A reading from the Book of Satan!

CONGREG. (*responds*): Glory to thee, Prince of Darkness!

SELECTED CONGREGANT READS BOOK IV.

# VII. AVE SATANAS

CELEBRANT: To us, thy devoted disciples, oh Infernal
Lord, who celebrate our iniquity and trust
in your boundless might, grant thy bond
of Stygian sodality. It is through you that
lavish gifts come to us; knowledge, vigor,
and wealth are yours to bestow.
We renounce the spiritual paradise of
the desperate and gullible. You have won
our trust, oh God of the Flesh, for you
champion the satisfaction of all our desires
and provide abundant fulfillment in the
land of the living. Shemhamforash!

CONGREG. (*responds*): Shemhamforash!

CELEBRANT: Deliver us, Dark Lord, from every
hindrance and grant us joy in our lives. By
your munificence you ensure our freedom
and protect us from injustice as we indulge
in our heart's desires. The kingdom, the
power, and the glory are eternally yours.

CELEBRANT (*CONGREG. repeats*): Hail Satan full of might!
Our allegiance is with thee!
Cursed are they, the God adorers,
and cursed are the worshippers
of the Nazarene Eunuch!
Unholy Satan, bringer of enlightenment,
lend us thy power,
Now and throughout the hours of our lives!
Shemhamforash!

# VIII. THE WEDDING INVOCATION

CELEBRANT (*addressing couple*): Arise and come forward!
(*or* "Come forward!" *if they are standing*)

COUPLE STANDS IN FRONT OF CELEBRANT.

Glory to Thee, almighty Satan, highest and ineffable King of Hell; and on Earth joy to the followers of the Left-Hand Path. Oh potent Prince of Darkness, Thou grantest us vital existence and undefiled wisdom.

Ever living Lord of the Pit, who has willed that all the pleasures of the flesh shall be made manifest, grant abundance to Thy advocates, [*first names of couple to be wed*] who revel in thy truth. Shemhamforash!

CONGREG. (*responds*): Shemhamforash!

CELEBRANT: In the name of Satan, I welcome you on this night of nights. Our hall has become a chamber wherein the culmination of your courtship shall be honored. Each of you, in your unique manner, has woven the sorcery of fascination upon the other and so wishes an acclamation of this mastery. Your consummation is not a minor victory, for ardent lust seeking lasting dedication is not always satisfied. By the power of your love and the essence of your selves, you have attained this fusion. As each truly living creature upon the Earth seeks enhancement, so you have grown greater together. May the children of the night join with us, singing your praises, for life and love abound! Shemhamforash!

CONGREG. (*responds*): Shemhamforash!

CELEBRANT: Hail Satan!

CONGREG. (*responds*): Hail Satan!

GONG IS STRUCK.

# IX. THE VOWS

CELEBRANT: I ask you [*name of groom*], is she your chosen mate, decreed by your deepest ardor, the image of your fantasy incarnate?

GROOM: She is indeed.

CELEBRANT: I ask you, [*name of bride*], is he your chosen mate, decreed by your deepest ardor, the image of your fantasy incarnate?

BRIDE: He is indeed.

CELEBRANT: It is time to express your vows.

BRIDE AND GROOM FACE EACH OTHER AND JOIN HANDS.

GROOM: [*name of bride*], I desire to live with you just as you are. I choose you above all others, to share my life with me. I promise to always speak the truth to you, to honor and to tenderly care for you.

I love you for yourself, in trust that you will become all that you can be, and in turn I promise to be as great as my Nature and Will allow. I will honor this pledge as long as life and love endure.

**BRIDE:** [*name of groom*], I desire to live with you just as you are. I choose you above all others, to share my life with me. I promise to always speak the truth to you, to honor and to tenderly care for you.

I love you for yourself, in trust that you will become all that you can be, and in turn I promise to be as great as my Nature and Will allow. I will honor this pledge as long as life and love endure.

# X. THE JOINING

CELEBRANT: Behold the rings, symbol of the covenant
between [*names of bride and groom*].

CELEBRANT CONSECRATES RINGS WITH MUDRA OF FLAME,
GONG IS STRUCK. CELEBRANT HOLDS OUT PILLOW/TRAY
WITH RINGS TO COUPLE.

GROOM (*takes ring*): [*name of bride*], with this ring I
marry you and join my life with yours.

BRIDE (*takes ring*): [*name of groom*], with this ring I
marry you and join my life with yours.

CELEBRANT: You stand before me now as consorts.
By your volition, you have declared your
vows in the presence of these witnesses. I
therefore consecrate this union under the
aegis of the Lord of the Earth, whose priest
I am. In the name of Satan, I proclaim
you husband and wife. May your bliss be
unbounded, and may your love wax ever
stronger during your journey together.
Embrace and be as one.

AS THEY DO SO, PRIEST RECITES THE SECOND ENOCHIAN KEY.

CELEBRANT: You may seal your bond with a kiss.

AS THEY KISS, CELEBRANT BEGINS TO CLAP
AND CONGREGATION JOINS IN WITH APPLAUSE.
CONTINUE AFTER THE OVATION CONCLUDES.

# XI. THE CLOSING RITE

**CELEBRANT:** I bid thee rise and give the Sign of the Horns. (If standing, "I bid thee give the Sign of the Horns.")

**CELEBRANT:** Almighty Satan, open wide the Gates of Hell! Reveal the mysteries of your creation for we are partakers of your undefiled wisdom!

Forget ye not what was and is to be! Flesh without sin! World without end!

**CELEBRANT** (*CONGREG. repeats*): Shemhamforash!
Hail [*names of bride and groom*]!
Hail Satan!
Hail Satan!
Hail Satan!

# XII. POLLUTIONARY

Celebrant rings bell as at the beginning, while "Hymn to
Satan" or other appropriate music is played.
When the sounds have decayed into silence
the Celebrant concludes:

**CELEBRANT:** So it is done!

Celebrant extinguishes candles, any other lighting is
blacked-out. All experience the darkness for a moment.
Conventional illumination is restored,
ending the ceremony.

# XIII. LET THE WEDDING FEAST NOW BEGIN!

A SATANIC WEDDING

# A Satanic Funeral Rite

SATANISM IS FOR THE LIVING, and so are the Satanic obsequies. We are a life-centered philosophy. We fight against the unnatural cutting short of one's vital existence. We resist leaving the joyful experience of the one life we have to live. If we can, we will cheat death at every turn, to continue living well. But we also understand that our lives will eventually cease. When someone we cherish dies, we regret the loss of a worthy companion. When we die, the end of consciousness is upon us and we cannot experience what happens amongst those who succeed us. Life cycles endlessly, and we are part of this process. So we enjoy the here and now, and do not look for a fictive afterlife.

Unlike death-centered religions, from ancient Egypt with its elaborate funerary customs to contemporary Christianity and its stultified platitudes, Satanism acknowledges that death is the end. As is written in *The Satanic Bible*: "There is no Heaven of glory bright, and no Hell where sinners roast. Here and now is our day of torment! Here and now is our day of joy!" The Church of Satan therefore does not require that words be spoken over the remains of our members. The Satanist is dead; he or she will not know the difference. We do not believe that we need an "insurance policy" for the dead to get what is deserved from whatever supposed Gods control justice in the hereafter. We are our own Gods, and we know that such ceremonials have no benefit for us once we've died. Many Satanists may decide not to plan on any sort of services or memorials, leaving that up to those who survive them. Others, particularly our members who have friends and acquaintances who share their Satanic values, may wish for their cohorts to gather and commemorate the life that has come to a conclusion.

The purpose of this rite is to provide a framework in which the participants may acknowledge and mourn the death of someone they esteemed, after which they celebrate and concretize what meaning that person's life had and will continue to have for them. We believe that immortality lies only in the memories of the people whom the deceased touched in some way during their lives, or whomsoever they influence *post mortem* via their lives' creative output. This rite is thus a tribute to the achievements of the deceased.

As always, this is not a dogmatic rite; it is a suggestion for a possible ceremony, which may be adapted to suit the needs of the situation.

In order to make the text more readable, we have placed a revered name in brackets that should be replaced by the name of the individual for whom this rite is performed. We have also placed gender specific words in brackets, having selected the male version for this rite but which should be substituted to suit the gender of the deceased.

# PRELIMINARY:

The rite will vary depending upon what is to be done with the body of the deceased. That decision is in the power of whoever was deemed to be legally responsible—the family, loved ones, or the desires of the deceased as stated in a legally acceptable instrument. Do not place your funeral plans in your will, as that is not usually read until after your funeral. It is wise to write a letter of intent to your executor and send copies to anyone who might have a role in the handling of your after death affairs. The Church of Satan accepts burial of the remains in a private or national cemetery (and this may be accompanied by a marker suitable to the aesthetics of the deceased) and can even include burial at sea as well as cremation. If the latter is chosen, the remains may be kept by the family and loved ones, or scattered in a place that was special to the deceased. There are other means available for the disposal or preservation of remains, and such are up to the will of the deceased and the remaining family and loved ones. Embalming is also a matter of taste.

If the deceased is in a casket, it may be either open or closed at the discretion of the responsible parties. Likewise, the clothing of the deceased is up to their discretion, but we suggest that they reflect the nature and self-image of the decedent.

Since a funeral will bring together people who have varying religious or philosophical beliefs, we note that they each may have a means of dress that would seem suitable for their own expression of grief and remembrance. The Satanist participants may wear the standard black robes, or may dress in black clothing and should be wearing a Sigil of Baphomet. Each should also include some item of clothing colored white (the color of death and sterility), which may simply be a white armband. Armbands may be provided for attendees. The Celebrant may wear a chasuble or sash, black in color, upon which is emblazoned a skull and crossed bones in white (a traditional symbol of mortality).

At the place for the rite—which can be in a ritual chamber of one of the family or friends of the deceased, or at a funeral home—devices standard to Satanic ritual are assembled (bell, sword, gong, chalice, phallus, elixir) and placed on a table set within reach of the Celebrant's position for officiating. A copy of *The Satanic Bible* is required for the "Invocation to Satan," passages from the "Book of Satan," and the "Enochian Key" referenced below.

An additional table is used as the main Shrine Altar, which serves as a gathering place for memorial objects as well as two black candles in holders (used for illumination). It may be draped in cloth of a color or colors admired by the deceased, and should be placed centrally, perhaps in front of the casket. Consider the geometry of the chamber and decide accordingly. A Sigil of Baphomet should be placed above or upon this altar. Cloths or banners bearing this sigil may be draped over the casket. If there is an urn, it may be placed upon the Shrine Altar and be either draped with or set upon a cloth bearing this Sigil. Layouts will vary according to the space being used.

If the remains of the deceased are not present for the rite, an actual (or replica) human skull and crossed bones may be placed upon the Shrine Altar to represent them.

A black pillar candle in an appropriate holder is placed near the head of the deceased if the body is present in a casket or next to the container of ashes if the body has been cremated or in front of the representational skull and bones. This candle, when lit, symbolizes the Black Flame—the essence of the deceased. Enough smaller black candles are present for each of the mourners. These may be candles in glass holders, which prevent the dripping of wax and resist the wind or they may be smaller, slender candles with some provision made for catching the dripping wax. These candles are placed on a small table near to the Black Flame candle in some proper receptacle such as a tray, basket, or bowl containing sand in which candles may be stood. Some black tapers or long wooden matches may be needed to transfer the flame from the Black Flame candle to the mourner's candles. Make certain that the Celebrant has mastered functional techniques for lighting these candles from the Black Flame candle before beginning the rite.

Items dear to the deceased should be present in the chamber as well as things created by the deceased during his/her life. Photographs depicting the rich and varied life of the deceased are also appropriate. All of these items should be placed on or near the Shrine Altar, which must be easily accessible to the mourners, so that they may have time to experience these tokens of the fullness of the deceased's life.

Flowers may also be present—this is up to the tastes of those who arrange the funeral. Proper Satanic symbolism should be utilized in any floral tributes.

Prior to the commencement of the formal rite, the mourners should have a span of time to meditate at the Shrine Altar, experiencing their emotions and coming to accept the reality of their loss. During this period of reflection they should compose their statements for the memorial part of the liturgy. If it may take some time for all of the mourners to gather, there may then be several days allotted for this period of meditative remembrance. During this interval the mourners may bring items to place upon the Shrine Altar. They are welcome to retrieve these items at the conclusion of the rite or they may choose to donate them to other mourners whom they feel should have them. Someone should be appointed to oversee the aesthetic placement of objects on the Shrine Altar. Once all of the mourners have had this opportunity, the rite may begin.

All words are spoken by the Celebrant unless otherwise noted. Infernal names have been chosen which have a particular association with mythology of death or the Underworld, but the Celebrant may choose to use names that held particular resonance for the deceased.

The Black Flame candle is ignited. External light sources are shut out. If a censer is used, the coals should be ignited. The congregation is seated. Lights are then extinguished and decompression music is begun. This music should be something that had significance for the deceased. The Celebrant proceeds to the altar and lights the two basic black altar candles (he should use the Black Flame candle as the source for this lighting, perhaps lighting a long match or taper from this candle). If other black candles are needed for illumination, they are now lit, or if it is more practical to have electric lighting for the proceedings, this is now brought to a proper level.

# I. PURIFICATION OF THE AIR

RING BELL 9 TIMES, DIRECTING TOLLING TO THE FOUR CARDINAL
COMPASS POINTS WHILE TURNING COUNTER-CLOCKWISE. THE
"HYMN TO SATAN" MAY BE PLAYED SIMULTANEOUSLY.


# II. INVOCATION TO SATAN

INVOCATION FROM *THE SATANIC BIBLE*
IS INTONED BY THE CELEBRANT.

THE INFERNAL NAMES:
Gorgo, Mormo, Tezcatlipoca, Nija, Hecate, Mictian, Pluto,
Proserpine, Mania, Yaotzin, Supay, Mantus, Emma-o,
Nergal, Yen-lo-Wang

CONGREGATION REPEATS EACH NAME AFTER CELEBRANT.

CELEBRANT: Arise, oh Gods of the abyss, and bear
witness to these testimonials that celebrate
the life of one who was thy kith and kin.

A SATANIC FUNERAL RITE

# III. RITE OF THE CHALICE

*Use of incense and words accompanying it are optional.*
*If incense is not used, proceed directly to*
*the blessing of the chalice.*

CELEBRANT ADDS INCENSE TO THE CENSER.

CELEBRANT: As our incense ascends to thee,
Infernal Lord, so shall your blessings
descend upon us.

CELEBRANT CENSES CHALICE THRICE, BOWS. CENSES
BAPHOMET THRICE, BOWS. CIRCUMAMBULATES CHAMBER
COUNTERCLOCKWISE AND DIRECTS INCENSE TO THE CARDINAL
POINTS, AS WELL AS THE REMAINS OF THE DECEASED.

BLESS CHALICE WITH MUDRA OF FLAME.

Lord Satan, Imperator of Fire, Hell and
Earth are filled with your glory. Hosanna in
profundis!

CELEBRANT ELEVATES CHALICE. GONG IS STRUCK.

Behold the chalice of ecstasy filled with the
elixir of life. As kindred to the undefiled
beasts, I drink and celebrate the Black
Flame within.

CELEBRANT DRINKS AND SAYS:

Satan, thy strength is mine!

CELEBRANT TURNS TO OFFER CHALICE TO MOURNERS
WITH THESE WORDS:

Drink and honor thy true nature.

MOURNERS WHO WISH TO PARTAKE APPROACH.
THEY EACH DRINK AND REPLY:

MOURNER:  The Black Flame burns within me.
Satan, thy strength is mine!

CELEBRANT FACES ALTAR, ELEVATES CHALICE A FINAL TIME
THEN REPLACES IT ON ALTAR.

# IV. SUMMONING THE PRINCES OF HELL

CELEBRANT TAKES SWORD AND POINTS TOWARD THE DOMAIN OF THE PRINCE TO BE CALLED.

CELEBRANT: From the south I summon thee almighty Satan. Come forth oh Lord of the Inferno, I bid thee welcome!

From the east I summon thee great Lucifer. Come forth oh Bearer of Light, I bid thee welcome!

From the north I summon thee fearsome Belial. Come forth oh King of the Earth, I bid thee welcome!

From the west I summon thee dread Leviathan. Come forth oh Dragon of the Abyss, I bid thee welcome!

Shemhamforash!

CONGREG. (*responds*): Shemhamforash!

CELEBRANT: Hail Satan!

CONGREG. (*responds*): Hail Satan!

GONG IS STRUCK.

CELEBRANT REPLACES SWORD ON ALTAR.

# V. BENEDICTION

CELEBRANT ELEVATES PHALLUS:

CELEBRANT: For thou art a mighty Lord, oh Satan, and from thee arises all potency, justice, and dominion. Let our visions become reality and our creations endure, for we are your kindred, demon brethren, scions of carnal joy.

CELEBRANT SHAKES PHALLUS TOWARDS
APPROPRIATE COMPASS POINTS SAYING:

Satan, give to us thy blessing.
Lucifer, grant to us thy favor.
Belial, confer upon us thy benisons.
Leviathan, bestow to us thy treasures.

CELEBRANT REPLACES PHALLUS ON THE ALTAR.

# VI. THE READING

CELEBRANT: A reading from the Book of Satan!

CONGREG. (*responds*): Glory to thee, Prince of Darkness!

SELECTED CONGREGANT READS BOOK V,
NUMBERS 1 THROUGH 6, AND 13.

# VII. AVE SATANAS

**CELEBRANT:** To us, thy devoted disciples, oh Infernal Lord, who celebrate our iniquity and trust in your boundless might, grant thy bond of Stygian sodality. It is through you that lavish gifts come to us; knowledge, vigor, and wealth are yours to bestow.
We renounce the spiritual paradise of the desperate and gullible. You have won our trust, oh God of the Flesh, for you champion the satisfaction of all our desires and provide abundant fulfillment in the land of the living. Shemhamforash!

**CONGREG.** (*responds*): Shemhamforash!

**CELEBRANT:** Deliver us, Dark Lord, from every hindrance and grant us joy in our lives. By your munificence you ensure our freedom and protect us from injustice as we indulge in our heart's desires. The kingdom, the power, and the glory are eternally yours.

**CELEBRANT** (*CONGREG. repeats*): Hail Satan full of might!
Our allegiance is with thee!
Cursed are they, the God adorers,
and cursed are the worshippers
of the Nazarene Eunuch!
Unholy Satan, bringer of enlightenment,
lend us thy power, Now and throughout
the hours of our lives!
Shemhamforash!

# VIII. THE FUNERARY INVOCATION

**CELEBRANT:** Glory to thee, almighty Satan, highest and ineffable King of Hell; and on Earth, joy to the followers of the Left-Hand Path. Oh potent Prince of Darkness, thou grantest us vital existence and undefiled wisdom.

Ever living Lord of the Pit, who has willed that all the pleasures of the flesh shall be made manifest, grant to thy disciples remembrance of [*Anton*], one of the children of the night who reveled in thy truth, who was truly born to be among thy chosen. Hail [*Anton*]!

**CONGREG.** (*responds*): Hail [*Anton*]!

**CELEBRANT:** Tonight we mourn the loss of a friend and [*brother*], a fellow God. Without you, our worlds are lessened indeed.

We celebrate [*Anton Szandor LaVey*] and all [*his*] extraordinary works. [*He*] embraced the title of Satanist because [*he*] chose to be [*his*] own God in the face of the vastness of indifferent Nature. [*Anton*] took command of [*his*] life, moving from victory to victory in triumphant succession. [*He*] was a beneficent deity to [*his*] allies and associates. [*He*] was a ruthless adversary to any who stood against [*his*] true friends, who were far more important to [*him*] than any mythological deities. Indeed, [*he*] chose wisely, according to the nature of [*his*] flesh. Our world is ever in need of outstanding individuals like [*Anton*]. Shemhamforash!

CONGREG. (*responds*): Shemhamforash!

CELEBRANT: Hail Satan!

CONGREG. (*responds*): Hail Satan!

GONG IS STRUCK.

# IX. THE MEMORIAL

CELEBRANT: Come forth, cherished friends and lovers, admirers of [*Anton*] and share some of what [*he*] has given to you.

THE CELEBRANT HAS THUS INVITED THE MOURNERS TO APPROACH HIM AT THE ALTAR SHRINE. ONE AT A TIME, THOSE WHO WISH TO MAY COME UP, EACH FACING THE CONGREGATION, AND SPEAK ABOUT THEIR MEMORIES AND LOVE AND RESPECT FOR THE DECEASED.

*This part of the rite may include spoken testimonials, the reading of passages from books which were important to the deceased, the playing of music of significance (recorded or performed live), the reading of poetry, telling of favored jokes, showing of video, and so on. Any presentation, which brings the memories of the deceased most vividly to mind, is acceptable. The intent is to bring an emotional catharsis wherein weeping is expected, as the loss is felt most deeply. But also, finally, we mean to incite joy, as each congregant treasures the memories of the person whose life has ended, as well as the marvelous things produced during that life, and shares this with the other mourners.*

# X. PASSING OF THE BLACK FLAME

WHEN ALL OF THE MEMORIALS HAVE BEEN PRESENTED, THE
CELEBRANT INVITES ALL THE MOURNERS TO APPROACH THE
SHRINE ALTAR WITH THESE WORDS:

CELEBRANT: Unholy brethren, these many deeds and creations wrought by [*Anton Szandor LaVey*] remain with us. Come forward and accept this token of [*Anton*]'s gifts to you.

AS THEY DO, HE HANDS EACH OF THEM A BLACK CANDLE, WHICH THEY THEN PROCEED TO LIGHT AT THE BLACK FLAME CANDLE (CELEBRANT OR AN ASSISTANT MAY HELP THEM). APPROPRIATE MUSIC MAY BE PLAYED DURING THIS PROCESS. AFTER RECEIVING THE CANDLE, EACH MOURNER QUIETLY SAYS "HAIL [ANTON]!" THE MOURNERS RETURN TO THEIR PLACES AND STAND, HOLDING THE BURNING CANDLES, MEDITATING ON THE THOUGHT THAT THIS FLAME SYMBOLIZES THE VITALITY THAT WAS SHARED WITH THEM BY THE DECEASED.

AFTER THE FINAL MOURNER HAS RETURNED TO HIS PLACE THE CELEBRANT CONTINUES:

Dear [*Anton*], long shall you live in the hearts of those you inspired.

You enjoyed life to the fullest—fanning the fires about you, igniting in those fortunate enough to be near a part of your passion for the pleasures of this world.

As you are borne out upon the Ebon river, to be embraced by Darkness Eternal, you continue to touch us with your magic.

We shall always cherish the gifts you have bestown upon us, as they bring us deep satisfaction, and spur us on to our own achievements.

We salute thee, [*Anton Szandor LaVey*], comrade of the Left-Hand Path, one who is truly numbered among Hell's chosen, who moved with elegance and might within the Devil's fane.

<small>Celebrant now moves to the Black Flame Candle:</small>

Good night, sweet [*Prince*].

<small>Celebrant extinguishes the candle.</small>

Your flame has been spent, yet it burns ever brightly within our hearts.

<small>congreg.:</small> Good night, [*Anton*].

<small>Mourners now extinguish their candles. They may keep these to use for future meditations upon the gifts from the deceased.</small>

# TRANSITIONAL:

*A. If there is to be a burial, the rite is not closed but will end at the gravesite when the mourners re-assemble. It would be preferable for this to take place at night, or twilight.*

CELEBRANT: Kinsmen of [*Anton Szandor LaVey*], we go now to gather at the appointed place.

THE MOURNERS NOW LEAVE THE CHAMBER QUIETLY AND GO TO THE PLACE OF BURIAL. IF IT IS NECESSARY TO DRIVE, A TRADITIONAL FUNERARY PROCESSION OF VEHICLES MAY NOW TAKE PLACE. IT IS PREFERABLE FOR THE VEHICLES TO BE WHITE IN COLOR. WHEN ALL HAVE ASSEMBLED AT THE GRAVESIDE, THE RITE MAY CONTINUE WITH THE CLOSING.

*B. If the body has been cremated and the remains are kept, then the closing rite follows immediately.*

*C. If the remains are to be scattered now, the rite is not closed but is concluded when the mourners have assembled at the spot for the scattering. The Celebrant uses the same words of invitation to re-assemble as above in "A."*

*If the scattering will take place at an indeterminate later time, the closing rite is followed, and those present at the scattering may repeat the closing rite, or other appropriate words, at that time.*

# XI. THE CLOSING RITE

CELEBRANT: Attend, dear fellows. We give a sign of our allegiance to the Powers of Darkness with these words received from an unknown hand.

THE ELEVENTH ENOCHIAN KEY IS READ BY THE CELEBRANT.

> I bid thee rise and give the Sign of the Horns.
> (*If standing,* "I bid thee give the Sign of the Horns.")

CONGREGATION RESPONDS AS BIDDEN WITH THE SALUTE, GIVEN WITH THE LEFT HAND.

CELEBRANT: The gates of Hell have opened and the Lords of the Netherworld have drawn near! [*Anton Szandor LaVey*] reveled in this world of worlds, and as a true exemplar of Satanism [*he*] shall live in the hearts and memories of those who adored [*him*] throughout [*his*] lifetime, as long as the breath of life shall sustain them.

By all the powers of Satan let [*Anton*] walk this beloved Earth to which I bind [*him*] forever and ever; and may [*his*] final place of rest lie all the way to Hell.

CELEBRANT (*CONGREG. repeats*): Shemhamforash!
Hail Satan!

Hail [*Anton*]!
Hail [*Anton*]!
Hail [*Anton*]!

GONG, IF PRESENT, IS STRUCK FOLLOWING CONGREGANT'S
REPETITION OF "HAIL SATAN!" AND "HAIL [*ANTON*]!"

A SATANIC FUNERAL RITE

# XII. POLLUTIONARY

Celebrant rings bell as at the beginning, while "Hymn
to Satan" or music dear to the deceased is played.
When the sounds have decayed into silence
the Celebrant concludes:

**CELEBRANT:** So it is done!

Celebrant extinguishes remaining illuminating candles
(or other light sources if this is out of doors), and all
experience the darkness for a moment. Conventional
illumination is then restored, ending the ceremony.

# XIII. REPASS

*It is then traditional for the mourners to gather for food and
drink, as this signifies the continuance of vital existence.*

# RITE OF RAGNARÖK

SATANISTS TAKE THE POSITION that Man has invented his gods. We find world mythology to be our field from which to harvest symbols and metaphors that we find to resonate most strongly with our Satanic natures. When exploring a particular historical mythology, we do not simply pick something that is NOT Christian, or not a part of Christianity's various antecedents and offshoots; we look instead to a myth system and ferret out its unique dark side, the taboo and forbidden regions that its adherents held in awe and terror. That's where the Devils are to be found.

This rite is an exercise in "exoticism"—an old practice in the West for purloining elements from foreign cultures that might seem too alien to be comprehended in their foreign form. Thus they become palatable and enjoyable in an adulterated state. Such absorptions launch trends in the arts. Art Deco had been influenced by the discovery of Tutankhamun's tomb in 1922. Musically it happened in the classical realm when composers like Beethoven imported into his Ninth Symphony the trumpets, drums, and cymbals used by marching Turkish Janissaries. Closer to our own time was the explosion of the "Tiki Lounge" fad. In the 1950s, a faux version of Pacific tribal culture was created to transport Western viewers into a state of blissful otherworldliness. Statues of gods were made into mugs for exotic cocktails; Asian food was garnished with pineapple; elements of primitive island architecture were implemented to create total environments that entertained, but had little relationship to original uses. So, only curmudgeons demand that you must experience such imports in their original forms—authenticity be damned!

I've chosen to import elements from ancient Northern European pagan beliefs to flavor the "stew" that is our traditional ritual practice in the Church of Satan. This is not to be construed as pretending to be authentic, or to be in any way representative of ancient or neo-pagan beliefs or practices. It is solely a means to explore the symbolism of Darkness from a distinct cultural milieu by adopting it into the context of contemporary Satanism. The same could be done with other non-Christian cultural traditions such as rituals utilizing Greek and Roman deities. Asian cthonic imagery can provide rich source material. Eastern art abounds with resonant demonic representations from the pantheons of China, Japan and Tibet.

The purpose of this rite is to expedite the shattering of a social order that has become moribund, seeing it cleared away to prepare for a new society based on values that will bring prosperity and satisfaction to the celebrants. This Norse apocalypse, Ragnarök, is depicted in various literary works handed down to the present. In the prose and poetic Eddas, there are vivid descriptions of the events casting down the old Gods, and I've used these as source material to fuel the litany.

Satanists, regardless of their ethnic or cultural heritage, are seen as one meta-tribe, and so we feel free to absorb appropriate examples of Satanism from whatever source in which they are discovered. When Anton LaVey released *The Satanic Rituals*, he included rites that had German, Russian, Middle Eastern, and French roots, and so Satanists who perform these workings freely identify with their ancestral fellows from all of these traditions. Likewise, you need not be descended from Northern European stock to appreciate and participate in this powerful ritual—you need only be a Satanist.

Originally written in the late 1980s, this is a militant rite, not for the timid, and it is exaggerated in its cataclysmic dramatics. Some might note that some of this mythology has been used dramatically by the Third Reich. However, they should also see that while we appreciate the drama of the mass rallies of the past, we are invoking and embracing the gods that were considered enemies by those who tried to create a neo-pagan culture for Nazi Germany. They wanted to resurrect Valhalla—our rite sends it crashing down in flames.

Our members have used this ritual to purge emotions raised by the terrorist attacks of 9/11, as well as to release their hatred of the current creeping theocracy imposed by right wing fundamentalist Christians in Western nations. You too may find it a powerful cathartic to eliminate feelings of repression induced by parts of society that are distinctly anti-individualistic and utterly un-Satanic.

It may be used as well to cast a vision of the future, a societal Is-To-Be that moves the world in directions of greater freedom, abundant secularism, and utter elimination of fundamentalist fanaticism. Here's to a glorious world of abundant joy. Hail Ragnarök!

## Sowulo (Sig) Pentagram

## Nauthiz (Not)

## Teiwaz (Tyr)
*Posture: arms at 45 degree angle from sides.*

## Sowulo (Sig)
*Mudra: hands flat, palms facing each other, left hand half a hand higher; left thumb at 45 degree angle touches fingertips of right hand.*

## Isa (Is)
*Posture: Stand straight, feet together, arms at sides.*

## Eihwaz (Eh)

## Ragnarök Rune

## Mannaz (Man)
*Posture: legs together, arms extended upwards to the sides.*

## Fehu (Fa)
*Posture: arms raised to front at 45 degree angle, left slightly higher.*

## Dagaz (Dag)
*Posture: arms crossed with hands touching opposite shoulders.*

## Gebo (Gibor)
*Mudra: hands flat, fingers interlaced making an "X" with thum tips touching.*

# PRELIMINARY:

All of the accouterments standard to Satanic ritual may be employed here; however, we suggest certain substitutions which will add a greater resonance to the rite. The Baphomet Sigil may be replaced with an inverse pentagram thrust through with the SIG rune (ᚺ,victory), as was seen in the Sigil worn by Anton LaVey. For the sword of power you may choose one that is of Viking design, or you may substitute a spear or even a battle hammer. Participants may also carry daggers, decorated with runic symbols, with which they echo the Celebrant's gestures according to the rubrics. In place of the chalice, one may substitute a drinking horn, filled with a strong ale or mead. Amulets of significant runes may be worn. Particularly effective is the symbol I designed called the Ragnarok Rune, which consists of a variant on the rune of outward radiating power with a wolf's cross (sign of Hel and unchangeable fate) at the center. Clothing may be the standard black robes, but one can also adopt a warrior-like appearance, creating a "Satanic Soldier" image since traditional northern gear today tends to bring to mind Anna Russell, Hägar the Horrible, or refugees from SCA gatherings.

In addition, a flame source will be needed on your altar, to be ignited during the Conflagration. This can be a small brazier filled with either charcoal, treated to easily ignite, or some form of jellied petroleum fuel like Sterno. If performed out of doors, this can be replaced with a bonfire, but it will require an attendant, and you must be certain of the laws regarding open fires in the locale of your performance. Flash powder or paper is also called for. Incense is not required, but if used should commence with a bitter smell during the Condemnation and Conflagration, and then change to something pleasing during the Victory. On a parchment, the Nauthiz rune (ᚾ) must be depicted, or a three-dimensional one may be constructed of papier-mâché. The ritual area may be decorated with runic symbols that should be displayed on banners or shields. Wolf imagery is also welcomed. Out of doors, one may employ torches for lighting, instead of the traditional black candles. The rite begins with a procession to the place of the working, and outdoors this must be accompanied by the sound of drums (hand drums of a deep tone—no bongos!) repeating the given rhythms (see examples), in succession, or any repetition/combination that you find to be satisfactory.

Music is of paramount importance to this working. I have found a particular recording, when cued correctly, will serve quite well (*Wagner: The Ring Without Words*; Berlin Philharmonic conducted by Lorin Maazel). During the Conflagration one may also play recordings of thunder and windstorms, or if exterior, have several drummers playing arrhythmically to approximate thunder. If desired, lightning generators may also be employed at this stage (van de Graf generators or Tesla coils), As a closing anthem, we have found Dr. LaVey's "Hymn of the Satanic Empire" to be eminently suitable.

There are several runic systems that have varied and evolved over time, as living languages tend to do. In the text, I have mixed older and newer names for these symbols, according to personal preferences and the varied shades of meaning evoked by these names. Resonance is more important than "purism."

In the preceeding list, I give the Elder Futhark name first, followed by the Armanen Futhork name in parenthesis. I encourage the reader to explore some of the numerous books concerning the runes which are now available.

THE SATANIC SCRIPTURES

# ENTRANCE PROCESSIONAL:

**Indoors:** *Participants should file into the totally darkened chamber, lead by an acolyte bearing a lit black candle. Proper music would be "Total War" by NON or march rhythms on the drums. When all have entered and taken their places, the candle is extinguished, and all stand in darkness for several minutes. Next, the ritual music is commenced, and about five minutes should be spent in darkness before lighting the altar candles.*

**Outdoors:** *The congregation should be led by a torchbearer and deep-toned hand drums play a march rhythm. Upon arrival at the ritual site, all assemble in appropriate order and the rite is begun.*

*Possible rhythms for drummers:*

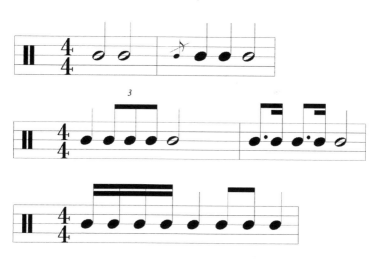

# PURIFICATION:

THE BELL IS RUNG NINE TIMES. THE CELEBRANT TURNING
COUNTER-CLOCKWISE, DIRECTS THE TOLLING TOWARDS
THE FOUR COMPASS POINTS.

# INVOCATION OF THE NETHER GODS:

CELEBRANT TAKES UP HIS SWORD AND POINTS IT
TOWARDS THE SIG PENTAGRAM.

CELEBRANT: Hear me, Gods of the abyss and attend! I command thee, Infernal Lords, to witness mighty deeds done in Thy name. Come forth and greet those numbered among thy pack. The time has come for redress. Justice shall reign through the rule of fang and claw, as it was in the beginning, and as it shall be again!

We smash open the gates to Musspellsheim, Nifelheim and the very depths of Hel's domain and summon thee forth to climax this age of fire!

CELEBRANT (*CONGREG. repeats*): Heija! Hail Loki!

GONG IS STRUCK.

# THE SUMMONS:

SOUTH

**CELEBRANT:** Surt! Master of Fire, I summon thee to come forth from Musspellsheim and kindle thy unquenchable flame! Attend us!

EAST

Loki! Ancient Lord, I summon thee to slaughter the foul ones who stand against nature! Attend us!

NORTH

Fenris! Almighty Wolf, I summon thee to rend the flesh of those who oppose thy children! Attend us!

WEST

Jormungandr, venomous sea dragon, I summon thee to smash the halls of Valhalla with thy crashing waves! Attend us!

With thy power and presence, our hour of victory is at hand!

Sword is replaced on the altar.

# RECOGNITION OF KINSHIP AND DECLARATION OF ALLEGIANCE

CELEBRANT: From the nighted halls of the netherworlds, I call my kindred to witness my oath.

CELEBRANT (*CONGREG. repeats*): I pledge my troth to the honor of my brethren. I reclaim this soil, hallowed by the blood of my folk. Grandfather Loki, Lord of the Inferno, Thy flame burns deep in my heart. Father Fenris, mighty wolf, my teeth are your fangs tearing our enemies. My blood burns with irresistible rage for the murder of our kind by the filthy minions of the gods of death. Thou tasted their flesh when thou wert bound and shall now feast upon their corrupt remains.
Heija! Hail Fenris!

GONG IS STRUCK.

# TOAST

Celebrant fills drinking horn,
forms the SIG rune (ᛋ) over it with his hands.

Fenris! Thy might shall bring me victory.

Celebrant raises the horn up to the SIG Pentagram.

**CELEBRANT** (*CONGREG. repeats*): Hail Victory!

Gong is struck.

Celebrant drinks.

As each congregant stands before Celebrant, he offers
the horn with the words: "Partake of the might of
Fenris." Congregant responds: "Hail Victory!" and drinks
from the horn. When all have drunk,
drained horn is replaced on altar.

# CONDEMNATION OF THE POLLUTION OF THE WORLD

CELEBRANT STANDS IN ISA POSITION (I), ARMS AT SIDES.

**CELEBRANT:** Behold! We are deep in the frigid wasteland of Fimbulvetr, our culture choked with the glacial tread of mediocrity. The weak govern the strong, perverting natural law. Witness the reign of the gods of death! Yahweh, Christ, Buddha, Mohammed—all you have touched has spawned corruption! Dwarves of mind and spirit have swept the globe as a pestilence, stifling higher Man. We have seen the forward motion of the ruthless life-force slow to a crawl, mired in a bog of despicable refuse. Discipline is banished; idiocy enshrined. The world is ruled by crippled and twisted thralls, groveling before their idols of renunciation, wallowing in the filth of desire denied. Aspiration and advancement are mocked by pox-ridden beggars, whose festering sores are THEIR signs of honor. A pall of guilt smothers the visage of pride! Justice is hamstrung! The very living treasure of Midgard, our precious lair, is soiled by the massed swarm of worthless, subhuman dross.

**CELEBRANT** (*CONGREG. repeats*): Woe! – Woe! – Woe!

GONG IS STRUCK, *MEZZO FORTE*, AFTER PARTICIPANTS REPETITION OF EACH "WOE!"

# RENUNCIATION OF THE CORRUPT

Celebrant strikes MAN rune posture (ᛘ).

CELEBRANT: ENOUGH! The time is now to sound the clarion of rejection! Hear me, oh warriors! Men and women of mighty minds, I call the very whirlwinds to be our steeds! Time to shatter the bonds of OUR Gods, to loose the primal powers that bore our ancestors. March forth to total war. Smite the worshippers of the weak and frail! Fill your hearts with berserker frenzy! Mind and force shall reign supreme. The time has come, to cleanse and purify, a time for birth, spilling an ocean of blood!

CELEBRANT (*CONGREG. repeats*): Heija! Hail Loki!

Gong is struck.

# THE NINETEENTH ENOCHIAN KEY

To be read in Enochian.

# THE CONFLAGRATION

CELEBRANT STRIKES FA POSTURE (ᛕ).

**CELEBRANT:** It is now AMOK time!
Baldur has been slain and Heimdall sounds
his call.

CELEBRANT TRACES EH (ᛖ), THE DEATH RUNE, IN THE AIR
WHILE GONG IS ROLLED TO *FORTISSIMO*.

Brothers battle, slaying one another.
Siblings writhe in incestuous embrace.
Men know misery with all their hearts.
Treacheries abound. Harsh is the world.
Behold an age of axes, of swords, of
shattered shields;
An age of tempests, an age of wolves!
Now ends the age of sterility!

Look upon Nauthiz, rune of binding!

SIGIL IS ELEVATED BY CELEBRANT.

Loki, we sunder thy bonds and loose the
ravening wolf of Hel!

SIGIL ON PARCHMENT IS THRUST INTO THE FLAME OF A
CANDLE, THEN CAST DOWN INTO THE BRAZIER WHERE IT
IGNITES THE FLAME SOURCE. AS THIS IS DONE, THE GONG IS
STRUCK, *FORTISSIMO*, AND THE DRUMMERS COMMENCE THEIR
CONFLICTING THUNDER RHYTHMS. RECORDED THUNDER
SOUNDS, IF USED, ARE NOW ACTIVATED. IF THE NAUTHIZ RUNE IS
CONSTRUCTED, RATHER THAN PARCHMENT, IT IS SMASHED BY A
BATTLE HAMMER BEFORE BEING BURNED.

**CELEBRANT** (*Congreg. repeats*): Hail Loki! Hail Fenris!

Gong is struck.

Celebrant strikes DAGAZ posture (ᛞ).

**CELEBRANT:** Hear the glad tidings!
A torrent of swords and daggers
runs from the east through vales of venom.
Below the earth, a soot red cock crows in
the halls of Hel.
Fearsome Garm and savage Freke are free
to plunder.
Comes the dragon of darkness flying,
might from beneath the mountains of night.
With a roar in the ancient tree,
the giant is loosed.
Yggdrasil quakes where it stands;
is overturned.
Jormungandr writhes in titanic rage,
whipping the waves to froth.
His venom splatters the very sea and sky.

Nagelfar, dread ship of doom, casts off.
From the east, over the boiling waters,
comes Muspell's folk with Loki at the helm.
His allies, the Frost Giants, thirst for battle.
Fierce Garm devours Tyr, the one-handed.
From out the south,
mighty Surt's flames blaze before and after.

His sword, conflagration, touches all.
The embattled gods' sun is skewered
on the blade.
Mountains burst. Hags hurry hence.
The Bifrost span is smashed to shards.
Fenris slavers, jaws stretching
from earth to sky.
Odin, Loki-betrayer, is swallowed whole.
Men tread Hel's road; the skies are sundered.
Black is the sun as the earth sinks in waters
stained crimson with blood.
The sparkling stars are stripped from the
firmament.
Smoke rages and leaping flames lick
heaven itself.
At Loki's command, Surt's fires consume
all, a righteous pyre!
The old order is done.

CELEBRANT FORMS GIBOR MUDRA (✦).


## HAIL RAGNARÖK!

FLASH POWDER IS CAST INTO THE BRAZIER
WHILE GONG IS STRUCK FORTISSIMO.

CONGREG. (*salute with daggers*): HAIL RAGNARÖK!

THUNDER AND ARRHYTHMIC DRUMMING END.
DRUMS BEGIN SOLEMN MARCH TREAD.

# THE VICTORY

CELEBRANT STRIKES FA POSTURE (ᛜ).

**CELEBRANT:** Behold, Valhalla is ablaze!
The flames herald a new dawn.
The gods of weakness are vanquished!
Their ashes and blood, fuel for our future.
Now begins the age of Feral Man.
Multiply, sons and daughters of Fenris.
Fill our darkling halls with Iron Youth.
We glory in discipline and strength
through joy.

**CELEBRANT** (*CONGREG. repeats*): Hail Feral warriors!
Hail Iron Youth!
Behold, the world is ours!

CELEBRANT MAKES THE SIGN OF THE HORNS.

Hail Fenris! (GONG *FORTE*)
Hail Loki! (GONG *FORTISSIMO*)
Hail Victory! (GONG *FORTISSISSIMO*)

DAGGERS ARE LOWERED. DRUMS STOP. GONG FADES TO SILENCE.

BELL IS RUNG AS POLLUTIONARY.

**CELEBRANT:** So it is done!

LIGHTS ARE EXTINGUISHED.

RECESSIONAL MUSIC IS PLAYED.

END OF RITE.

# NOCTURNE:
# TO THE DEVIL BORN

PETER H. GILMORE was born in Paterson, New Jersey, America's first planned industrial city; he shares his birthplace with Colt Firearms and the first practical submarine, the Fenian Ram, built by inventor and Paterson schoolteacher John Holland in 1879. Peter's family background, however, is not industrial but artistic. His grandfather David trod the boards as a vaudevillian with his own traveling minstrel show; he played different ethnic characters and made a few recordings. Peter's maternal grandfather, William, was a pastry chef much in demand at the resorts along the Atlantic seaboard; he created large architectural representations in pastry, and ice sculptures that dominated the buffet tables at the fanciest parties and banquets. Donald, Peter's father, was a dog groomer and handler as well as a small businessman and entrepreneur; he established several shops, kennels and facilities around the tri-state area, and handled champions at Westminster as well as other major competitions. Peter's Mom, Frances, painted and decorated; she exercised her artistic abilities in her home by creating things to make it beautiful, and encouraged her children to do the same. She is also a self-taught organist and enjoys playing the old standards for her own pleasure and that of her friends and family.

This early exposure to the business of dog breeding and

champion bloodlines quickly gave Peter an adult's perspective on the biological sciences in general. Puppies came from breeding dogs before they got to those newspaper-strewn bins at the pet shop, and Peter concluded that babies had a similar source; he confirmed this by checking out a few biology books at the library. His parents allowed Peter to explore his early interest in animals and nature in general; his bedroom gurgled with several aquariums, tanks and terrariums, and he took over the backyard with a wading pool for captured turtles, frogs, snakes and other squishy things he found in the woods. Peter was independent, inquisitive and fearless of the non-human inhabitants of the forests of the lower Hudson Valley where he grew up; he'd wander on his own for hours and knew the location of hidden lakes, caves and waterfalls.

He was a smart kid, learned to read quite early and began exploring books. Books fed his imagination, and his imagination pushed him to create the things with his hands that did not exist for purchase. He made forts, models, and miniature cities as well as creating and recording the histories, political systems, and urban planning that went along with them. And he read, read, read as much as he could of the myths and pantheons of the Roman, Greek, and Hindu gods, being fascinated by the ruins of "lost civilizations" as well as looking into the strange beliefs of present-day world religions. Peter quickly concluded that all these myth-systems were on the same footing: interesting stories made up to help people feel more important in the vast scheme of things, when in fact they were no higher or lower than the bears he observed in the woods, or the hawks that soared overhead. The animals he admired didn't need gods, and neither did he.

By rote and custom, however, Peter's parents required him to learn their loose Roman Catholicism and he participated in this religious instruction for as long as necessary, acting as an anthropologist studying an odd primitive culture. He has a clear memory of officially declaring his atheism on the day of his First Holy Communion at age eight. After weeks of "studying" to receive this sacrament—the purported transubstantiation of bread and wine into the body and blood of Christ—Peter insisted it was just another myth, and not as interesting as the Greek ones filled with heroes and monsters. Over twenty years later I was sorting though a shelf of his books from childhood and I found his Communion Missal; he had inscribed his name and the date of that milestone: May 1st, 1966, the day after the founding of the Church of Satan.

Science, art, books, movies and the wonderful toys that went with them were his burning interests as he grew up. Like many boys in the Sixties, Peter was fascinated by space exploration, robots, and all the futuristic developments these things promised. He never missed Star Trek or a NASA launch on television; he carefully combed the TV Guide for late-night broadcasts of horror movies, especially those involving vampires or giant Japanese monsters. Without the convenience of videotapes and DVRs, Peter relied on his own imagination and drew pictures of scenes from his favorite movies and shows from memory so he could enjoy these magical images over and over again. He also illustrated favorite myths and events from the histories he'd invented for his sci-fi civilizations.

Peter never developed a taste for popular music. As he entered high school and concentrated more on painting and drawing along with his academic studies, he didn't adopt rock music as a mode of rebellion, unlike many other boys his age. Instead, his interest was sparked by the music of Beethoven; it was strong, bombastic, and complex, engaging both his emotions and his intellect. And it was much more like the film music he'd also grown to love. Peter began haunting the Newburgh Library, housed in a Victorian building with its collection of LPs, and eventually discovered another favorite composer, Gustav Mahler. He would blast the music of Mahler and Beethoven for hours while he worked on his surrealistic paintings inspired by Bosch, Dali, and Ernst; sometimes he'd miss school for days staying awake around the clock while he worked on something that was absorbing him.

Despite these absences, Peter was the Valedictorian for our graduating class and at the top of our school's National Honor Society. One of his innovations while participating in the NHS was to make the induction ceremony more gothic and atmospheric with darkness and candles and a very secular, individualist oath. He did an Easter presentation in a social studies class in opposition to some "born-agains" reading from Christian scriptures. He chose texts from *The Satanic Bible* and read them dramatically over recordings of Mussorgsky's "Night on Bald Mountain" and Stravinsky's "The Rite of Spring." Parents who heard from their kids about this complained to the board of education but when the principal confronted him, Peter stood his ground explaining that there should be pluralism of viewpoints—and the man agreed. The 70s were far more liberal times than now. Peter also worked as the Editor-in-Chief of our yearbook and created the painting that wraps around the cover; the twisted bodies and bizarre landscape were a bit of a surprise to many of our uptight classmates who made a point of encasing the book in brown paper as a method of protest—even then Peter was making waves and challenging the status quo.

Peter's painting is what brought us together. When we were both in our junior year, the school's Art Department had a festival highlighting the work of the student body's most prominent young artists and I came across Peter's self-portrait in one of the display cases. "Wow, this is weird!" I commented to Lori, who was with me at the moment as she usually was, being my best friend and co-conspirator.

"I know that guy—that's Peter Gilmore. He's in my Social Studies class. I think he's a Satanist, or something. It's a pretty good self-portrait, because it looks just like him."

"I have to meet him," I replied. And I did meet him. We were married in 1981; Lori was my honor attendant, and now that self-portrait hangs in our living room.

As the end of high school approached, painting had already become too static an art form for Peter; his interests in music, foreign films and the works of Ayn Rand had coalesced into a desire to tell stories on a larger scale and so upon graduation he enrolled in the film program at the School of Visual Arts. The collectivist political attitudes and agendas of his professors quickly became apparent, and this, along with the necessity of committee efforts in the making of films, quickly convinced Peter to transfer out. Despite his lack of early training, he decided to pursue what had become his great passion: music. He began studying music from the ground up and in a few short years had received both Bachelor's and Master's degrees in musical composition from New York University and began writing music. Peter contributed musical introductions for albums by the black metal band Acheron and he has created electronic musical scores for some independent film productions. Several of these latter pieces, along with other original compositions, are collected on the album, "Threnody for Humanity." Peter is in the process of rebuilding his music studio with modern computer technology in anticipation of releasing his Symphony No. 1, "Ragnarök."

So, you may well ask, if Peter was first an artist, then a filmmaker, and ultimately a composer, why is it a book of essays that you're holding right now?

Because Peter H. Gilmore is also a writer.

One of Peter's favorite activities when he was growing up was taking the commuter bus with a friend down to New York City and then riding the subway up to the American Museum of Natural History to look at the dinosaur bones and other displays in this vast and dusty old mother-lode of biological artifacts. On one occasion, when Peter was 13, the boys returned to the Port Authority bus terminal a little too early and decided to kill some time browsing the many shops along the main floor. One of these was the Book Bar, a tiny bookstore sandwiched in near Teepee Town and the coffee shop, and this was where Peter first picked up *The Satanic Bible* by Anton Szandor LaVey. At first Peter wanted to reject the paperback with its dark, forbidding cover and Ming-esque author photo on the back, thinking that it was probably just a lot of silly, spooky language directing the reader toward some mythical entity who promised to answer your prayers, or spells, or whatnot. But the black-bound tome kept pulling him back; the very simplicity of its title, that left no room for misinterpretation of the author's point-of-view, was strangely compelling. The book went home with him, and the rest is history.

Like so many other Satanists before and after him, Peter read through *The Satanic Bible* in a single sitting and knew that he was a Satanist. He read each subsequent book by Dr. LaVey as soon as it hit the stands. Historically, he was living right in the middle of the Church of Satan's early phases and began seeing news reports and print media articles about LaVey and his disciples. When *The Devil's Avenger* appeared on the paperback racks, Peter bought a copy and was enthralled to learn that the man who had changed history with his little black book, was just as interesting and colorful as Peter hoped he'd be. At 15, Peter wrote to the Church of Satan and his letter was referred to a local Grotto. He was politely turned away because of his age, but was provided with some written materials and encouraged to continue his studies and come back when he was old enough. He did—in fact, we did it together in 1982 while we were both in college. Our Active Applications were submitted and accepted in 1984, when we both felt that we might have some time to contribute to the Church itself. Peter was asked to serve as a local contact for other members because of his thorough grasp of the Church and its philosophy. Then in 1986, we were ready to accept an earlier invitation to the Black House on California Street to meet the great man.

Anton LaVey was everything we'd hoped he'd be, and more. We were treated to hours of conversation in the infamous Purple Parlor, a midnight tour of San Francisco from the backseat of the black Jaguar, and an intimate concert by this infernal keyboard wizard in the chilly kitchen of the old Victorian house-on-the-way-to-the-sea. And it turned out that Anton LaVey was suitably impressed with us, too. When a media opportunity presented itself soon after our first visit to San Francisco, Peter was asked by Dr. LaVey to represent his ideas and his Church on national television.

Thus began a career with the Church of Satan that included media representation on national, international, and local television, radio, newspapers and magazines. This was during the turbulent heyday of the Satanic Panic, when TV talk show hosts like Geraldo were exploiting the public's misconceptions about Satanism and Christian cops were making big bucks "educating" other law enforcement agencies with misinformation and outright fantasies. Peter made his media chops fielding questions, accusations, hostile hosts and crazy religious basket-case panelists in the furor of this media frenzy. His pleasant voice, ever-present humor and complete confidence in his knowledge of Satanic philosophy and the way Satanists apply it to their lives, has made Peter the consummate Satanic representative for almost 20 years. In this day of podcasts and Internet radio, it shows no signs of slowing down.

Peter also assisted with the administration and management of our growing organization and sent out a clarion call in 1988 when he founded *The Black Flame*, the first newsstand magazine for and by Satanists. His interest in exploring the implications of our philosophy, as well as presenting the ideas of other intelligent Satanists doing the same, sparked the need for this journal which began to draw a circle of those who would become our friends and co-conspirators for years to come. In the same manner that a tidal wave follows a drawing-down and receding of the waters, a renewed cross-fertilization of ideas and projects among Satanists followed the Satanic Panic, much of it in response to *The Black Flame* and Blanche Barton's books, *The Secret Life of a Satanist* (a new biography of LaVey) and *The Church of Satan, a history of the world's most notorious religion*. Peter began writing essays to clarify and clear up misconceptions, to quash rumors and myths about our organization and its founder, and to explore areas of modern culture where our ideas were creating change and the evolution that LaVey had predicted. Many of those essays have been collected here.

In addition to expanding on Satanic philosophy and explaining the attitudes and actions of Satanists, Peter has also explored the use of Greater Magic over the years, creating new rituals and invocations. Together with our friends, we've attempted ceremonies in different settings and spaces; we've collaborated on carefully-rehearsed and scheduled workings such as thunderous versions of "Die Elektrischen Vorspiel" as well as breaking into spontaneous rituals as the mood arose—one held in the total darkness deep in a lava tube beneath Mt. St. Helens. On the first anniversary of the passing of Anton LaVey, Peter and I organized and hosted a memorial piano concert in LaVey's memory, with the idea that our founder was first and foremost a musician, and this was the best way to remember him in a group setting. Years later, on June 6th, 2006, in recognition of the public's misconceptions about the numerical significance of this date, Peter presided over the largest group ritual ever celebrated by members of the Church of Satan, at the Steve Allen Theater in Los Angeles. By exploiting popular culture's prejudices and fears about the dreaded 6-6-6, our present High Priest has continued the Church of Satan's long history as the profane world's cosmic joy buzzer. And so by reason of all of the above, this volume contains rituals by Peter H. Gilmore, as well as his essays.

What else can I tell you about the man who succeeded Anton LaVey as High Priest of the Church of Satan, appointed to that position in 2001 by High Priestess Blanche Barton? He enjoys fine wine as well as good music; he's lived the majority of his adult life here in New York City, taking full advantage of our proximity to the greatest concert halls and classical music venues in the world. Our living spaces are clogged with the evidence of a lifetime of voracious reading and book and film collecting, along with models, toys, paintings and figurines of the monsters who occupy his imagination. He wears mostly-black, and likes red meat; he takes wonderful care of our Chow dog, Contessa Bella Lugosi, and her coat gleams as a result. He is a great husband—or I wouldn't be around to celebrate 25 years of marriage with him, and we are definitely celebrating.

But the most important thing I have to tell you about Peter H. Gilmore, is that he is just like any other Satanist—in one very significant way. He found Satanism on the shelf of a bookstore; the words in *The Satanic Bible* spoke to the very center of Peter's dark, Satanic soul. He wasn't born into a "traditional Satanic family"; he wasn't initiated by his Granny during the dark of the moon. Peter H. Gilmore is a Satanist-born because of who he is—and what he does. He's shaped his life and his destiny by his own wits, will and desires—and according to *The Satanic Bible*, we all possess the power to do that.

**Magistra Peggy Nadramia, High Priestess**
October 31, XLI A.S.
Hell's Kitchen, New York City

"To a new world of gods and monsters!"

"Sometimes I have wondered whether life wouldn't be much more amusing if we were all devils, and no nonsense about angels and being good."

Doctor Pretorius,
*The Bride of Frankenstein*

# Church of Satan
P.O. Box 666
Poughkeepsie, NY 12602-0666

WWW.CHURCHOFSATAN.COM

Printed in Great Britain
by Amazon

47441320R00184